Supporting
ENGLISH
LEARNERS
in the **Classroom**

Supporting ENGLISH LEARNERS in the **Classroom**

Best Practices for Distinguishing Language Acquisition from Learning Disabilities

Eric M. Haas
Julie Esparza Brown

TEACHERS COLLEGE PRESS

TEACHERS COLLEGE | COLUMBIA UNIVERSITY

NEW YORK AND LONDON

Published by Teachers College Press, 1234 Amsterdam Avenue, New York, NY 10027

Cover insets (top to bottom) courtesy of MediaProduction, FatCamera, and shironosov, all via iStock by GettyImages.

Figure 3.3 adapted with permission of Wiley. Copyright © Brown, Ortiz, and Turner. Figure 4.4 reprinted with permission of Behavioral Research and Teaching, University of Oregon. Copyright © 2017 Hasbrouck & Tindal.

Library of Congress Cataloging-in-Publication Data is available at loc.gov
Names: Haas, Eric (Eric M.), author. | Brown, Julie Esparza, author.
Title: Supporting English learners in the classroom : best practices for distinguishing language acquisition from learning disabilities / Eric M. Haas and Julie Esparza Brown.
Description: First edition. | New York : Teachers College Press, [2019] | Includes bibliographical references and index. |
Identifiers: LCCN 2018059843 (print) | LCCN 2019014697 (ebook) | ISBN 9780807777862 (ebook)
ISBN 9780807759530 (pbk. : alk. paper)
Subjects: LCSH: English language–Study and teaching–Foreign speakers. | Learning disabled children—Education. | English language—Remedial teaching.
Classification: LCC PE1128.A2 (ebook) | LCC PE1128.A2 H225 2019 (print) | DDC 428.0071—dc23
LC record available at https://lccn.loc.gov/2018059843

ISBN 978-0-8077-5953-0 (paper)
ISBN 978-0-8077-6174-8 (hardcover)
ISBN 978-0-8077-7786-2 (ebook)

Printed on acid-free paper
Manufactured in the United States of America

26 25 24 23 22 21 20 19   8 7 6 5 4 3 2 1

Contents

Acknowledgments

Thank you to my wife, Leslie, whose expertise on second language literacy development and writing greatly informs my thinking and research in these areas. You are a wonderfully patient, wise, and supportive listener and guide in every aspect of my life. Thank you, too, to my daughter, Michaela, whose adventurous life continually inspires me to take chances so that I am better tomorrow than I am today. I am constantly grateful for having you as my family.

Thank you also to my colleagues in English learner research and practice. To my former REL West English Learner Alliance team at WestEd: Min Huang, Loan Tran, Min Chen-Gaddini, and Elizabeth Burr—our studies form the foundation of my understanding about the large-scale educational experiences of English learner students. To Julie Goldman, Chris Faltis, and Jamal Abedi: Your knowledge, generosity, curiosity, energy, and commitment during our work together on the WRITE Institute evaluation have shown me how to thoughtfully connect practice to research to improve the everyday classroom learning of English learner students. To Julie Esparza Brown: Thank you for taking a chance on this writing partnership—we really made this work.

I hope this book reflects all the best that I have learned from each of you.

—EMH

First and foremost, I am grateful for the neverending support of my three children, Nathan Brown, Liana Richey, and Danae Brown and their partners Janai Schubert Brown, Matt Richey, and Chris Merrill. Without their faith, love, and encouragement this work may not have happened.

The inspiration for my work is my two young grandchildren, Zach Richey and Morgan Brown, whom I adore beyond words. They are the reason for my continuing commitment to improving our educational systems so that *all* children, no matter their color, language, abilities, or zip code, have equitable opportunities to learn and grow.

I am also eternally grateful for the undying support of my parents, Frank and Florence Esparza, sister and brother-in-law Maureen and Patrick Pierce, and my niece, Caylee Pierce, and nephew, Nicholas Pierce. Without their support, particularly my parents, this Chicana educator would likely not have believed she could pursue college and have doors open to a world of education I only imagined.

I am also grateful to colleagues Amanda Sanford (who coauthored two chapters with me), Maria Tenorio, and Mickey Caskey, who offered encouragement, edits, and suggestions, and my colleagues at Portland State. Thank you, Eric Haas, for inviting me to be a part of this publication.

Finally, this book is for all of the students who need that one person to believe in them. My hope is that educators will read this book and heed the call for building those relationships students need so their futures will be a "universe of possibilities" (a favorite saying of the late Dr. Valerie Cook-Morales, a very wise woman and one of my mentors).

—JEB

CHAPTER 1

Introduction

An English learner student is struggling in school. How do you enable her to succeed? Nearly all educators—elementary teachers, secondary teachers, English learner specialists, special education specialists, counselors, principals, and district superintendents—will face this dilemma. In a large school, many English learner students may be struggling, all at the same time. How do you determine whether an English learner (EL) student's struggles are typical, because learning science, math, history, and poetry in a new language is hard work, or are also due to something more, such as poor teaching practices, cultural differences between the student and the school, or a learning disability? And further, how do you go from helping struggling EL students to promoting the success of EL students *before* they struggle?

This book answers these questions with research data and effective practice information on how to support EL students at the first sign of struggle; provide the appropriate intensity of supports in consideration of EL students' cultural and linguistic backgrounds; determine which EL students should be referred for a special education evaluation; and make the appropriate special education eligibility and placement decisions, when needed. This book is a resource for anyone trying to figure out what to do when you suspect that one (or many) of your EL students would benefit from a referral for special education services. We describe effective, evidence-based, everyday practices for determining whether an EL student's rate of progress is typical for a second language learner in their grade, with their experience, and in their classroom environment, or whether their progress rate may indicate a learning difference or disability. We also offer guidance about how to view and understand *dual identified* students—EL students who have been identified as having a learning difference such as dyslexia, ADHD, hearing loss, or other disabilities as defined by the IDEIA (2004).[1] We intend this book to enable teams of educators and caregivers (parents and guardians) to effectively determine what EL students need to succeed and the best ways to provide these supports and activities in their own classrooms, schools, and districts, adapting and implementing them for individual contexts.

We structured this book around seven main principles. First and foremost, this book takes a collaborative approach to supporting EL students who do or may have a learning difference or disability.[2] Identifying, assessing, and supporting dual identified students requires an efficient team and systems

1

approach involving multiple areas of expertise and multiple levels of support and intervention. For example, one should call on expertise in subject matter content and pedagogy, second language acquisition and pedagogy, and learning differences and pedagogy, plus extensive knowledge of the life experience of each individual student. General and targeted assessments in English proficiency and learning differences and pull-out and push-in supports in English language development and learning disabilities are available and should be considered. Cross-grade and even multischool systems need to operate accurately and efficiently every day with each student. Finally, the legal rights and responsibilities set forth in federal and state laws must be considered. Few people are expert in all these areas, but schools and districts have experts in each and, in partnership with caregivers[3] (and students), educators and policymakers can address these influences on an EL student's success in school. This book provides guidance and resources so that those knowledgeable in one area can understand the influence of the other areas on the educational experience of potential and identified dual identified students.

Second, this book approaches bilingualism, language diversity, and the contributions of individuals with special learning needs as resources that should be promoted, and we firmly believe that individual success contributes to the prosperity of the entire community (Haas, Fischman, & Brewer, 2014; Ruiz, 1984). We believe educators should proactively promote asset-based learning pedagogies that begin with, "What can this student do well?" This book provides ideas and tools for teaching and learning to promote the success of EL and dual identified students by building on their advantages and helping them overcome areas of difficulty. When EL and dual identified students experience this type of schooling, they can thrive and achieve at high levels in academics and other areas of their lives (see, e.g., ACTFL, n.d.; Butrymowicz & Mader, 2017).

Third, as educators, we must provide rich learning environments (caring, engaging, rigorous, and scaffolded) for our students, where we seek out ways to help them thrive, including catching them early on in their struggles. Further, rich learning environments especially for EL and dual identified students must include activities that regularly encourage deep content-based conversations because "reading and writing float on a sea of talk" (Britton, 1983, p. 11; see also Fisher, Frey, & Rothenberg, 2008; Haas, Goldman, & Faltis, 2018). Every student struggles at some point in their K–12 schooling, but while struggles are inevitable, and healthy struggles may be necessary for high achievement, failure should not be. Gone are the days when we wait for students to fail before providing additional supports. Now, a Multi-Tiered System of Supports (MTSS) is fundamental to providing the structure necessary for integrating high-quality instruction in rich learning environments with timely interventions in ways that are effective with heterogeneous students, including EL and dual identified students. When you use an MTSS built on evidence-based practices, it becomes easier to determine whether a student's difficulties are due to a learning difference or disability. This book provides guidance and resources for effectively implementing this type of MTSS.

Fourth, students are heterogeneous. EL students are heterogeneous. Students with disabilities are heterogeneous. Dual identified students are heterogeneous. Further, students and their experiences with school change from kindergarten through 12th grade, with key transition periods along the way. Student literacy development changes from *learning to read* to *reading to learn*; native language speakers usually make this transition around 3rd grade, but second language learners often make the transition later. Adolescence generally sees heightened peer group influence, among other social and emotional changes, and schooling that is more academically demanding with teachers who have content area expertise rather than literacy development expertise. Because each EL student's school experience is different and changeable over time, their learning activities and supports need to evolve with them as they progress toward high school graduation. This book provides guidance, resources, and examples that can be differentiated for elementary and secondary students and between EL students with different life experiences.

Fifth, this book builds on an age-old tradition in education: Borrow from your successful colleagues. You are not alone in looking for ways to improve the education of EL and dual identified students. Throughout this book, we describe existing successes and the resources for finding out more about them: collaborative school teams, evidence-based best pedagogy and assessment practices, and state-level processes for scaling up these improvements. Specifically in Chapter 6, we describe state manuals that form a thoughtful base of practice for supporting EL and dual identified students. There is no need to reinvent the wheel when you can tweak and tinker with existing models to make them fit your context.

Sixth, this book includes practical resources and guidance, along with the evidence and research for why they are effective. There are checklists, protocol examples, and resource links throughout the chapters, and in the Appendix, a sample of a brief but thorough matrix for information-gathering. This book provides what you need to get started today and suggests where you can go tomorrow for more.

Finally, our experience is consistent with the leading research in systems change: Fundamental improvements in practice, especially on the scale of schools and districts, require simultaneous improvements in understandings, activities, resources, and procedures, promoted by ongoing evaluation, reflection, and professional practice and learning cycles over multiple years. It is the nature of a book to present topics linearly, but we intend educators to address these topics together. You will find discussion of some topics from different viewpoints in more than one chapter.

In Chapter 2, we describe the challenges involved in providing potential and actual dual identified students an education that will enable them to succeed in school. We describe the heterogeneity of EL students created by their individual combinations of life experiences and current school contexts, as well as learning disability (if applicable), and how this makes each EL student unique. We describe how difficult it can be for educators and caregivers to understand how the interactive web of life experience, school context, learning English as a second language, and learning differences impacts the struggles of potential dual identified students and how this has led, despite the seeming contradiction, to both over- and underrepresentation of EL students in special education. We use the lens of *Critical Disability Theory* to show that our individual understandings of the intersection of race and disability can collectively limit the effectiveness of the systems we create for identifying and supporting students who are English learners and students with a learning difference or disability in need of special education. Finally, we recommend that you read the remainder of the book as suggestions for improving how you think and act both individually and within collective systems of teams and institutions.

Chapter 3 begins the discussion of evidence-based practices, starting with the key elements of high-quality teaching within a Multi-Tiered System of Supports (MTSS), a version of Response to Intervention (RTI), and how this instructional structure can be tailored for the unique needs of EL students. Using the MTSS framework, we describe ways for educators to provide culturally and linguistically appropriate instruction, intervention, and assessment, matching a student's needs to appropriate levels of intensity so as to ensure "opportunity to learn" before considering a referral to special education. We describe effective second language literacy and culturally responsive pedagogy practices in general education classrooms (Tier 1 of an MTSS) to minimize the influence of ineffective instruction on the struggles of an EL student. Next, we outline the role of school teams in determining which students need support and in planning targeted interventions that align with students' language, cultural, and experiential needs. We emphasize using multiple data sources to determine the extent to which school context and the EL student's life and educational experiences may be impacting their academic progress and to decide what additional interventions and supports are needed to enable the student to be more successful (Tiers 2 and 3). Whether students' difficulties are rooted in a disability or not, we provide protocols and checklists for educators and caregivers to use to implement high-quality instruction, ongoing monitoring, and evolving supports to accurately identify and fulfill the needs of EL students. Finally, we introduce the PLUSS framework (Sanford, Brown, & Turner, 2012) to use as an overlay to evidence-based literacy interventions that have not been designed for EL students and that often assume mainstream knowledge and lack adequate language supports.

In Chapter 4, we focus on assessment across the three levels or tiers of an MTSS structure. We describe how to effectively conduct ongoing monitoring of EL students, suggesting specific tools and checklists for gathering and interpreting the multiple forms of evidence needed to accurately gauge English language proficiency and academic progress and to identify the likely influences on areas of struggle and strength. We describe what to consider in choosing progress monitoring instruments, including validity and reliability criteria, and how to interpret and use the results for formative instructional and program improvements and summative placement and intervention determinations for individual students. We describe how to use "true peers"—students who are similar to the EL student(s) being assessed—as the comparison, rather than the default norm of White, native English-speaking students from socioeconomically privileged families, in order to make more accurate progress estimates and goal and intervention decisions, including special education eligibility. We provide charts and tables of examples of true peer progress for EL and dual identified students.

In Chapter 5, we delve into the implications of the heterogeneity of EL students for special education identification and instructional strategies. Appropriate special education referral for EL students is described here as a process, rather than an event, and we outline the steps across the MTSS tiers in this process. Special education eligibility decisions are based on data collected throughout the MTSS process and, often, from standardized tests. Such tests can be biased against nonmajority populations or can simply fail to take their differences into account, rendering them inaccurate. We will share an interpretive framework that considers the cultural loading and linguistic demand inherent in standardized tests that can help teams reduce bias. Next, we describe collaborative approaches for ensuring that an EL student with learning disabilities receives an appropriate and meaningful education through the implementation of their Individual Education Program (IEP) as prescribed by best practice evidence and as required by law. We provide checklists and interpretive guidance for IEP teams on how to incorporate support for both the language-learning and special education needs of a child with limited English proficiency based on how the student's English language proficiency level interacts with the academic demands of their grade level and their learning disability. This chapter provides models of IEPs for EL students with disabilities, and suggestions, as well as legal entitlements, for enabling diverse families to be equal partners in the education of their child (see also Chapters 6 and 7 for more details). Finally, the chapter will share the emerging policies regarding the use of differing standards and criteria for reclassifying EL students with learning disabilities as fluent English proficient (RFEP) and exiting EL support programs (CCSSO, 2016a, 2016b). This chapter will be especially relevant for administrators, general education teachers, and English language development (ELD) teachers, who may have less direct experience with special education students.

To effectively realize the practices described in Chapters 3 through 5, education agencies from schools to states will need to systematically improve their materials, professional development training, and data management and decisionmaking processes; the roles and processes educators and administrators work through; and the beliefs educators, administrators, and policymakers have about dual identified students and how best to support their academic success. To aid these efforts, Chapter 6 describes key elements of the systems needed to support these best programs and practices for potential and actual dual identified students as recommended by system change research in education and as presented in current state manuals on how they are implementing these improvements. Currently, seven states have publicly available manuals: Connecticut, Illinois, Michigan, Minnesota, Oklahoma, Oregon, and Vermont. We describe the key elements of each manual, including resources and action steps, and how they fit with the research literature on how to make school-, district-, and state-level improvements in education. In the References, we also provide links for accessing these manuals.

In Chapter 7, we describe the legal rights of EL students and students with disabilities and the mandated responsibilities for educators (from teachers to paraprofessional staff to administrators), including relevant definitions and federal guidance on required practices, and how these rights and responsibilities can (and should) be used to promote the effective practices previously described in this book. We present the most relevant sections of the Every Student Succeeds Act (ESSA), the Equal Educational Opportunity Act of 1974, the Individuals with Disabilities Education Improvement Act (IDEIA, 2004), and Section 504 of the Rehabilitation Act of 1973, along with key court cases that have interpreted or promoted their provisions, such as *Castañeda v. Pickard* (1981), and *Lau v. Nichols* (1974). We describe the legal requirements for determining whether a student is an English learner and when an EL student is exited from an English language development (ELD) program. We then describe the legal requirements for identifying and providing services for students with learning disabilities, including new requirements related to EL students. Throughout the chapter, we present both the poor outcomes of following the bare-minimum letter of the law and the benefits of instead using these rights and responsibilities to promote evidence-based practices.

Chapter 8 concludes the main text with an inventory of needs assessment questions for understanding the current state of one's program (strengths and weaknesses) as the first step toward improvement. The needs assessment inventory includes questions for key actors at each of three levels: classroom (teachers), support team (teachers, counselors, EL experts, special education experts, and administrators), and system (building-level administrators, district personnel, and state and national policymakers). We then point out areas where future research and practice development are needed and areas where new research is being initiated, including accommodations on state English language proficiency (ELP) tests and/or differing criteria for exiting ELD support programs for EL students with learning disabilities, and comprehensive professional development for current and preservice teachers.

Finally, our Appendix includes a multipage Collaborative Problem-Solving Form (CPSF) to help you determine which evidence to gather to determine the efficacy of your core general education instruction for EL and dual identified students (Tier 1 of MTSS). Further, if needed, the CPSF information can inform which interventions will best support your EL and dual identified students from within Tier 1 to more focused and intensive interventions in Tiers 2 and 3, through to the beginning of making special education determinations in collaboration with an IEP or 504 team.

From our work with educators and policymakers in states throughout the United States, we know the improvements we describe can be made. We are seeing it happen. We hope this book can assist you in making these improvements, too.

Problems in Identifying English Learner Students at Risk for Learning Disabilities and in Need of Special Education

Millions of students in American schools are now, or once were, designated as English learner (EL) students. Beyond the difficulties they experience due to the poor fit between their everyday learning experiences and their reduced English fluency, EL students may face a wide range of additional circumstantial obstacles both inside and outside school. They may also be affected by learning differences or disabilities, or by physical disabilities. EL students' success in school will depend on educators' correct analysis of these factors and consequent application of interventions (up to and including placement in special education services) to support the students. This analysis is difficult, and educators often do not get it right. It appears, paradoxically, that EL students are both over- and underrepresented in special education. In this chapter, we analyze the data that shows these difficulties and perverse results, pull out what seem to be the chief issues, and suggest some practical and policy responses.

ENGLISH LEARNER STUDENT STATISTICS

In 2015, the most recent year of data available, the National Center for Education Statistics at the U.S. Department of Education indicated that about 9.5% of K–12 students in the United States are currently designated as English learner (EL) students, which is approximately 4.8 million students (U.S. Department of Education Statistics, National Center for Education Statistics, 2018). The percentage of students who have ever been an EL student is much higher, as "ever EL" students include former EL students who have been reclassified as fluent English proficient (RFEP) as well as current EL students. Currently, there are no national statistics on ever EL students. However, we know that the percentage and number of students who are currently designated as EL students varies by state and likely so does the percent and number of ever EL students. Using California as an example, in 2015, 21% of students were designated as current EL students (U.S. Department of Education Statistics, National Center for Education Statistics, 2018) and the California Department of Education estimates that 42% of all students were ever EL students, which equals about 1.3 million and 2.6 million students, respectively (California Department of Education, 2018). Thus, using California as an example metric, a state's ever EL population may be approximately twice the size of its EL student population. EL and ever EL students attend schools in every U.S. state, with the largest numbers in California, Texas, Florida, and New York. EL student populations were 10% or higher in seven states: Alaska, California, Kansas, Nevada, New Mexico, Texas, and Washington (U.S. Department of Education Statistics, National Center for Education Statistics, 2018).

EL AND DUAL IDENTIFIED STUDENT DIVERSITY

The EL student designation and RFEP (former EL student) designation encompass a heterogeneous group of boys and girls. EL students are in every grade from kindergarten through 12th. They come from every major racial and ethnic group and every socioeconomic level (Takanishi & Menestrel, 2017; U.S. Department of Education Statistics, National Center for Education Statistics, 2018); however, over three-fourths of EL students are of Hispanic/Latino heritage (U.S. Department of Education Statistics, National Center for Education Statistics, 2018). Approximately one-third of the families of EL students live at or below the federal poverty level of $25,100 for a family of four (compare U.S. Department of Health & Human Services, n.d., and Takanishi & Menestrel, 2017). Further, by 2020 some researchers project the Latinx K–12 student population will rise by another 25% (Herrera, Perez, & Escamilla, 2015). EL students speak over 150 languages, with more than 77% speaking Spanish. EL students who speak Arabic are the second largest EL group at 2.4% (U.S. Department of Education Statistics, National Center for Education Statistics, 2018).

Both EL and RFEP categories include students with a range of home language and English language fluencies. Ever EL students range from being fully academically fluent in their native language to conversationally fluent to knowing very little of their native language, even though it may be spoken frequently in their homes. In English, ever EL students can range from a student who was RFEPed many years ago and is fully academically fluent in English to one who was recently RFEPed and is still transitioning to being fully academically fluent in English. Further, EL students can range from one who is brand new to U.S. schools and who speaks little to no English to one who has been in a U.S. school for many years and is nearly ready to score well enough to RFEP and exit some or all of their EL support programs. Some students spend 1 year or less as an EL student in a support program, while other EL students spend 6 or more years in an EL support program, including some who graduate from high school without ever being RFEPed (see, e.g., Haas, Huang, Tran, & Yu, 2016a, b; Haas, Tran, Huang, & Yu, 2015). In general, EL students who are in their sixth or higher year in an EL support program are referred to as "long-term English learners" (U.S. Department of Education, 2016a); however, formal definitions vary by state and by the federal government. Naturally, nearly every long-term English learner student is in middle or high school. There is one characteristic, however, that most EL students share: The vast majority of our EL students—approximately 77% in 2013—were born in the United States (Zong & Batalova, 2015).

FACTORS INFLUENCING EL AND DUAL IDENTIFIED STUDENT SUCCESS

Many, and likely most, EL students struggle at some point in school. Most students struggle in school at one time or another. These struggles may be due to any number of possible reasons. An EL student's struggles in school may be due to unqualified teachers and other school staff; teachers, staff, and other students who have biases about EL students; or poor curricula, pedagogy, and school resources. EL students may struggle because of trauma they have experienced from war and being a refugee and immigrant, an experience that few U.S. natives can fully comprehend. Many EL students may struggle due to personal trauma in their own families, something many native English-speaking students experience as well. EL students may struggle in school due to interrupted schooling prior to or after entering a U.S. school and differences between their home culture and norms and those of the school they attend. EL students may struggle because they do not have the level of home support that the school expects, which, again, many native English-speaking students also experience. They may struggle due to developmental changes, especially during adolescence and puberty, which all students experience to some extent. EL students likely also struggle because they are learning both English and subject matter content, so they have at least twice the work that a native English speaker does to do well in school. EL students may struggle because learning is often hard and "doing school" is often stressful. And they may struggle because they have a learning difference, learning disability, or physical disability that impacts their learning. An EL student's learning difference, learning disability, or physical disability could range from those that are considered mild and are not readily physically visible, such as dyslexia and auditory processing disorder, to those considered more severe and that have more observable physical manifestations, such as ADHD and dyspraxia (Learning Disabilities of America, 2018).

To enable an EL student to succeed, especially a struggling one, educators must sift through all these factors to find those most likely to be the cause (or causes) and respond effectively. Educators must examine school factors as well as factors related to the student and their caregivers in order to enable EL students to succeed (Hibel, Farkas, & Morgan, 2010; Morgan et al., 2015). An EL student, like any student, will struggle when there is a disconnect between what they need to do the hard work of learning and how the school operates, what it demands, and what supports it provides (or not) to students and their families.

This long list of possible causes for an EL student's struggles, as well as their interactive or overlapping influence on language expression, can make an accurate determination and an effective response quite difficult for educators, as well as for caregivers and the student. For example, a new student in kindergarten who was born in the United States and whose caregivers are not fluent in English may score below proficient on the state's required English language proficiency (ELP) test and be designated as an EL student; however, the actual cause for the low test performance is dyslexia, poor eyesight, or hearing loss. Or a 9th-grade student who was recently RFEPed and now placed entirely in English-only math, literature, science, and history classes might start getting low grades and misbehaving. The teachers then might recommend special education services to deal with what they perceive to be some type of emotional disturbance issue. However, the student actually needs continued EL support services and more time to make the full transition to the higher level of academic English fluency required in high school content classes. These decisions can be further complicated by the fact that the students themselves and their caregivers, just like seasoned educators, may have difficulty separating second language issues from learning difference and disability issues and other issues and so cannot state what should be done on their behalf, especially when English is their second language. Add caregiver distrust or misunderstanding of the school system, and the result may be caregivers and students adamantly demanding, supporting, or acquiescing to incorrect determinations and placements.

MISIDENTIFICATION AND MISPLACEMENT OF STRUGGLING EL STUDENTS

Unfortunately, it appears the U.S. education system makes many incorrect determinations about struggling EL students. We know that schools have identified approximately 14.7% of EL students as also having a learning disability under IDEA (dual identified students), which is about 713,000 students. By comparison, approximately 12% of the general population have been identified as having a learning disability (U.S. Department of Education Statistics, National Center for Education Statistics, 2018).[1] Neither of these statistics includes additional students who receive support services under Section 504 of the Rehabilitation Act of 1973. Since there is no physiological link between learning disabilities and the need to learn English as a second language, some other factors are influencing the higher rate at which educators determine that individual EL students have a learning disability. Further, studies report that EL students are both over- and underrepresented in special education and that the variation in representation levels as compared to the general student population often depends on grade level and other contextual factors (Artiles,

Rueda, Salazar, & Higareda, 2005; Greenberg Motamedi et al., 2016; Rueda & Windmueller, 2006; Sullivan, 2011; Sullivan & Bal, 2013; Zehler, Fleischman, Hopstock, Pendzick, & Stephenson, 2003).

The misdiagnosis and then misplacement of EL students in special education programs when they do not have a learning disability, and their misplacement only in general education classes without special education supports when they do indeed have a learning disability, appear to result from many factors. These misdiagnoses and misplacements can occur even when the EL student is experiencing reasonably good curriculum and pedagogy in their general education classes. One factor is the difficulty of understanding the extent to which an EL student's struggles are due to the additional work that an EL student does to learn English as a second language, which slows their literacy development progress as compared to a similar native English speaker who is learning to read and write in English. Is it a little, some, a lot? And to what extent is any additional level of slower progress due to a learning disability, as opposed to one or more other factors, including low-quality instruction? This difficulty in knowing what range of progress should be expected as typical both generally for EL students and for each individual student has been shown to lead to the underrepresentation of EL students in special education, especially in earlier grades (Counts, Katsyannis, & Whitford, 2018; Zehler et al., 2003). Teachers in these early grades have been shown to wait to refer EL students for a special education evaluation until they can better communicate with the EL students in English, especially when the EL student's caregivers are also English learners (Shifrer, Muller, & Callahan, 2011). This waiting to diagnose for a learning disability may occur more often and for a longer period when the teacher does not speak the EL student's home language, if for no other reason than to ensure that the results of the disability diagnostic tests—usually given in English—are accurate (Shifrer et al., 2011). A second factor is educators' frustration at their long-term EL (LTEL) students' lack of progress; they may place them in special education classes, in an (to our judgment, misguided) effort to help them, because nothing has yet worked to enable them to be successful in school. This "last resort" placement results in the overrepresentation of LTEL students in special education, especially in high school (Sullivan, 2011).

Another factor in the misdiagnosis of EL students as having, or conversely not having, a learning disability is that the many possible reasons for an EL student's struggles are neither discrete nor static. Instead, the causes are mutually affecting or intersectional and can change over time. For example, misdiagnosis can result from educator misunderstandings. Researchers who critically examine racial disproportionality in special education placements, a scholarly lens sometimes referred to as Disability Critical Race Theory or DisCrit (Annamma, Connor, & Ferri, 2013), contend that this disproportionality results, in often large part, from systemic racism based on an inaccurately simplistic view of the relationship between disability, race, and school and societal contexts. This systemic racism, they contend, emerges from the typical process of disability diagnosis and remediation, which focuses primarily on deficits in individual students, with little consideration of the beliefs and practices of educators and members of society that promote viewing some students as inherently different (or worse) and then blaming these students as the sole cause of their struggles (Annamma, Morrison, & Jackson, 2014; Blanchett & Schealey, 2016). Instead, they continue, we must view disability determinations and remediation as at least partially constructed and influenced by inaccurate beliefs and norms about race that pervade people generally, including, of course, school personnel (Annamma, Morrison, & Jackson, 2014; Blanchett & Schealey, 2016). In other words, we must critically examine the extent to which we view typical White, middle- and upper-class behaviors as normal (as well as male, heterosexual, cisgendered, and native English-speaking behaviors, among others).

The danger is that this normalization process has a flip side. Logically, if these behaviors are "objectively normal" in all circumstances, then other behaviors, especially when done by students of color, whose home language is not English, and who are eligible for free or reduced-price lunch, must be or should be considered "inherently abnormal" and in need of fixing. Extending this misplaced logic further, fixing these "inherent abnormalities" must focus on fixing the student as these "misbehaviors" or the lack of school success are most likely the result of either cultural or physical deficits that require changes only in students and their individual education program, and not changes in the beliefs and practices of the educators and the schools (Blanchett & Schealey, 2016). For example, researchers have documented that more physically obvious disabilities or low-incidence disabilities, such as autism, visual impairments, and hearing impairments, are designated at about the same rates across races (Sullivan & Bal, 2013). However, researchers have also documented that designations of more subjective or less obvious disabilities, such as specific learning disabilities, intellectual disabilities, and some speech and language impairments, occur at a significantly higher rate among students of color than among White students and among EL students than native English speakers (Artiles et al., 2005; Sullivan, 2011; Sullivan & Bal, 2013). Applying a DisCrit lens to the IEP or 504 plan process for a struggling EL student as a means for understanding these conflicting disability rates suggests that educators should consider all the intertwined influences, including the general education curriculum, pedagogy, resources, and teacher skills; cultural differences between the student's family and the school; the student's individual English proficiency and prior schooling; and the extent of systemic and individual beliefs and practices that are implicitly biased or explicitly racist, to at least the same extent to which they consider a learning disability. Then, having done this fuller examination, the support plan for the EL student must be a holistic response that includes acknowledgment of and supports for improvements related to *all* the relevant contributing factors.

In short, two-way accountability enables a good fit between each student and the schooling system. Schools must be accountable to students and their families for providing the resources and supports needed to do the hard work of learning (especially in a new language) and then, once these are provided, the schools can look to the student and caregivers to ensure that they are meeting their responsibilities as well. This level of diagnosis and support determination can be a daunting, though necessary, task as sorting out influences such as the extent of systemic racism, as well as other biases, will require the additional work of collecting and analyzing data to discern patterns in outcomes across large groups of students, often referred to as equity audits or as organizational change to promote equity (Dowd & Liera, 2018; McKenzie & Scheurich, 2004). Yet few districts and schools (or states) have systems and processes for collecting, analyzing, and using these data to inform their everyday practices.

CHANGING ACHIEVEMENT AND CONTEXTS FOR EL AND DUAL IDENTIFIED STUDENTS K–12

Further complicating matters are the results of a recent study (Haas, Tran, & Huang, 2016) that suggests the degree and type of struggles EL students face generally changes from elementary school to secondary school. The minimum level of academic English fluency needed for RFEP and exiting an English support program, and the level of academic English fluency needed to succeed in subject matter content classes, is much greater in secondary school than in elementary school (Haas, Tran, & Huang, 2016). In our study, we compared the English language proficiency (ELP) scores of EL students to their scores on state standardized content tests in math and English language arts (ELA) in Arizona and Nevada, two states with very different approaches to EL support programs and with different ELP and state content tests during the study period. We examined how high an EL student had to score on their ELP test to have at least a 50% probability of passing their math and ELA content tests at least once during the next 2 school years. We wanted to know if there was a difference in this probability between students taking their ELP test in 3rd grade and students taking their ELP test in 6th grade. We picked these grade levels because the English literacy demands are different. In 3rd grade, students, both EL students and native English-speaking students, are expected to be just finishing learning how to read. By 6th grade, all students are expected to know how to read well enough that they can read to learn new content, to have moved from "learn to read" to "read to learn." Thus, the English literacy demands for the students starting in 6th grade are considered greater than those of students starting in 3rd grade.

The results from Arizona and Nevada were quite similar: EL students had to score much higher on their ELP tests in 6th grade than in 3rd grade to have at least a 50% probability of passing their math or their ELA content tests (Table 2.1). Third-grade students could score below the minimum level of English fluency required for RFEP and exiting their EL support program and still have

Table 2.1. Difference between the minimum ELP score for reclassification and the score needed for at least a 50% probability of passing the state content test in ELA and math in at least one of the subsequent 2 years in Arizona and Nevada.

	Grade 3		Grade 6	
State	ELA	Math	ELA	Math
Arizona	-29	-15	+15	+46
Nevada	-25	-46	+41	+1

Note: For this analysis, EL students took their state's ELP test in 2009–2010 and their state's content tests in ELA and math in 2010–2011 and 2011–2012 (adapted from Haas, Tran, & Huang, 2016, Figure 1).

Table 2.2. Probability of passing the state content test in ELA and math in at least one of the subsequent 2 years when scoring at the ELP proficiency level for reclassification in Arizona and Nevada.

	Grade 3		Grade 6	
State	ELA	Math	ELA	Math
Arizona	87	69	32	15
Nevada	83	88	14	49

Note: For this analysis, EL students took their state's ELP test in 2009–2010 and their state's content tests in ELA and math in 2010–2011 and 2011–2012 (adapted from Haas, Tran, & Huang, 2016, Tables 3–6).

at least a 50% probability of passing their state content tests. In contrast, EL students in 6th grade had to score much higher than the minimum level of English fluency for RFEP and exiting their EL support program to have the same 50% probability of passing their state content tests (Table 2.2).

Tables 2.1 and 2.2 show that when EL students in 3rd grade were exited from their EL support programs because they scored at or above the minimum levels for RFEP on their state ELP test, generally, they were ready for academic success in their English-dominant or English-only general education classes in 4th and 5th grade. In math, for example, 3rd grade EL students who scored at the minimum RFEP level on their ELP test had a 69% probability in Arizona and an 88% probability in Nevada of passing their state standardized math content test at least once in 4th or 5th grade (Table 2.2). However, the story for 6th grade EL students was much different. In math, when 6th grade EL students scored at the minimum RFEP level they had just a 15% probability in Arizona and 49% probability in Nevada of passing their state standardized math content test in 7th and 8th grades (Table 2.2). It appears that most 6th grade EL students were not ready for academic success in general education classes in 7th and 8th grade even though they had been reclassified as being "fluent English proficient" or RFEP. Thus, we must view secondary EL students' literacy and academic struggles differently than we do those of elementary EL students and treat them differently as well.

Tables 2.1 and 2.2 show that the academic fluency demands in middle school are much greater than those of elementary school, which further suggests that the struggles of EL students in secondary school will likely be greater and perhaps occur more frequently than the struggles of elementary school EL students. Further, adolescent EL students often deal with other issues that influence their academic achievement that elementary EL students do not deal with. These issues include greater sensitivity to differences with their peers and additional family obligations, including greater familialism—the idea that family support comes before individual success—which researchers contend occurs more frequently in Latino and other non-European-based cultures than in European-based ones (see, e.g., Comeau, 2012). In addition, teachers in middle and high school generally are not trained to teach students how to read and write at the most basic level, even though secondary EL students still need this type of teaching if they are to become fluent in the additional subject matter specific genres they encounter. In short, effective strategies that worked to support EL students to be academically successful in elementary schools will likely not be sufficient for secondary EL students. Similarly, the determination of whether a struggling secondary EL student has a learning disability and the extent to which their struggle is due to their learning disability as well as all the other possible influences will need to be different than that determination for an elementary EL student.

Relatedly, the trends in over- and underrepresentation of EL students in special education appear to be due to three intersecting issues: understanding how the second language acquisition process impacts learning within early grades when students are learning to read and later when students are reading to learn, understanding other influences on learning—including adolescence, family, culture, and prior schooling—and understanding the manifestations of a true learning disability. Further, the capacity to accurately make this determination and then effectively respond to each child's individual situation must occur at both the individual and systemic levels. Currently, however, at each level, educators and educational agencies (EAs) often lack this capacity to accurately identify and address these heterogeneous and changing needs (Abedi, 2008, 2009).

Beyond identification, our research (Haas, Huang, & Tran, 2014a, b, c; Haas, Huang, Tran, & Yu, 2016a, 2016b; Haas, Tran, Huang, & Yu, 2015) and the research of others (Greenberg Motamedi et al., 2016; Thompson, 2015) suggest that dual diagnosed students (those designated as EL students and with a learning disability) are not getting the supports they need to succeed in school, especially in middle and high school. We conducted three parallel studies: two analyses each in the states of Arizona, Nevada, and Utah. We followed cohorts of EL students in each of the states over 6 years—from 2006–2007 through 2011–2012—and assessed their progress in English proficiency as well as academic content knowledge in English language arts (ELA) and math, as measured by their state standardized tests. We analyzed three cohorts of EL students, one from kindergarten through grade 5, one from grade 3 through grade 8, and one from grade 6 through grade 11. For each grade-level cohort in each state, we tracked the progress of the EL students as a group and by eligibility for special education services, as well as by their level of English language proficiency at the start of the study, eligibility for free or reduced-price lunch (as a proxy for low-income status), and gender.

For each grade-level cohort for each state, using each state's own standardized tests and criteria for RFEP, we conducted two types of analyses, each the inverse of the other. For the first analysis, summarized in Table 2.3 (Haas, Huang, & Tran, 2014a, b, c), we calculated which EL students scored high enough to RFEP and which EL students did not during the 6-year period and then compared the percentage of EL students eligible for special education services in each group: the group that was RFEPed and the LTEL students who were not. In the second analysis, summarized in Table 2.4 (Haas, Huang, Tran, & Yu, 2015; Haas, Huang, Tran, & Yu, 2016a, 2016b), we grouped students by whether they were eligible to receive special education services and then calculated the cumulative percentage of EL students who reached each of three milestones: being RFEPed, passing the ELA content test for the first time, and passing the math content test for the first time during the 6-year study period. We compared the progress rates for EL students who were and were not eligible to receive special education services.

Unsurprisingly in our current educational system, EL students who were eligible for special education services were less successful academically than the students who were not. This difference in performance was consistent across the grade levels and in all three states. What may be surprising is how extensive the struggles of the dual identified students were, especially at the secondary level. The results from the first analysis (Table 2.3) showed that the percentage of EL students eligible for special education services was three to five times higher in the LTEL group than in the RFEP group. Further, the percentage of dual identified students in the LTEL group in the late elementary to middle school cohort (grades 3–8) and the middle school to high school cohort (grades 6–11) were three to four times higher than the percentage of dual identified students in the early elementary cohort (grades K–5). In the two older cohorts, at least one-fourth, and sometimes over half, of the LTEL students were dual identified students.

In the second analysis (Table 2.4), the dual identified students had lower cumulative passing rates on all three tests than their EL peers who were not eligible for special education. What was somewhat surprising here was how low the cumulative passing rates were, regardless of grade level, for two of the three states. In Nevada and Utah, in only one group of dual identified students did the RFEP rate exceed 50% (Utah, K–5 cohort, 52%). The remaining cohorts had dual identified RFEP rates below 44%. In Arizona, the dual identified RFEP rates were much higher than those in Nevada and Utah, as were the RFEP rates for the EL only students. The gaps in RFEP rates between the EL only and the dual

Table 2.3. Percent of English learner students eligible for special education (dual identified) by grade-level cohort and language proficiency classification in Arizona, Nevada, and Utah.

Grade Cohort	Arizona		Nevada		Utah	
	RFEP	LTEL	RFEP	LTEL	RFEP	LTEL
K–5	5	13	3	8	4	9
3–8	11	57	5	26	10	28
6–11	14	54	11	33	14	40

Note: This analysis was conducted during a 6-year study period from 2006–2007 to 2011–2012. (adapted from Haas, Huang, & Tran, 2014a, 2014b, 2014c).

Table 2.4. RFEP percentages by grade-level cohort, state, and English learner classification.

Grade Cohort	Arizona		Nevada		Utah	
	EL only	Dual	EL only	Dual	EL only	Dual
K–5	91	77	67	34	74	52
3–8	99	88	85	43	70	37
6–11	96	80	75	39	68	34

Note: This analysis was conducted during a 6-year study period from 2006–2007 to 2011–2012. RFEP means reclassified fluent English proficient. EL only means those EL students who were not designated as eligible for special education services. Dual means those EL students who were also designated as eligible for special education services. (Adapted from Haas, Huang, Tran, & Yu, 2016a, b; Haas, Tran, Huang, & Yu, 2015.)

identified students were also smaller in Arizona than those in Nevada and Utah. Still, the RFEP rates for the dual identified students, even in Arizona, were 12 to 20 percentage points below those of the EL only students.

We were not able to study why Arizona had higher pass rates of dual identified students and also higher percentages of LTEL students who were dual identified than either Nevada or Utah, whose results were more similar to each other. The differences between the results in Arizona and those in Nevada and Utah may have been due to differences in the test difficulty, the curriculum being taught in the EL support programs, or the differences in special education services, among other possible factors. But what did stand out consistently is that EL students who were identified as receiving special education services were struggling, even with these additional services, especially during the middle and high school years. The greater struggles of the dual identified students as compared to the EL only students occurred across the three states with different tests, curricula, school systems, and populations. It seems that fundamental improvements need to be made in how we educate our heterogeneous dual identified students if they are going to succeed (Takanishi & Menestrel, 2017; Wagner, Francis, & Morris, 2005).

WE NEED TO IMPROVE EL AND DUAL IDENTIFIED STUDENT EDUCATION

As a nation and as individual educators, we need to improve our systemic and individual capacities for effectively identifying and supporting EL students at risk for or having a learning difference or disability. For example, districts and states often lack data systems, structures, and procedures that allow them to easily track patterns in the identification, assessment, and support services for dual identified students and thus highlight problems and implement solutions (Burr, Haas, & Ferriere, 2015). To the extent that these data systems do exist, their effectiveness in identifying areas of policy, program, or practice strengths and weaknesses is often hampered by differences in district and state procedures. States differ in their definitions of EL and LTEL students, and some of these definitions differ from those used in federal legislation (Linquanti & Cook, 2013; Thompson, 2015). States, and even districts within many states, also differ in their processes for identifying EL students and placing them in English language development programs as well as in their processes for re-classifying EL students as fluent English proficient and moving them full-time into English-dominant general education classes (Burr, Haas, & Ferriere, 2015; Linquanti & Cook, 2013). They also vary in the extent to which the fundamental approaches they use to educate EL students are guided by the best practice literature (Haas & Gort, 2009). Similar variations in the application of special education procedures can exist down to the level of individual schools (see Linn, 2011). Although special education identification, placement, and exiting are governed by well-established federal laws and regulations, including IDEA, ADA, and Section 504 of the Rehabilitation Act of 1973, the quality of their everyday application with individual students and their families can vary tremendously. The quality and effectiveness of these special education processes can be very low in schools where the dominant communities are people of color, people living in poverty, and people whose home language is not English (Counts, Katsiyannis, & Whitford, 2018). Further, school-, district-, and state-level experts in special education and English learners often work in separate organizational areas and come together mostly for IEP meetings, and less often for the development and implementation of system-wide best practices for EL students at risk for or having a learning difference or disability (Acosta, Rivera, & Shafer Willner, 2008; Gottlieb, 2016; Shafer Willner, Rivera, & Acosta, 2009; Ware, Lye, & Kyffin, 2015). In sum, the separate limitations in the systems for identifying and supporting EL students and students with learning differences or disabilities appear to doubly impact EL students.

Of course, systemic limitations exacerbate limitations in individual educator capacity. Individual educators or teams of educators—most notably classroom teachers and classified staff with expertise in English learners and special education—should have the capacity to understand the learning processes associated with second language acquisition as well as the learning needs of a variety of learning disabilities (Harry & Klingner, 2006, 2014). Educators should have the knowledge and skills needed to distinguish between the variety of possible reasons, already discussed, for the struggles of each individual ever EL student (Chu & Flores, 2011; Takanishi & Menestrel, 2017) and be prepared to adapt the supports so that they will be effective as the academic demands increase and the student's social–emotional development changes from kindergarten through grade 12. These capacities must be added to the content knowledge, child development knowledge, pedagogical skills, and classroom management skills that educators should possess. This is a lot to ask of educators who often work in underresourced schools, but it is not impossible.

Promoting bilingualism and language diversity in addition to strong English literacy abilities for every student benefits not only the individual students but also promotes the prosperity of our communities as a whole (Haas, Fischman, & Brewer, 2014; Ruiz, 1984). However, to meet these goals for our EL students who may have learning disabilities and our dual identified students, many states, districts, schools, and educators will need to make fundamental changes in what they do and how they do it. Fortunately, many best practices are available that can improve the success of struggling ever EL students. There are high-quality pedagogical practices—evidence-based and culturally and linguistically sensitive—for general education classes that can effectively support EL student success, both before and after identification for special education services and during and after classification as an EL student, which can also eliminate inappropriate instruction as a factor in an EL or dual identified student's struggles. With appropriate progress measures and assessment instruments and practices, educators can compare the progress of each ever EL or dual identified student to a true peer rather than to a generic native English-speaking student, increasing the number of accurately identified and properly placed students. Educators can make use of existing collaborative models to bring together the expertise in second language acquisition, special education, and large-scale formative data analysis that already exists, usually in separate departments, to create systemic capacities that are greater than the sum of the capacities of the individuals—and by doing so, actually increase the individual capacities as well. There are a growing number of states that are implementing these improvements, providing motivational examples and lessons to be gained for those coming next.

The rest of this book provides specific details about these practices, models, and resources necessary for making fundamental reforms.

Culturally and Linguistically Responsive Multi-Tiered Support Systems for English Learners

High-Quality Teaching Practices Across the Tiers

with Amanda K. Sanford

English learner and dual identified students, like other students, spend much of their school hours in general education classrooms. Teachers need assistance developing the additional skills and understandings (over and above their deep portfolio of teaching capacities) needed to provide all students in their diverse classrooms with high-quality instruction. Multi-Tiered Systems of Support can structure collaboration among educators and discipline experts to help assess, intervene, and monitor the progress of EL and dual identified students. This chapter will explain how.

As noted in Chapter 2, every region of our country is rapidly diversifying, with the overall ever English learner population growing from approximately 14 million in 1990 to 25.1 million in 2013 (Zong & Batalova, 2015). Ever ELs include both students who presently qualify for federally mandated English language development programs and students who were formerly identified as qualifying for these programs but who have since been reclassified as English proficient (RFEP) and no longer receive those services. This increase in the EL population represents a staggering 86% growth in under a quarter century, with over half of these ever EL students not yet designated as fluent in English. Of the English learner students, 77% were born in the United States (Zong & Batalova, 2015). These students still qualify for federally mandated language assistance programs, English language development (ELD), to access instruction that is often provided only in English. Between 2014 and 2015, 14.7% of EL students were also identified as having a disability (U.S. Department of Education Statistics, National Center for Education Statistics, 2018); these are dual identified students.

Even when an EL student is enrolled in special education, gifted and talented, or other special programs, they typically spend some portion of their day in the general education classroom. Thus, providing effective educational opportunities for EL and dual identified students, as with every other student, begins with and is anchored in high-quality general education instruction (Alton-Lee, 2003; Goe & Stickler, 2008; Goldhaber, 2016). Given the diversity of languages, cultures, and life experiences of EL students, teachers are more challenged than ever to address their range of instructional needs. Further, because they are not yet fluent in academic English and not enough teachers allow EL students to use their combination of languages in class, EL students typically lag behind their native English-speaking (and usually White) peers in academic achievement measures at every grade level (Hemphill & Vanneman, 2011). Also, students receiving special education services typically have lower achievement measure scores than their non–special education peers. For both sets of learners, we often fail to capture the full set of their knowledge in our assessment practices. For example, according to the nation's report card, the National Assessment of Educational Progress (NAEP), in 2017, there was a 37-point difference in 4th-grade reading between EL students and non-EL students and a 40-point difference between students with disabilities and those without disabilities (U.S. Department of Education Statistics, National Center for Education Statistics, 2018). These data reinforce the conclusion that our educational systems are not aligned to equitably support achievement for ELs and students with disabilities or to assess their total reservoir of knowledge. We can conclude that every teacher in every subject at every grade level will have classrooms full of heterogeneous students with a range of achievement levels, and all of these young people need and deserve high-quality instruction *and* the ability to maintain and grow their heritage or community practices. In order to provide high-quality instructional experiences, teachers will need to carefully consider and plan for the unique contexts of English learners and students with dis/abilities. (We acknowledge that the term *disability* is commonly used; however, we choose the more current use of *dis/ability* because it recognizes differing abilities not as an individual trait, but rather as an artifact of our cultural, political, and economic practices [Davis, 1995]. Therefore, unless quoting or referring to a specific legal right or responsibility that uses *disability*, we will use *dis/ability* from this point forward.)

Providing high-quality instruction that enables a wide range of students to each be successful is a daunting task for a classroom teacher (Bettini, Park, Benedict, Kimerling, & Leite, 2016) and, therefore, providing high-quality instruction must be approached as a collaborative, system-wide effort. In order to provide high-quality educational experiences for this heterogeneous group of students, it is essential to understand how their educational needs change as they progress from kindergarten through 12th grade. To accomplish this goal will require new alliances among educators and partnerships with students and their caregivers. These collaborative teams must include experts in key disciplines (e.g., subject matter content, second language literacy development, special education, and culturally responsive pedagogy).

While this charge appears daunting, these collaborative teams do exist and operate successfully in many schools. This chapter describes how using a Multi-Tiered System of Supports (MTSS) structures an integrated system-wide set of instruction, monitoring, and interventions, and how educator and caregiver teams can support the process of making this system effective. MTSS enables teams of educators to provide effectively targeted supports for EL and dual identified students that are integrated with general education, ELD, and special education programs. We describe how to maximize MTSS effectiveness for EL and dual identified students across the three tiers from Tier 1 (core, general education) to Tier 2 (focused group interventions) to Tier 3 (intensive individualized interventions). We then look at students' contexts: language, educational background, culture, life experiences, and personal traits and characteristics. By understanding these aspects of student context, teachers can provide more meaningful and truly democratic instruction. With a better understanding of the unique challenges of EL students in our schools, a culturally and linguistically responsive MTSS will be presented that includes: (1) culturally and linguistically appropriate instruction and interventions, (2) valid and reliable screening and progress monitoring assessments, and (3) data-based problem solving and resources to support this work.

A MULTI-TIERED SYSTEM OF SUPPORTS (MTSS)

This section details the features of the traditional MTSS. In many schools across the nation, students in need of additional support in academics or behavior are referred to a support team (sometimes known as a Collaborative Problem-Solving Team [CPST]) within a framework formerly called Response to Intervention (RTI) and more commonly known now as a Multi-Tiered System of Supports (MTSS).[1] When the Individuals with Disabilities Education Improvement Act (2004) was reauthorized, use of the longstanding discrepancy formula (a significant difference between a child's ability, usually an IQ score, and academic performance) as the criterion to determine a student's eligibility for special education services under the category of Specific Learning Disability (SLD) was discouraged (Griffiths, Parson, Burns, VanDerHeyden, & Tilly, 2007). Instead, a process of analyzing a student's response to scientific, research-based interventions was recommended and has evolved into MTSS (Batsche, Castillo, Dixon, & Forde, 2005; Fuchs & Fuchs, 2006).

MTSS is a prevention-focused model where interventions are matched to students' needs. For all students, but especially when serving EL students, understanding students and their context is critical. Critical components of MTSS include: universal screening, progress monitoring, evidence-based instruction, evidence-based interventions, data-based problem-solving and decisionmaking, shared teaming and leadership, and fidelity of implementation of the evidence-based practices. *Universal screening* involves screening all students at least three times per year to determine which students need additional support. Needing additional support should in no way imply that these students do not have the capacity to learn school content. Rather, the need for additional supports means only that their backgrounds may not have privileged them in the ways of or knowledge expected in U.S. schools.

Students who require additional support to learn foundational skills that will be critical to their future success receive additional *progress monitoring* to evaluate the effectiveness of instructional supports and to match new and additional supports to their need. Instruction and interventions are *evidence-based*, which means that there is rigorous research and/or strong, consistent *effectiveness data* from practice, and educators provide these instruction and intervention practices across three or four tiers of increasingly intensive interventions matched to students' need. School teams, such as a Collaborative Problem-Solving Team (CPST), involve *shared teaming and leadership*. Educators collaboratively engage in planning interventions to target a student's academic difficulties based on a variety of student assessment data (data-based decisionmaking) and reconvene at regular intervals to determine if more intensive support is needed. *Fidelity of implementation* deals with both fidelity at the instructional level and also at the systems level. It refers to the degree to which interventions and features of MTSS are implemented consistently and as recommended (Griffiths, Parson, Burns, VanDerHeyden, & Tilly, 2007).

The MTSS framework is most commonly conceptualized as a triangle divided into three (or sometimes four) tiers (Figure 3.1). All students are provided core evidence-based instruction in general education classes and the idea is that the largest portion of students, approximately 80%, will meet grade-level expectations with this level of support in the core curriculum within general education classes. The 20% of students whose screening data indicate they are at risk of failure or extensive struggles will be provided additional interventions through more intensive instruction (Tier 2). For approximately three-quarters of this 20%, this level of intervention will be sufficient for them to meet grade-level expectations. The instructional focus in Tier 2 is to provide a "double dose" of the same concepts they are learning in their classroom. About 5% of students, those who are far below grade level and/or for whom the Tier 2 intervention was not sufficient to enable them to meet grade-level expectations or make expected gains, will require the most intensive instruction, Tier 3. Tier 3 may include special education. (In four-tier MTSS models, special education is the fourth tier.[2]) Each component of MTSS will be described along with the factors to be considered to ensure the model is culturally and linguistically responsive to the needs of EL students (discussed in a later section). Figure 3.1 provides a diagram of an MTSS model that responds to EL students' cultural and language contexts.

Students who do not make sufficient progress toward instructional targets after receiving these increasing levels of interventions may, at that point, be referred for a special education evaluation.[3] Further, this referral for a special

Figure 3.1. Generic MTSS triangle.

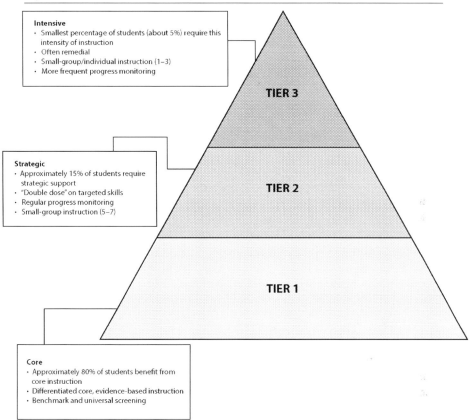

Intensive
- Smallest percentage of students (about 5%) require this intensity of instruction
- Often remedial
- Small-group/individual instruction (1–3)
- More frequent progress monitoring

Strategic
- Approximately 15% of students require strategic support
- "Double dose" on targeted skills
- Regular progress monitoring
- Small-group instruction (5–7)

Core
- Approximately 80% of students benefit from core instruction
- Differentiated core, evidence-based instruction
- Benchmark and universal screening

TIER 3

TIER 2

TIER 1

education evaluation can occur at any point in the progress monitoring and at any tier level; it does not have to wait until a student spends any specific amount of time at Tier 2 or 3 (IDEA, 2004).

While this model is intended to support all students and has been called an instructional equalizer with the potential to narrow achievement gaps, many of its inherent assumptions do not hold true for EL students (Brown & Doolittle, 2008; Haager, 2007). For example, assessments and instruction may not have been designed for or normed and researched with EL students. Further, teachers are often unfamiliar with diverse students' backgrounds (including the impact of issues such as language proficiency in both the native language [L1] and second language [L2], cultural beliefs, life experiences, and personal traits) and so may apply interventions and tier placements based only on what has worked with native English-speaking and White students. In the following section, we explore these important considerations of EL student context and discuss adaptations needed to create culturally and linguistically responsive MTSS.

UNDERSTANDING TODAY'S LEARNERS

Given the achievement gaps in large-scale achievement measures such as NAEP, we know our field is not consistently successful in teaching students coming from diverse backgrounds. It is common to first look to intrinsic student factors for the cause of poor achievement, rather than examining instructional practices. Even educators familiar with the three-tier MTSS triangle often mischaracterize poor student achievement as a deficiency within the student rather than first looking for a deficiency with the Tier 1 instructional practices. For example, we have heard educators state that their classroom (or school or district) is an inverted MTSS 80-15-5 pyramid of success levels since all their students are English learners and a majority of students are performing far below grade level, some students are slightly below grade level, and only a small number of students are at grade level. This might make initial intuitive sense, but it is incorrect. When an entire group of students with similar instructional needs is not meeting grade-level benchmarks, it is not an individual student problem, but rather an instructional problem. This situation demands an examination of core instruction and its alignment to students' backgrounds, contexts, and instructional profiles. Another example is when an educator comments that since the bottom 20% of students within their class are all English learners, the entire EL group should receive Tier 2 supports in the school's MTSS. If the entire population of EL students is characterized as needing additional support, it is important both to provide appropriate instructional supports and to evaluate the core instruction to understand how it is failing EL students. This should not be considered an individual student problem solved only by referral to more intensive instructional Tiers 2 and 3. The problem is not the students, but rather the school's fit for the students. Schools and educators bear the initial and primary responsibility for creating a good fit for their EL and dual identified students. The first critical component of teaching today's diverse range of learners is to ensure educators have the knowledge and skills to create this fit: to know their students, understand their learning and development contexts, and to adjust instruction to their students' specific needs, and, for the purposes of this book, specifically the needs of EL and dual identified students.

It is critical that schools are mindful of both implementing high-quality instruction in general education for diverse learners, and of investigating individual student needs when their achievement is different than their "true peers"—students with similar language profiles, educational experiences, and cultural backgrounds (Brown & Doolittle, 2008). If we do not understand the students' context and figure out how to use their existing knowledge as assets for learning important foundational and academic skills, we doom many to failure. Some systems, lacking an understanding of students' backgrounds, initially attempt to support struggling EL students by placing them into special education programs, even when eligibility teams do not have sufficient data to suggest an intrinsic dis/ability. Providing a struggling EL student with intensive, small-group support through special education may seem a reasonable form of catch-all intervention, but in reality this practice is rarely effective. It also results in segregating EL students from necessary general education instruction, which may violate their civil rights (see Chapter 7 for more discussion of legal rights and responsibilities). Recently, the U.S. Department of Education's Office for Civil Rights issued guidance on this practice in a *Dear Colleague* letter about racial discrimination, which is relevant for EL students, who are predominantly students of color. They stated:

> Racial discrimination that leads to inappropriate identification in special education, and the provision of unnecessary special education services and inappropriate placement into more restrictive special education settings, not only unlawfully limits the educational opportunities of individual students who are subject to inappropriate identification or inappropriate placement, but also deprives all students in that school, who are thereby consigned to learn in a discriminatory and more racially segregated environment. (USDOE, 2016a, p. 5)

Though often difficult to do in practice, it is now well accepted that it is both an instructional best practice and a legal obligation to effectively teach EL students in general education classes as well as their ELD support classes; this requires both knowing your students and accurately and consistently differentiating between difference and dis/ability.

Distinguishing difference from dis/ability is a complex process and, to reiterate, hinges on a student first receiving effective and appropriate education in the general education setting (Collier, 2005; Figueroa & Newsome, 2006; Klingner & Eppolito, 2014). To avoid inappropriate placement, all instruction must be aligned to EL students' level of language proficiency and connect to their cultural and experiential backgrounds. The process of targeted, appropriate instruction and interventions and regular progress monitoring provides important data to assist in determining who may ultimately need a special education referral. Even if a student is found eligible for special education services, their academic progress will also be influenced by the quality of instruction they receive in their general education classes, which is also a legal requirement under the Least Restrictive Environment (LRE) provision in IDEA (2004). (A full discussion of the legal rights of EL and special education students and the responsibilities of educators is presented in Chapter 7.) We have found MTSS to be an effective whole school approach to providing high-quality education for EL students who experience academic difficulties, when the traditional approach of MTSS is adapted for their specific contexts.

MULTI-TIERED SYSTEM OF SUPPORTS FOR ENGLISH LEARNERS: UNIQUE CONSIDERATIONS

MTSS begins in Tier 1 with general education classrooms that utilize evidence-based instructional practices and are culturally and linguistically responsive, inviting every student to engage in meaningful, rewarding learning in a caring and nurturing environment. All students, from kindergarten children to young adult high school seniors, deserve to be seen as capable learners. All students can be brilliant in their own unique ways (see Goodman, 2018). Consequently, classrooms must be welcoming and safe places in order to nurture students' gifts. Teachers must know their students and care about them if they are to empower them to grow and achieve at high levels. Further, teachers must provide the explicit instructional support that allows a broad range of learners to be successful, including the integration of all four language domains (listing, speaking, reading, and writing), direct and interactive approaches to teaching literacy, provision of English oral language development, and high-quality instruction in the components of reading (Project ELITE, Project ESTRE²LLA, & Project REME, 2015). These features are discussed in more detail later in this chapter.

Classrooms that are culturally and linguistically responsive invite students to explore, engage and interact with all their linguistic resources in authentic activities. They may have classroom staples such as libraries filled with colorful books that represent the students in the room; display texts in multiple languages; keep tubs of journals and portfolios documenting evidence of emerging writing practices about children's lives and their classroom projects out for easy access; and display collages of fabrics from student's cultures as a colorful visual backdrop. Aisles are kept clear to provide easy access to all students, including those that may have mobility challenges. These classrooms and school spaces invite students to learn in a variety of active ways that are anchored in content-based conversations (Fisher, Frey, & Rothenberg, 2008; Haas, Goldman, & Faltis, 2018). These classrooms promote continual literacy and content knowledge development and can occur in middle and high schools as well as elementary schools (see Faltis & Coulter, 2008; Goodman, 2018; Nieto, 2010).

Within each classroom, however, some students may need additional more explicit and systematic instruction to learn academic skills. The instructional interventions and framework that we describe are a powerful approach to supporting learners with more intensive instructional support needs. It should not be misconstrued, however, that the explicit and systematic instruction that characterizes effective intervention is provided to the exclusion of rich content and literacy opportunities. Students who require extra support must continue to engage as full members of a classroom, and they should also receive supplemental intervention support to accelerate their learning. After all, beautiful literature is experienced in its fullness when students can read it independently (as well as having choices in what they read). In the following sections, we highlight factors to learn about students that help create inclusive classrooms that respect and respond to all learners.

The Context: Know Your Students

The variety and complexity of students' backgrounds and experiences means learning must be situated around students' social-contextual factors and backgrounds in order to allow them access to learning in U.S. schools. As discussed above, we know that EL students underperform in many academic skills as compared to native English-speaking students.[4] Unless you believe that EL students are simply genetically inferior to monocultural students, it is essential to understand student-level factors that facilitate or impede achievement—in other words, we need to get to know our students if we are to teach them effectively.

In MTSS, when any students' academic progress in the Tier 1 general education setting is consistently below grade-level benchmarks, they are typically referred first to an intervention team. If the team determines the student is not making adequate progress in this Tier 1 core instruction, the student receives Tier 2 interventions (the double dose) and their progress is closely monitored. If Tier 2 instruction, including perhaps multiple rounds, has not conferred the expected benefits, the student is referred to an individual problem-solving team. This team is charged with documenting background information, identifying the problem, planning appropriate support, and monitoring progress. The Collaborative Problem-Solving Form (CPSF) (Appendix) is an organizational tool for teams to document the critical data needed to appropriately support all students, but particularly EL students. One key data component on the CPSF is caregiver and student interviews, a simple, though often overlooked, strategy for getting to know our students and their families. The following sections delve more deeply into five important student factors that should be examined, specifically: language, educational background, cultural experiences, life experiences, and personal traits and interests (Figure 3.2). We offer this in acknowledgment of the need for culturally sustaining pedagogies and practices throughout our educational system, defined as follows:

> [C]ulturally sustaining pedagogy seeks to perpetuate and foster—to sustain— linguistic, literate, and cultural pluralism as part of the democratic project of schooling. (Paris, 2012, p. 95)

The CPSF, found in the Appendix, will help teams collect the data discussed in the remainder of this chapter.

Language

Language is a unique gift that makes one human; it shapes the way we view our world and how we think. For all peoples, the cultural values and beliefs of their community—commonly referred to as one's worldview—is found in its

Figure 3.2. Five things to know about your students.

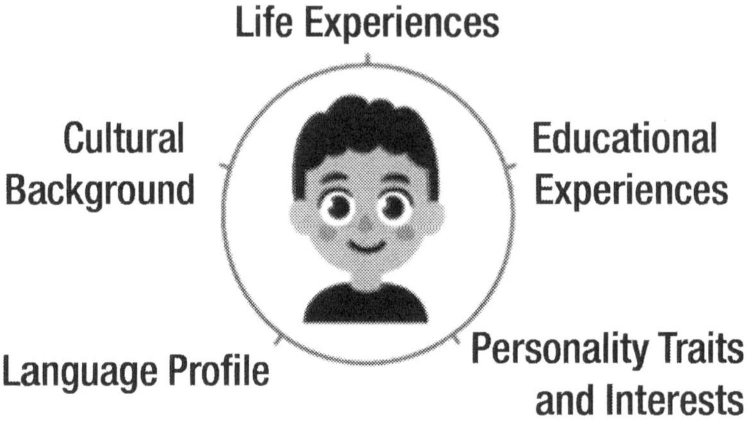

Life Experiences

Cultural
Background

Educational
Experiences

Language Profile

Personality Traits
and Interests

language (Keehne, Wai'ale'ale Sarsona, Kawakami, & Au, 2018). It has been said that language is a verbal expression of culture. Thus, acquiring a language can have profound effects on the learner. This is particularly true for EL students who enter school with varying levels of their heritage or native language and English. We must understand the challenges that beset EL students as they acquire their languages, the impact of early dual language exposure, and the cognitive demands inherent in learning new content in one or both languages as the student is developing, in order to provide appropriate instruction.

Recent advancements in brain research contribute to a deeper understanding of language and the bilingual brain. Petitto et al. (2012) found that babies from birth to around 4 months of age can discriminate the smallest building blocks of language, or phonetic units or sounds, such as "ba" and "da," from any language found in the world. By about 14 months of age, they lose this ability and focus on the phonetics of the language they have been exposed to—their native language. Early exposure to multiple languages seems to provide a "bilingual advantage" and perhaps a "perceptual wedge" that lengthens the timeline and capacity to discriminate phonetic units that, in monolingual children, is hardwired at about 14 months of age. Early bilingual language exposure, particularly before the age of 3, appears optimal for dual language development (Kovelman & Petitto, 2002).

Children exposed to two languages from birth appear to achieve typical language milestones in both languages. In contrast, later exposure to a second language, after the age of 3, changes the brain's neural organization with specific areas of the brain forming for each language. Kovelman, Baker, and Petitto (2008) studied the impact of early first bilingual exposure on literacy and found a positive effect on reading and phonological awareness in both languages. Late bilinguals (exposed between the ages of 3 and 9), on the other hand, were still catching up in reading and speaking as compared to monolingual peers as many as 7 years after second language exposure. Understanding that the time it takes for children to develop mastery of multiple languages relates to both how early and the extent to which they were exposed to English (or any other second language) is critical to setting realistic expectations and in deciding which children present with typical or atypical bilingual development.

As they do in developing their first language, children acquiring a second language progress through five predictable stages with varying timelines for each child as they develop two language registers (i.e., levels of formality). For school purposes, we generally discuss two registers: informal/social and formal/academic. While children can develop initial informal oral fluency fairly rapidly, it takes much longer, including many years of explicit language instruction, to develop the more complex structures of formal/academic languages. Pause to think about the many years of literacy training we provide students from kindergarten through high school and often through graduate school in all four domains (listening, speaking, reading, and writing) in order for them to be strong writers and speakers and thinkers in just one academic discipline in their native or home language. Now, imagine doing that when English is your second language or in two languages simultaneously. When we think about learning to be literate in this way, we expect *at least* 6 years for an EL student to reach formal academic fluency in English (Hakuta, 2011; Hakuta, Butler, & Witt, 2000; Thomas & Collier, 2003), and we are pleasantly surprised in the rare instances when an EL student's progress is more rapid. Figure 3.3 identifies the five stages of second language acquisition and describes the learner characteristics and appropriate instructional strategies at each stage of proficiency.

Translanguaging. Translanguaging is the practice where students use their linguistic resources in one language to understand and communicate in another language through strategies such as code-switching, translating and interpreting, and language brokering (Daniel & Pacheco, 2017). In English-only settings, multiple language knowledge is seldom valued or leveraged as a learning tool. This has to change. Instead, educators must understand that by mediating multiple language use, teachers facilitate deeper learning. This is accomplished by first understanding students' language use in their homes and communities and leveraging these experiences. In many cases, students frequently interpret for family members in business transactions, for healthcare purposes, and in the community at large. Many are also skilled in interpreting letters and other written communication. Knowing the linguistic resources the students use in their communities, teachers can then utilize, reinforce, and strengthen students' translanguaging abilities at school. Perhaps the most important aspect of translanguaging, however, is to value students' multiple

Figure 3.3. Second language use across the language development stages.

Stage	Learner characteristics	How will they gain language?	Do they understand me?	What can they do?
1	Can be silent for an initial period Recognize basic vocabulary and high-frequency words May begin to speak with few words or imitate	Multiple repetitions of language Simple sentences Practice with partners Use visual and realia model Check for understanding Build on cultural and linguistic history	Use instructions such as: listen; line up, point to, list; say; repeat; color, tell, touch, circle; draw, match, label	Use gestures Assistance from other native speakers High-frequency phrases Common nouns Basic needs Survival language
2	Understand phrases and short sentences Beginning to use general vocabulary and everyday expressions Grammatical forms may include present, present progressive, and imperative	Multiple repetitions of language Visual supports for vocabulary Preteach content vocabulary Link to prior knowledge	Present and past tense School related topics Comparatives/ superlatives Routine questions Imperative tense Simple sequence words	Routine expressions Simple phrases Subject–verb agreement Ask for help
3	Increased comprehension in context May sound proficient but have social (not academic) language Inconsistent use of standard grammatical structures	Multiple repetitions of language Use synonyms/antonyms Use word banks Demonstrate sample sentences Link to prior knowledge	Past progressive tense Contractions Auxiliary verbs/verb phrases Basic idioms General meaning Relationship between words	Formulate questions Compound sentences Use precise adjectives Use synonyms Expanded responses

(Adapted from Brown, Ortiz, & Turner, 2016)

Figure 3.3. Second language use across the language development stages. (continued)

Stage	Learner characteristics	How will they gain language?	Do they understand me?	What can they do?
4	Very good comprehension More complex speech with fewer errors Engages in conversation on a variety of topics and skills Can manipulate language to represent their thinking but may have difficulty with abstract academic concepts Continues to need academic language development	Multiple repetitions of language Authentic practice opportunities to develop fluency and automaticity in communication Explicit instruction in the use of language Specific feedback Continued vocabulary development in all content areas	Present/perfect continuous General and implied meaning Varied sentences Figurative language Connecting ideas Tag questions	Range of purpose Increased cultural competence (USA) Standard grammar Solicit information
5	Communicate effectively on a wide range of topics Participate fully in all content areas at grade level but may still require curricular adjustments Comprehend concrete and abstract concepts Produce extended interactions to a variety of audiences	May not be fully English proficient in all domains Have mastered formal and informal language conventions Multiple opportunities to practice complex grammatical forms Meaningful opportunities to engage in conversations Explicit instruction in the smaller details of English usage Focus on "gaps" or areas still needing instruction in English Focus on comprehension instruction in all language domains	Analyze, defend, debate, predict, evaluate, justify, hypothesize, synthesize, restate, critique	May not be fully proficient across all domains Comprehend concrete and abstract topics Communicate effectively on a wide range of topics and purposes Produce extended interactions to a variety of audiences Participate fully in all content areas at grade level but may still require curricular adjustments Increasing understanding of meaning, including figurative language Read grade-level text with academic language support Support their own point of view Use humor in native-like way

(Adapted from Brown, Ortiz, & Turner, 2016)

language abilities rather than overlooking or negating them when emphasizing or requiring only English.[5]

Educational Background

In 2010, Common Core State Standards (CCSS) were created to provide instructional consistency across the states. Yet we know that students' educational experiences vary greatly among districts and schools. Educational differences are particularly striking when the student has immigrated here. General information may be available from students' records, but formal records will likely provide an incomplete picture. Also, it is not always possible to acquire a student's educational file. In both cases, parents, other relatives, and caregivers can be great sources of information. The CPSF allows teams to document relevant background information on all aspects of a student's educational experiences, including preschool. It is important to know whether EL students have received rigorous and consistent formal English language development (ELD) programs and native language instruction. What follows is a discussion of the various types of educational experiences that may need to be considered in understanding an EL student's educational history.

English language development instruction. It is important to know the type and quantity of prior English language development instruction a new EL student has experienced. When enrolling any student into one of the nation's public schools, a requisite Home Language Survey asks several questions about language use in the home. If a family answers that a language other than English is spoken in the home, the child will be administered a state-approved English language proficiency (ELP) assessment. If they meet the criteria for second language supports (usually not scoring sufficiently high on the ELP assessment for their grade level), they will receive instruction in English language development. These ELD programs are funded by Title III of the Every Student Succeeds Act (ESSA, 2015b). Title III provides federally funded state formula grants for supplemental language programs and services aimed at improving the English language proficiency and academic achievement of EL students. Once qualified, students are automatically enrolled in the program and parents are notified. Parents have the right to refuse services if they so desire. EL students will stay in the ELD program until they meet the reclassification criteria, which, like the initial placement, is typically heavily dependent on their scores on a state ELP assessment. EL students may be in an ELD program for 1 year up to many years, with students considered long-term ELs (LTELs) if they are in an ELD program for 6 or more years.

While every district and school must provide their EL students these language services, the particular instructional model is left to the discretion of each state and district.[6] These programs and services are commonly referred to as English Language Development (ELD) or (formerly) English

Figure 3.4. English language development instructional models.

ELD Model	Description	Comments
Traditional ESL/ELD pull-out	The instructional goal is to build communicative competence; skill-based and task-oriented lessons focus on meaning over form	Content is often watered down; curriculum is inauthentic and disconnected from classroom content; instruction is in a segregated setting
Content-based ELD pull-out	The instructional goal is to prepare students for grade-level curriculum. Language and content learning are linked, greater focus on academic vocabulary and overall academic achievement	Language learning is linked to content learning; vocabulary needed in core curriculum explicitly taught; instruction is in a segregated setting
ELD push-in to general education classroom	Small-group ESL/ELD instruction occurs in the general education setting, often a separate curriculum is taught,	EL students are not removed from their classroom during essential learning time; students often feel more connected to their classroom and peers; may be difficult to appropriately group students if there is a range of language proficiencies
Co-teaching (general and ELD teacher)	Teachers instruct side-by-side to both grade-level content and ELD standards within a general education classroom; each is responsible for their area of expertise; equal instruction and responsibility are key	Sometimes one teacher may prefer to be lead instructor over the other; good communication between the partners is essential

as a Second Language (ESL). In general, there are four instructional models used to teach ELD. These models are described in Figure 3.4 and include: (1) traditional ESL/ELD pull-out; (2) content-based ELD pull-out; (3) ELD push-in to general education classroom; and (4) co-teaching (general and ELD teachers).

As the field has progressed, the focus has moved from traditional models focusing on improving conversational English to increasing a student's academic language and content achievement. More and more ELD instruction has moved to the co-teaching model in which a general education teacher and an ELD specialist plan together and then teach at least part of the time in the same classroom. One benefit of co-teaching is that a greater number of general education teachers are learning about second language acquisition and best practices in ELD instruction. Further, including all students in instruction benefits English learners and native English-speaking peers. English learners benefit because they are not segregated from their peers, and native English-speaking students benefit because they receive language supports that they also may need to develop their own mastery of the English language. One thing is clear—no matter the program model, becoming proficient in a second language takes time. Robust research suggests "even the most effective programs require five to six years to bring English learners to full parity with average native English speakers in English proficiency and in mastery of the curriculum to high standards" (Thomas & Collier, 2003, p. 63).

Native language instruction. Native language instruction programs are shifting perceptions of second language learners as being somehow deficient to a new narrative of language as capital in an empowerment perspective (DeMatthews & Izquierdo, 2018). As with ELD programs, there are several native language models whose goal is to provide access to grade-level content as the students develop their English skills. *One-way bilingual models* provide native language and English content instruction. The programs often begin with 90% native language, 10% English, in kindergarten and progress to 30% native language and 70% English in upper elementary grades. In *dual language models* (also known as two-way immersion models or TWI) instruction is in English and the target second language and students are generally an equal mix of monocultural English and native language students. In this model, most or all of the native language/EL students are speakers of the same native language. It must be emphasized that research shows the academic benefit incurred in this model is most evident beyond the early grades, so schools must commit to providing such instruction at least through elementary grades and preferably into secondary grades. However, it is important to note that it is difficult for students to enter such programs after kindergarten or 1st grade unless they enter the program with grade-level skills in the target, non-English language (e.g., Spanish).

Prior formal educational opportunities. Immigrant EL students may have received formal education in their native country in their home language. While general information may be gathered from students' records, crossing international borders often limits the usefulness of this information. Information is often incomplete, and unfamiliar curricula and pedagogical practices may not be properly interpreted by U.S. teachers. Non-U.S. educational records often provide an incomplete picture and so they should be supplemented with information gathered directly from caregivers and the student.

A NEW IMMIGRANT STUDENT
Several years ago, a 3rd-grade student who had recently arrived from rural Mexico was referred to our school team with reports that "he did not belong in 3rd grade." Examination of the records indicated consistent school attendance in Mexico leaving us puzzled as to why this young man was unable to write his own name or numbers. Two team members met with the family, who reported that during most of the boy's schooling in their village, a years-long teacher strike resulted in very little actual classroom time. Yet even during the times school was in session, his teachers repeatedly asked the family to work with him at home, explaining that he was behind his peers. This was critical information for the team in considering "difference or dis/ ability" and showed that he was struggling even in his native language. After a few meetings with the family, they shared that the boy had fallen out of his walker when he was 8 months old and suffered brain trauma. Unless we had taken the time to build a relationship with the family, it is doubtful we would have learned of this significant event. The child, in fact, had a disability known as traumatic brain injury.

Cultural Experiences

Whichever instructional model EL students receive, the curriculum must link to the knowledge and lived experiences from the students' cultural roots (Bartolomé, 2000, 2004, 2008). It is not enough to provide native language instruction; education must work to empower minoritized students through access to high-quality instruction grounded in their lived experiences. Culture is defined as a set of values, beliefs, behaviors, and worldviews shared by a group of people (Matsumoto, 1996). Language is the way a culture's members learn and express these phenomena. Culture is not static, but a complex interplay between family culture, country of origin culture, and other systems in which the student belongs.

Why is it important for educators to know about students' cultures? Isn't it enough that schools hold an annual Multicultural Night where students and families can share their art, food, and music? While such events are fun, they are not enough; schools must learn about and truly work to understand students' cultural backgrounds, including their beliefs, values, and worldviews, and to reckon with the complex links among language, culture, and content knowledge in order to continually use these elements of thinking as bridges to all aspects of teaching and learning. It is not enough to teach the technical aspects of literacy and math without inviting children into the community of learners by making instruction meaningful. It is critical that children see others who look and sound like them within stories and reading themes for these texts to be understood as relevant to their lives. When they do, they are more likely to read for pleasure and on their own, which research consistently shows will greatly boost literacy development (Krashen, 2004).

Such instruction invites EL students, students with disabilities, and other diverse learners into the center of instruction rather than sentencing them to the margins.

Culturally responsive and culturally sustaining pedagogy. Educators actualize their understanding of students' cultures and experiences by using culturally responsive pedagogy. Gay (2000) describes culturally responsive pedagogy as using the cultural knowledge, prior experiences, and performance styles of diverse students to ensure appropriate instruction for each one. Culturally responsive pedagogy recognizes the importance of including students' cultural references in all aspects of learning (Ladson-Billings, 1994). To act as a culturally responsive educator requires intentional awareness of one's own cultural identity, views about differences, socialized beliefs, norms, and biases, and then a commitment to learning their students' worldviews. Recently, Paris (2012) introduced the concept of *culturally sustaining pedagogy,* writing that educators need to be more than merely responsive to students. Instead, we need to meaningfully value and maintain the practices that students bring with them. Then, using students' own cultural knowledge, we can extend their repertoires to include their home language and English, multiple literacies and cultural practices (Paris, 2012). It is only from this perspective that we can ensure that our learners benefit from the gift of cultural, linguistic, and individual differences. This is crucial in today's political context, where EL and immigrant students can feel particularly vulnerable.

Cultural groups also vary on their views related to disabilities. While it is not possible to list the beliefs of all cultural groups, Figure 3.5 outlines some general guidelines to consider in learning about families' cultural beliefs regarding dis/ability.

INCLUSIVE CULTURAL REPRESENTATION

A popular elementary reading textbook includes a story about citizen rights and women's right to vote. The illustrations do not contain one picture of a person of color, even though the reading discusses the Civil War and the 15th Amendment giving African American men the right to vote. Culturally responsive teachers would understand that the topics of citizenship and voting may be sensitive for some students given the current political context regarding immigration. Planning ways to create a safe environment for students to voice their experiences, perspectives, and views is crucial while ensuring that students know they should not and will not be asked to divulge sensitive legal information (see Goodman, 2018). Students must actively participate in order to learn. So, when topics that impact students' lives appear in the curriculum, they must not be glossed over. To do so only reinforces dominant perspectives. Instead, celebrate multiple voices and views (see Nieto, 2010).

Figure 3.5. Questions to ask yourself about your cultural beliefs and biases.

1. What are some of the values and beliefs you were raised with? To what extent have they changed over time?
2. Can you define your current key beliefs and values? Do you consider these the "norm"?
3. What is your relationship with your family? Who was the primary decisionmaker in your family? Who was the primary decisionmaker regarding education? Was extended family included in your families' activities?
4. What is your faith or spiritual belief? To what extent has it changed over time?
5. Can you identify your own personal biases and assumptions about people with different views and backgrounds?
6. Given your own socialized beliefs, are there any student groups for whom you may need to challenge your views, assumptions, or stereotypes?
7. Have you examined your classroom practices to determine if certain groups of students receive unintended preference?

Life Experiences. Educators need to understand the lives of the students outside of class, especially the lived experiences of their EL and dual identified students. We know that learning occurs beyond the school walls, with each student bringing unique experiences and therefore unique understandings with them to school and the classroom. Ample evidence illustrates children interact with their environment and familial relationships before entering formal school, and they become socialized in those behaviors and practices acceptable to the family/community. These lived experiences not only provide parents opportunity to transmit cultural values and beliefs so the family and community continue to thrive (LeVine, 1977), but also establish prosocial competencies for successful functioning in later years (Ogbu, 1981). Garcia Coll (1990) posits that the developmental goals of marginalized or minoritized families (families who do not come from the dominant culture) will differ from mainstream families (families who come from the dominant culture), influenced in part by culturally determined perceptions and behaviors. Thus, educators often must make an extra effort to learn about their students whose lives are different from their own or the dominant culture.

Although research on early childhood socialization suggests that differences in childrearing values and practices influence children's school performances in classrooms, the cultural knowledge, skills, and abilities shared among members of socially, culturally, and economically marginalized groups often go unrecognized, unacknowledged, and unappreciated by teachers and schools. Curriculum reviews and observations in many classrooms highlight that curriculum and teachers often assume mainstream knowledge and

---

MULTIPLE CODES OF CONDUCT

Unlike middle- and upper-class Euro-American families, families marginalized by race, ability, housing, police and educational institutions (among others) often have incorporated a set of conscious and unconscious adaptive strategies or defense mechanisms for how to safely act when they are in the dominant culture and outside of their home or personal culture. This additional "code of conduct" includes many unspoken rules that members of the dominant or "normalized" communities could ignore. The *Negro Motorist Green Book*, for example, was published from 1936 to 1966 during the time of Jim Crow laws as a guide for African American travelers, identifying places and services friendly to African Americans as they drove from New York to the rest of the country. African Americans had to know the places where they would be refused service or possibly assaulted for entering. This additional knowledge was not necessary for White travelers.

The *Negro Motorist Green Book* is an example of explicit additional knowledge; however, there are many examples of implicit additional knowledge that minoritized and marginalized communities regularly need to learn to be successful in the dominant culture. For example, the values of learning by observation and fostering of resiliency as social capital were meant to support diverse children's ability to navigate the mainstream culture. A description of these unspoken codes and the advantages they provide is presented by Peggy McIntosh in her seminal article, "White Privilege: Unpacking the Invisible Knapsack" (1989). Here, she speaks to the White privilege she is provided because of her race, listing examples to show the unearned entitlement and advantage, and access to social classes, that White people are able to use not due just to the color of their skin but also to the knowledge and skills they learned just from living in their dominant White culture.

---

experiences by all students. It is not uncommon that when some students do not possess this knowledge and these experiences, we default to a deficit view. Instead, we should familiarize ourselves about students' life experiences, beliefs, and values, collectively known as "funds of knowledge" (Moll, Amanti, Neff, & Gonzalez, 1992), and use what we learn to link our students to new learning to create a truly inclusive learning environment. The "funds of knowledge" theory (Gonzalez & Moll, 2002) holds that when teachers view diverse learners' backgrounds from a strength-based perspective, they can access this knowledge while teaching as they would access the mainstream cultural knowledge described earlier. In sum, immigrant and diverse students are not blank slates or empty vessels; rather, they bring rich and varied backgrounds with which they think and reason as they learn the content and social rules they experience in school. Culturally and linguistically diverse students can be successful in U.S. classrooms if their educators link past experiences and ways of knowing to new learning.

Topics related to learning differences and disabilities, like those concerning language and culture, should be represented and embraced in the learning resources and activities.

Invite families and communities as partners. These principles concerning culturally sustaining pedagogy also apply to working with families and communities. In the past, a common view was that culturally diverse families needed to understand the dominant cultural beliefs, attitudes, and behaviors of the school with no consideration of educators needing to learn those of the minoritized families they serve. A concept often discussed in international education, transculturalism, may be a useful consideration here. Transculturalism implies building bidirectional cultural knowledge. Creating spaces for the mutual sharing of cultural knowledge and worldviews will help diminish prevailing stereotypes, myths, and prejudices. All individuals, including educators, hold implicit biases, and a key to acting as a culturally sustaining educator is understanding one's own biases with the idea that recognizing these biases in one's self allows us to reduce the impact of these biases on the children and families we serve. Figure 3.6 suggests questions to ask yourself to consider the root of any implicit biases you may harbor that could create gulfs as you work with diverse families whose lives and cultures are different from your own or the dominant culture.

Personality traits and interests. While the above factors provide context for planning appropriate instruction for diverse students, this last area is perhaps the most important: Learning about a student's personality and interests is a way to understand how they conceptualize their own life and experiences. This is critical because learning builds upon a student's prior knowledge and involves the child's ability to make personal meaning of what they are learning and how this defines their identity—who they are. The wise teacher pays close attention to student beliefs based upon prior learning, including any misconceptions, and recognizes that learning is a continuous process in which students engage with content and others to develop increasingly complex understandings. In some cases, students from a diverse background may feel alienated from school because they are unsure that their interpersonal communication has yielded an understanding of their cultural identity. Research shows, however, that one adult taking an interest in them and developing an authentic relationship can transform the school experience. As the famed developmental psychologist Uri Bronfenbrenner stated, "Every child needs at least one adult who is irrationally crazy about him or her" (1991, p. 2). Even if the child is not one whom you are "crazy about," your understanding of how, for example, poverty may subject a student's family to deep structural inequities gives you a window into the context of how the student is affected by the difficult experiences they may encounter in their daily life.

Figure 3.6. Working with diverse families in the special education process.

1. Identify the family's attitudes, beliefs, and perceptions toward disabilities. Certain disability categories may be new concepts to parents.
2. Take the time to establish a relationship with the family; it takes time and communication to build trust. Communicate with the family on an ongoing basis.
3. Determine the family's home language and consistently communicate in this language with them (through an interpreter, if necessary) if they do not speak or have limited English.
4. Learn the interaction style of the family and consider how to bridge their style with those of the educational team.
5. Schedule meetings at optimal times for the family.
6. Use trained interpreters at all meetings and ensure that they are in attendance for the entire meeting.
7. Identify the key decisionmaker(s) in the child's life.
8. Encourage families to bring an ally with them to meetings as formal meetings and unfamiliar concepts can be overwhelming to them.
9. Learn about the services for children with disabilities in their culture/native country and use this as a bridge to explain services in the U.S.
10. Clearly and concisely explain special education to families and refrain from using jargon. The more precise and concise educators are in English, the better the interpretation will be understood.
11. Orally review parents' rights and responsibilities; provide clear explanation of the principles while allowing time to respond to parents' questions.
12. Determine culturally and linguistically appropriate IEP goals and service delivery.

Thus, educators should prioritize time for authentic dialogue with students in order to successfully engage them in learning. Student engagement is complex and dependent on several factors. Ryan and Deci (2010) identified four key elements that resulted in higher student engagement: (1) autonomy, (2) self-efficacy, (3) relatedness or relationships, and (4) relevance. "Students are much more likely to remember what they have learned" when the tasks are relevant and meaningful (Knight, 2013, p. 231). Learning other individual personality traits such as motivation, self-efficacy, and resilience, also facilitates creating connections. Komarraju and Karau (2005) suggest that matching personality traits to learning environment resulted in improved outcomes. While personality traits such as these were thought to be relatively stable, a recent meta-analysis supports their malleability, particularly before middle age (Roberts & DelVecchio, 2000). Thus, teachers can target strengthening those traits known to be predictors of positive academic outcomes and be able to employ a more dynamic approach of active engagement within a cultural context.

While these aspects of student contexts can be addressed individually, there are two practices that are vital for educators to address the contexts of EL and dual identified students in a holistic manner: culturally responsive pedagogy and family and community partnerships.

USING MTSS TO SUPPORT ALL STUDENTS

Even in the best instructional context where all the above student characteristics are considered and instruction is explicit, aligned linguistically, and culturally relevant, there will be some students who require more support than is available within the general education classroom. Within the context of MTSS, there is a systematic framework of support for students requiring more intensive supports, and this framework begins with valid and reliable universal screening. While these critical features of MTSS (i.e., universal screening, progress monitoring, and research-based instruction) were introduced earlier, here they are described within the context of EL students. Figure 3.7 compares the traditional features of MTSS and the unique considerations of the model for EL students.

We describe how the implementation of each element can be used effectively in instructional programs for EL students.

Universal Screening

Universal screening assessments are brief, easy-to-administer, timed grade-level probes of essential academic skills that are administered to all students usually three times per year (fall, winter, and spring). Curriculum-based measures (CBM) are most commonly used to screen students (Aceves & Orosco, 2014). CBMs assess skills from the curriculum and include a criterion for performance against grade-level peers or established benchmarks. The goal is to identify students who need support beyond what is available in the general education setting.

The benefits of using screening data to identify students needing more support are that decisions are based on data, rather than random teacher observations or anecdotes. There is evidence to suggest that the identification of students for additional support is less biased when using a systematic screening tool and problem-solving process (Griffiths, Parson, Burns, VanDerHeyden & Tilly, 2007). As in all assessment, screening tools must be valid (assess what they claim to measure) and reliable (results are consistent for the student group) for the population assessed (Aceves & Orosco, 2014), and match the language or languages of instruction. Research suggests that CBMs in English are generally reliable and valid for EL students (Baker, Cummings, Good, & Smolkowski, 2007; Kim, Vanderwood, & Lee, 2016; Muyskens, Betts, Lau, & Marston, 2009; Riedel, 2007; Vanderwood, Linklater, & Healy, 2008). Limited

Figure 3.7. Components of MTSS and unique considerations for EL students.

MTSS Components	Definition	Unique Considerations for EL Students
1. Universal screening	Universal screening assessments are brief, valid, reliable grade-level probes to determine appropriate levels of support for each student and are administered usually three times per year	Screening assessment(s) administered in the language(s) of instruction Data are disaggregated by student populations In dual language programs, screening data in both languages should be examined side-by-side to look holistically at the students' literacy skills Assessment instruments are valid and reliable for all student populations, including ELs
2. Evidence-based instruction	Core instructional programs demonstrate positive outcomes on the sample population included in the research	The research evidence on efficacy of instructional programs must include ELs in their research population A rigorous ESL/ELD program is provided to all students who qualify for Title III services All instruction is aligned to the students' language proficiency in the language(s) of instruction Materials used reflect the students' cultural and experiential backgrounds
3. Progress monitoring	Students' progress in target skill(s) is systematically gathered and analyzed, over time to evaluate their response to instruction and interventions	Progress monitoring is administered in the language of intervention EL students' progress is compared to "true peers" Educators maintain rigorous goals and support ELs in making progress toward grade-level standards Assessment instruments are valid and reliable for all student populations, including ELs
4. Evidence-based interventions	Intervention programs demonstrate positive outcomes on the sample population included in the research	The research evidence on efficacy of intervention programs must include ELs in their research population Interventions are recommended to be provided in one language; based on primary literacy instruction, language proficiency, and literacy assessment data

Figure 3.7. Components of MTSS and unique considerations for EL students. (continued)

MTSS Components	Definition	Unique Considerations for EL Students
5. Data-based decisionmaking	A formal process to analyze and evaluate information in planning and implementing effective instruction matched to students' levels of need	EL students' progress must be compared to grade level benchmarks and "true peers" Multiple data sources are used in all languages of instruction Parents may be consulted for background information on child's background, including cultural and linguistic experiences
6. Fidelity of implementation	Systematic monitoring of the degree to which interventions are implemented as recommended	Instruction and interventions must be adjusted to align with EL students' instructional language proficiency and cultural backgrounds Adjustments to evidence-based programs leave core elements in place that are implemented with fidelity
7. Shared teaming and leadership	Educator teams share decisionmaking responsibilities	Decisionmaking teams must include an EL specialist when the target student is an EL Team must include parents in decisionmaking, particularly for special education consideration If families do not speak English or have limited English, use trained interpreters throughout the process Clearly explain special education and all concepts

research also suggests the same is true for CBMs in Spanish for native Spanish speakers and English first language students in dual language programs (e.g. Baker, Cummings, Good, & Smolkowski, 2007).

Screening data can be used to identify students who need support and to provide initial information on appropriate instructional groupings, and it can also be used to evaluate the overall effectiveness of instruction for students. When reviewing and evaluating screening assessment data, it is critical that all data be disaggregated by student groups. That is, analyzing who is represented within the three tiers of instructional need provides an informal program evaluation of core instruction. If the students whose data place them at the bottom 20% of the class are all EL students, then this signifies an instructional problem, not a student problem. In other words, the instruction is likely not aligned with their linguistic and cultural contexts. In sum, typical CBM and other universal screening assessments can be used with EL students so long as educators critically examine the results for patterns that first point to general instructional needs and then the need for individual EL student supports.

Progress Monitoring

As described above, universal screening assessments identify which students may need more support. Once students are supported through targeted instruction or interventions, their growth must be gauged. The same assessments used to screen students are often used as progress monitoring tools. One difference between universal screening and progress monitoring is that growth is measured at shorter intervals, or more frequently based on the intensity of need, to monitor progress (McIntosh & Goodman, 2016). Thus, if students aren't growing as expected, instruction can be adjusted. Second, progress monitoring assessments are administered to match the one or two skills targeted for instruction/intervention instead of assessing a student on multiple skills. A third difference is while screening tools match students' grade level, progress monitoring measures match the approximate level of their instruction or interventions. As with screening assessments discussed earlier, progress monitoring assessments should match the language or languages of instruction and be valid and reliable for the population.

Evidence-Based Reading Instruction:
Helping EL Students Achieve School Success

A core principle of MTSS is that students receive research- or evidence-based instruction, with empirical evidence on its efficacy for that student population (D'Angiulli, Siegel, & Maggi, 2004; Klingner & Edwards, 2006; Saenz, Fuchs, & Fuchs, 2005). This fundamental principle is problematic for EL students, however. We know there are gaps between the reading achievement of EL students as compared to native English-speaking students. The question is: Why? Some researchers attribute this to EL students' lack of access to evidence-based practices in core instruction (Thorius & Sullivan, 2013; Vaughn, Mathes, Linan-Thompson, & Francis, 2005). However, a perusal of the What Works Clearinghouse (/ies.ed.gov/ncee/wwc/) finds very few evidence-based reading programs that include EL students in their research population. Thus, a program that is research-based may not be researched with EL students, and therefore may require adaptations by teachers to be effective in addressing the needs of EL students.

The "Big Five" Components of Reading Instruction and EL Learner Students

In 1997, Congress convened the National Reading Panel (NRP) to review reading research and make recommendations for the instruction of reading. They concluded their review of more than 100,000 studies and issued a report recommending instruction be explicit, systematic, and meaningful and identified five essential components of reading, most commonly known as the "Big Five" (NRP, 2000). This report was criticized for omitting the topic of teaching reading to English learners. In response, in 2002 the National Literacy Panel on Language-Minority Children and Youth was charged with compiling reading research related to English learner students. Their report, *Developing Literacy in Second-Language Learners* (August & Shanahan, 2006), found that the same five essential reading components, or the "big five," identified for English-only students also have positive influences on literacy development for English learner students learning to read in English. Other research reinforces these conclusions (Ehri et al., 2001; Shanahan, 2016). Although the five components are important in the reading instruction of EL students, some adjustments are needed. For example, EL students may need extra focus on the sounds of phonemes not found in their native language. Or, punctuation signs may be different across English and a student's native language. In other words, while instruction in the "big five" is essential, it is insufficient for EL students' success. One overarching area is the need for oral language development, particularly in the instructional language(s). The following sections will discuss the "big five" components of reading instruction and the instructional implications for EL students.

Phonemic awareness. Phonemic awareness (PA) is one predictor of future reading success (Gersten et al., 2007; Linan-Thompson & Vaughn, 2007; Shaywitz, 2003). Early reading research on the components identified by the National Reading Panel showed that 25% of middle-class 1st-graders had difficulty acquiring PA, as did an even greater percentage of EL students (Adams, 1990). The ability to distinguish individual sounds in English may be particularly challenging for EL students when the sounds are not native to their first language (Brown & Ortiz, 2014). The good news is that research shows EL students can develop PA in English before they are fluent in speaking English

(Durgunoğlu, Nagy, & Hancin-Bhatt, 1993; Geva & Zohreh, 2006) but the meaning of the vocabulary used to teach PA may need to be explicitly taught to EL students. Thus, language and literacy opportunities using culturally relevant materials should begin early in a child's school career and not be withheld until students develop some English proficiency.

Students transfer literacy skills from their first language to any new language they are learning. However, the transfer of literacy skills across languages depends upon the similarities and differences between the two, including whether they share an alphabet or not (Peregoy & Boyle, 2000). Further, although the stages of reading develop linearly, because of linguistic similarities and differences between their native language and English, EL students may develop their English skills differently than native English speakers. For some examples, Figure 3.8 presents some differences between the English and Spanish language while Figure 3.9 lists difficult English sounds for native Spanish speakers. This same information could be gathered for other languages your students speak.

Phonics. While phonemic awareness instruction helps children learn the sounds of a language, phonics instruction teaches them the sounds letters make and how to apply this knowledge to sound out words as a beginning strategy for learning to read. However, sounding out words they do not recognize is an abstract process and an ineffective one. If the words are not defined for or by students, decontextualized phonics exercises may actually hamper comprehension (Hoover, Klingner, Baca, & Patton, 2008). Studies suggest reading instruction that emphasizes comprehension along with systematic phonics instruction has positive effects on word reading for EL students (Gunn, Biglan, Smolkowski, & Ary, 2000; Gunn, Smolkowski, Biglan, & Black, 2002; Lesaux & Siegel, 2003; Stuart, 1999; Vaughn, Mathes, Linan-Thompson, & Francis, 2005). Consequently, EL phonics instruction should: (1) follow a defined sequence, (2) explicitly teach skills, (3) teach sets of letter–sound relationships, (4) teach linguistic patterns, (5) bring meaning to the vocabulary words used, and (6) include texts that are decodable (Brown & Ortiz, 2014). A recent study found a double-dose of phonics instruction for kindergarten EL students conferred increased comprehension (Vadasy & Sanders, 2010). When the language is meaningful and content is relevant, EL students are likely benefit from systematic phonics instruction. Therefore, prior to phonics instruction, unfamiliar content and concepts must be pretaught and instructional materials must include characters that look, act, and sound like our students for cultural alignment.

Fluency. Fluency is defined as reading quickly, accurately, and with expression; it is the bridge between word recognition and comprehension. If students can quickly and accurately decode text, known as automaticity, they will better comprehend what they read (Linan-Thompson, Vaughn, Hickman-Davis, & Kousekanani, 2003; Lingo, 2014; Marchand-Martella, Martella, Modderman,

Figure 3.8. Some differences between Spanish and English.

Spanish	English
Phonology	
Syllable-timed language; Spanish speakers flatten or even out the stress	Stress-timed language (some syllables longer; some shorter) where meaning is conveyed through the use of stress, pitch, and rhythm (e.g., "record" as in student files, "record" as in audiotaping)
Multisyllabic words are most common with many fewer monosyllabic words	The general range of syllables is from 1 to 10 with many one-syllable words and many monosyllable words
Only five consonant sounds—r, s, l, n, and d—appear at the end of words	The consonant sounds—v, b, d, t, g, h, j, l, r, w, v, and z—are difficult to pronounce for native Spanish speakers
Grammar	
Spanish word order is generally subject-verb-object, but is more flexible than English, so words can be placed at the end of a sentence for emphasis	English word order is strictly subject-verb-object
The adjective follows the noun as in "el libro verde" (the book green)	The adjective precedes the noun, as in "the green book"
An article reflects the gender of a noun as in "el libro, la mesa" (the book, the table)	Articles do not reflect gender
Orthography	
Spanish uses an upside-down question mark (¿) at the beginning of a question and ends with a right-side-up question mark (?)	English uses one question mark at the end of a question
Spanish uses an upside-down exclamation (¡) mark at the beginning of a question and ends with a right-side-up exclamation mark (!)	English uses one exclamation mark at the end of an exclamatory sentence
A possessive apostrophe is not used: "la bicicleta del muchacho" (the bicycle of the boy)	The boy's bike
Only the first word is capitalized in titles	All important words in titles are capitalized
Days of the week, months of the year, and names of different languages are not capitalized	Capitalize days of the week, months of the year, and names of different languages
Dates are written: el 8 de septiembre de 2018 (the 8th of September of 2018)	September 8, 2018

Adapted from August & Vockley (2002) and Lenters (2004)

Figure 3.9. Difficult English sounds for native Spanish speakers.

- Initial consonants of b, c as in "cinema," g as in "geode," h as in "happy," j as in "jump," p as in "pop," r (does not trill), and v (which is not distinguished from b), w, x, and y
- Final consonant sounds of t, d, k, g, and s
- Digraphs of ch as in "character," dg as in "fudge," sh as in "wash," th as in "the" or "fifth," and wh as in "who, what, when," wr as in "write," kn as in "know," ph as in "phone"
- Letter combinations of -ck, -ght, -nd, -ng, -nt, sc-, sch-, scr-, sk-, sl-, sm-, sp-, spl-, spr-, sq-, st-, str-, sw-, -tch, thr-, tw-
- Some long and some short vowel sounds /a/ as in "ace" or "apple," /e/ as in "eek" or "early," /i/ as in "ice" and "in," /o/ as in "ok" and "on," /u/ as in "use" or "up"
- Vowel combinations ai, ay, oo, ow, ea, oa, ew; ie, oi, oy, ee, ui, au, aw, ough, eigh, and controlled r and re
- Diphthongs au as in "audio," aw as in "paw," ew as in "sew," oi as in "point," ou as in "you," ow as in "owl," oy as in "boy," ue as in "sue"
- R-controlled vowels /ar/ as in "park," /er/ as in "perk," /ir/ as in "quirk," /or/ as in "cork," /ur/ as in "turk"
- Silent letters—gn- as in "gnu," kn- as in "know," -mb as in "dumb," wr- as in "write"
- Word endings -s and -ed (d as in "ended" and t as in "looked")

Peterson, & Pan, 2013). Oral reading fluency (ORF) assessments, where students are assessed for their ability to read passages aloud, are used as a proxy for comprehension, but for EL students, ORF assessments may overpredict their actual comprehension skills (Crosson & Lesaux, 2010; Quirk & Beem, 2012). One likely reason is that gaps in EL students' oral proficiency (ability to talk or converse) and vocabulary knowledge in the instruction and assessment language (English) may negatively impact comprehension (Crosson & Lesaux, 2010). In other words, an EL student's ORF score may result from their ability to sound fluent in English without actually understanding some or much of what they are saying. Proctor, Carlo, August, and Snow (2005) found oral language proficiency or the ability to converse well in English predicted or mediated reading comprehension more than automatic word reading in EL students. EL students with uneven language proficiency, even with good automaticity in sounding out words, may still not comprehend what they read. These students have been, unfortunately, termed "word callers" because they can decode but with little comprehension. This phenomenon can be particularly true for EL students if fluency interventions do not embed language support and comprehension instruction and strategies. Evidence-based fluency interventions include Repeated Readings (Therrien, 2004), Listening Passage Preview (Skinner, Cooper, & Cole, 1997), and Phrase-Drill Error Correction (Begeny, Daly, & Valleley, 2006). Below, the Repeated Reading strategy will be described along with modifications that target both fluency and word meaning thus reinforcing reading for understanding. Denton, Anthony, Parker, and Hasbrouck (2004) suggest that combining fluency- and vocabulary-based strategies can benefit EL students, so these types of language modifications shared below may be useful to include in other fluency strategies.

Repeated readings. The purpose of this strategy is to improve reading rate, accuracy, and prosody. Prosody refers to the ability to appropriately use phrasing, timing, emphasis, and intonation in reading, which is a defining feature of fluency. EL students need instruction and opportunities to practice prosody through meaningful and comprehensible language since both language and comprehension mediate fluency. To use this strategy, choose a text of between 50 and 200 words at the student's independent level and introduce the passage to the student. Additionally, the teacher may choose three to five unknown words to preteach. The student reads the passage orally for 1 minute while the teacher records errors (substitutions, omissions, or insertions) and marks where the student stops. When the student misreads a word or hesitates for more than 5 seconds, read the word aloud and have the student repeat it. If the student asks for help with a word, read it aloud. The student rereads the passage until they read it with fluency. Some modifications for EL students might include previewing the passage and providing background knowledge of the content, giving a quick definition (fast map) when students encounter unfamiliar words, or having students highlight unknown words during subsequent readings. Also effective is asking students to flag (by raising an index finger) unknown words they encounter in their individual or group read-aloud. The teacher provides a quick definition to ensure students comprehend the text, but the quick definition does not disrupt the continued reading. For older students who may be more reluctant to admit to not knowing some words, you may ask them to flag words they think their peers may have difficulty with.

These modifications support both fluency and comprehension by ensuring that unfamiliar content and language are not barriers to reading. To model prosody, teachers may read the passage aloud and ask the students to echo read with the same intonations. Once students have practiced reading with language supports, they will conduct a final hot-read, where the students read the passage, and the teacher listens, records, and marks errors. The students then graph their final reading in red to document their increased fluency as compared to their cold timing. This can be motivating to students, as well as increasing their reading comprehension through the repeated readings. Finally, some kind of check for comprehension, either retelling the passage, answering key questions, or applying a key comprehension skill or strategy, will help ensure that the students understand what they read.

Vocabulary. Most learning is accomplished through language. For EL students, the challenge is learning new concepts in a language they also are in the process of learning. To comprehend text, both conceptual and vocabulary knowledge are required; the two are highly correlated (Baumann, 2009; Helman, 2009). As explained earlier, while students acquire informal conversational language fairly rapidly, academic language vocabulary develops much more slowly and needs to be explicitly taught (Pasquarella, Chen, Gottardo, & Geva, 2014). Swanborn and de Glopper (1999) rank the probability of learning unknown words exclusively through reading at only about 15%, and likely much lower for EL students who are less able to use context clues to guess at unknown words. Readers, in general, must be familiar with about 95% of words in the text to have moderate comprehension (Nation, 2001). Consequently, it is apparent that EL students should be provided with rigorous, grade-appropriate vocabulary instruction beginning at school entry as part of authentic, engaging, and culturally relevant learning activities because vocabulary knowledge begets vocabulary knowledge. In other words, if you have fair comprehension because you understand most of the vocabulary in a text, you can use the context to understand unknown words. Conversely, limited vocabulary knowledge hinders the process of learning new vocabulary through reading because you register fewer of the context clues needed to do so. Plus, if reading is difficult, students often read less. Stanovich (1986) called this phenomenon of a widening gap between good readers and readers who struggle the "Matthew effect." In other words, in reading, evidence supports the phenomenon that the rich get richer and the poor get poorer (Share, McGee, & Silva, 1989; Share & Silva 1987).

It is estimated that by middle school, students must have a vocabulary bank of about 25,000 words to comprehend content-area texts (Graves, 2006). Other findings report that EL students whose vocabulary knowledge is 2 years below that of native English-speaking students' vocabulary often never catch up (Mancilla-Martinez & Lesaux, 2010). EL students generally know fewer words and their word knowledge is often superficial, thus differing from native English-speaking students' vocabulary knowledge in both breadth and depth (Dutro & Moran, 2003; Feldman & Kinsella, 2005). Consequently, as noted above, EL students need consistent, systematic, and explicit vocabulary instruction across the grades to support deep word learning in addition to authentic, engaging, and culturally appropriate learning activities if they are to catch up to the vocabulary levels of their peers, especially in middle and high school. Depth of word knowledge develops through multiple exposures (generally between 8 and 12) in multiple contexts, and for EL students, the opportunity to use the words learned. The key is to continually provide vocabulary support that is within each EL student's zone of proximal development or "Goldilocks" words—not too easy, not too hard, but just right (Baumann & Kame'ennui, 2004).

Vocabulary tiers. One helpful framework for structuring explicit vocabulary instruction is vocabulary tiers, where words are categorized into three tiers (Beck, McKeown, & Kucan, 2002). Tier 1 includes basic words that rarely require direct instruction. These words generally consist of nouns, verbs, adjectives, and early reading words; they rarely have multiple meanings. Tier 2 words are high-frequency words that students will encounter across content domains. Words in Tier 2 should be targeted for direct instruction and include polysemous words (multiple meanings) and descriptive words. Tier 3 words are low-frequency, domain- or content-specific words that are generally taught as students encounter them. The distinction between Tier 2 and 3 words is not always clear and can be dependent on a students' background knowledge. Vocabulary tiers, however, differ somewhat for EL students. Figure 3.10 is an adaptation of Beck, McKeown, and Kucan's (2002) framework that is targeted for EL students. As with instruction in other content areas, be sure to make personal and meaningful connections between new words and students' contexts.

Teaching word family structures. Since the vast amount of vocabulary required in school and found in texts cannot be directly taught, teaching word families, roots, and affixes facilitates word learning, particularly in content areas (Fisher & Frey, 2007). Teaching morphological structures strategies can confer exponential growth in EL students' vocabulary. Lists of common prefixes, suffixes, and roots are easily found from a simple Internet search.

Vocabulary routines. Explicit and systematic vocabulary instruction can be accomplished through the use of vocabulary routines. A common format is: (1) introduce the word by reading and pronouncing it, (2) provide a student-friendly explanation using concrete examples and cognates, (3) provide examples and (when appropriate) non-examples with visuals or actions, (4) model the word's use in a complete sentence, (5) have students orally repeat the sentence, (6) provide a sentence frame that supports students to use the target word and apply their knowledge to demonstrate understanding of the concept (e.g. if the target word is *banned,* then an appropriate frame might be "Cellphone use is banned at school because . . . "), and (7) finally have student pairs use the complete sentence with each other.

Strong vocabulary knowledge is needed to comprehend what is read. By carefully identifying words that need to be directly taught, using effective learning strategies with high levels of students' engagement and opportunities for oral practice, and teaching morphological awareness (prefixes, suffixes, affixes, roots), students will expand their vocabulary and be better equipped for learning.

Comprehension. Comprehension is understandably the most difficult and most important aspect of reading for both EL and native English-speaking students. Building on the understanding that oral language and vocabulary skills highly correlate to reading, we examine here their impact on comprehension. The simple view of reading conceives reading comprehension as a product of

Figure 3.10. Vocabulary tiers for English learner students.

Instructional Considerations: Direct instruction of vocabulary and demonstration is an effective strategy across all tiers. Some words, however, cannot be demonstrated but must be directly taught (i.e., *aunt*). If students know a word in their L1, providing a simple explanation or quick English translation is useful. Tier 2 words are the most important to teach because these are ones that students will frequently encounter across all content areas. Note: Some words are high frequency words in one language but low frequency in the other language.

Tier 1: Basic vocabulary and conversational words	Tier 2: High-frequency words found in texts that are used across the curriculum	Tier 3: Highly functional words used in a specific content area
Everyday words that ELs typically know in their L1; words used frequently such as *happy, good, run*	High-frequency, high-utility words that are important to comprehension such as *author, setting, character, plot*	Complex, technical and low-frequency words found in context books
Simple high-frequency words that are cognates such as *doctor/doctor, sofa/sofa*	Words with multiple meanings used across domains	Vocabulary of a specific discipline and domain
	Known concept in native language where you can provide a quick definition (fast map)	Unknown concepts in native language where you need to also teach the label (vocabulary word)
	Process words used across content (e.g., *describe, justify, explain, argue, predict*)	
Simple false cognates such as *rope/ropa* (clothing)	Idioms and common expressions	
	Roots, prefixes, and suffixes	
	Abstract concepts	
	Words that have connections to other words and concepts, such as *between, among, by*	

(Adapted from Beck, McKeown, & Kucan, 2002)

decoding and listening (or language) comprehension skills (Gough & Tunmer, 1986; Hoover & Gough, 1990). Evidence does suggest the key differences in reading comprehension between native English-speaking and EL students is best explained by language comprehension abilities (Bellocchi, Tobia, & Bonifacci, 2017; Linan-Thompson & Vaughn, 2007; Melby-Lervåg & Lervåg, 2011). However, the degree to which decoding and language comprehension contribute to reading comprehension depends on the age of the student and the transparency of orthography (Florit & Cain 2011). Transparent languages (e.g., Spanish, Italian, Finnish, and Turkish) have consistent one-to-one sound–symbol relationships and decoding abilities develop relatively early as compared to English, an opaque language. In opaque languages (e.g., English, Hungarian, and French), these relationships are less consistent, and readers must learn many irregular words.

For EL students, the lack of background knowledge about content, differing literacy experiences and developing language proficiency further exacerbate challenges with comprehension. EL students need explicit and integrated instruction of meaning-making strategies, language instruction, and content knowledge development through rich and inclusive curricular materials and activities.

Additional instructional element: Developing metacognitive strategies.

Good readers also rely on metacognitive (thinking about thinking) strategies such as planning before reading, monitoring understanding, and evaluating the reading experience to comprehend text (Auerbach & Paxton, 1997; Cornoldi & Oakhill, 1996). Metacognitive strategies are particularly useful for EL students, especially in middle and high school. Additionally, Nassaji (2003) found EL readers used both world knowledge and morphological knowledge to inform the metacognitive strategies they use to facilitate their reading comprehension. One problem for EL students, especially young ones, those with limited prior formal schooling, or those with low language proficiency in the instructional language, is that their background experiences and second language status may leave them ill-prepared to effectively use the various literacy development strategies just described, or intuit them from authentic, problem-based activities. Therefore, explicitly teaching and incorporating metacognitive strategies can further enable EL students to accelerate their literacy development. The good news is—as opposed to a negative "Matthew effect" where ELs struggle and use a reading strategy less often than more skilled readers in English—in this case, El students are rich in metacognitive strategies and so become richer in metacognitive and other reading strategies as they successfully use them more and more often. EL students tend to respond positively to metacognitive strategy instruction such as questioning, monitoring, summarizing, and making inferences (Jiménez, Garcia, & Pearson, 1996; Proctor, Dalton, & Grisham, 2007).

Evidence-Based Interventions

For any students who do not adequately respond to Tier 1 instruction, Tier 2 interventions should be provided. Tier 2 interventions should align with core instruction in terms of language, and skill but they should be more explicit, systematic, and intensive than Tier 1 instruction. Tier 2 instruction usually focuses on a narrower set of skills and teaches these skills in more depth to smaller groups of students so teachers can monitor students more closely. If students still require more intensive intervention, they may move to Tier 3, where the intensity of instruction is increased further, such as in time, frequency, and reduced group size.

When students are provided with appropriate and targeted interventions, their progress toward goals is monitored to determine whether to continue or adjust the interventions. This requires knowing how students are currently performing, setting a meaningful and ambitious goal, and monitoring growth at an appropriate frequency (perhaps once a month for students who require some additional support and weekly for students requiring intensive instructional support).

In dual language programs, we recommend providing interventions in the stronger language only, usually the native language. Although there is no research on this issue to date, we have two reasons for this recommendation. First, providing reading interventions in the student's stronger language builds on their language strengths; the link between language knowledge and literacy is well established (Fletcher et al., 1994; Stanovich, 1986; Vellutino, Scanlon, Small, & Tanzman, 1991). This also enables educators to get a clearer picture of whether the student's reading challenges are due to lack of full proficiency in English or really reflect a reading difficulty. Second, interventions are generally provided in a small-group pull-out model so providing them in one language will limit disruption in the student's instructional day. In circumstances where a student does not seem to be progressing in native language interventions, the team may choose to switch the language of intervention to English. This may be helpful for some students who are stronger in English than their native language. Progress should then be monitored in the language of intervention delivery. In a dual language core classroom, progress should be monitored in both languages of instruction. When reviewing these data, the English and Spanish data (assuming a Spanish-English dual language program) should be examined side by side to look holistically at a student's full repertoire of literacy skills.

Additionally, EL students' English language proficiency should also be monitored. At this time, unfortunately, there are no research-based tools for progress monitoring language skills, but various researchers are working to develop them (Ortiz, 2018). Until the tools are developed, language samples, oral story retells, and other informal language measures could be used. Monitoring language growth (across all of a student's languages) is essential because, as mentioned earlier, there is solid research suggesting the strong link between oral language and reading (Fletcher et al., 1994; Stanovich, 1986; Vellutino, Scanlon, Small, & Tanzman, 1991).

Data-Based Decisionmaking

Data-based decisionmaking involves the consideration of multiple data sources and is defined as a formal process to analyze and evaluate information in planning and implementing effective instruction matched to students' level of need. In evaluating the rate and level of progress achieved by EL students, it is essential to use the appropriate comparison group. Since native English-speaking students and EL students are very different populations with different backgrounds and experiences, including access to English, it is not appropriate to base expectations of academic growth and benchmarks for EL students on the standards created for native English-speaking students. Consequently, EL students' rate of progress is best compared to that of "true peers" or other individuals with similar backgrounds and developmental experiences (Brown & Doolittle, 2008). Evaluating the rate of progress is different from evaluating the growth needed to meet grade-level benchmarks that must be the goal for all students and student groups. EL students must be held to the same grade-level standards as native English-speaking students. At no time should the standards be lowered for EL students. Often, we find groups of EL students requiring extra support. In this scenario, the instructional program itself may need to better align with the EL groups' language proficiencies and cultural and experiential backgrounds. Contrarily, when a student's progress differs from their "true peer" group, it is essential that they receive interventions matched to their instructional need. This topic will be addressed in depth in the next chapter.

Shared Teaming and Leadership

To accomplish any systemic change requires a strong leader who is a collaborator, instructional leader, and able to generate the resources needed to accomplish this work (Griffiths, Parson, Burns, VanDerHeyden, & Tilly, 2007). (We discuss shared, collaborative leadership again in Chapter 6.) When creating a culturally and linguistically aligned MTSS model, leaders must also be familiar with best practices in the instruction and assessment of EL students. They will understand that teams need dedicated time to establish processes and procedures and learn together. Additionally, within this context, a leader understands that the best functioning teams include a variety of school professionals (e.g., general education teacher, EL specialist, reading specialist, school psychologist, special education teacher, counselor, and an administrator). Depending on the type of referral (i.e., referral to interventions, referral for a special education evaluation), the membership of meetings may change based on meeting purpose. At any point in the MTSS process, caregivers may be included in the problem-solving process. As discussed earlier, sometimes meeting with caregivers is the only way to gather critical information. When families or caregivers does not speak English fluently, they should be provided an interpreter along with scheduling additional time to meet since it may take twice the time as an English-only meeting to allow for interpretation.

Fidelity of Implementation

Fidelity of implementation is the systematic monitoring of the degree to which interventions are implemented, or taught, as recommended by the program. To reiterate a point made earlier, very few reading programs have included EL students in their research base. These programs, then, are not necessarily evidence-based for EL students, and implementing them with fidelity may still not ensure effectiveness for these students. Kearns, Lemons, Fuchs, and Fuchs (2014) acknowledge that there are times when adjustments to evidence-based programs may be called for; they recommend making adjustments after Tier 1 has been implemented with fidelity and that adjustments leave core elements of the program in place. It is worth reiterating here that Tier 1 instruction must be adapted for the range of proficiency levels of EL students. Below, we describe some adaptations that can maintain fidelity to the program being implemented, while considering the unique instructional needs of ELs.

PUTTING IT ALL TOGETHER: THE PLUSS FRAMEWORK

Due to the limited number of evidence-based reading programs for EL students, Sanford, Brown, and Turner (2012) developed the PLUSS framework: a conceptual framework for providing the linguistic and cultural supports to instruction and intervention programs to specifically address the needs of EL students (Figure 3.11). The components of PLUSS are:

> **P**reteaching critical vocabulary and priming background knowledge;
> **L**anguage modeling and opportunities for using academic language;
> **U**sing visuals and graphic organizers;
> **S**ystematic and explicit instruction; and
> **S**trategic use of native language and teaching for transfer.

The PLUSS framework merges the research foundation of effective instruction for EL students and MTSS to enhance existing instructional and intervention programs. Figure 3.12 is an enhanced MTSS triangle that includes the PLUSS components and specific attention to the cultural and linguistic instructional alignment EL students need in order to fully benefit from their instruction and interventions. What is unique about this triangle is that it focuses

Figure 3.11. PLUSS framework for research-based instructional practices for EL students.

Framework	Definition	Evidence
Preteach critical vocabulary and prime background knowledge	Identify and explicitly teach vocabulary and language structures that are unknown and critical to understanding a passage or unit of instruction; provide culturally relevant curriculum and make connections between new information and life experiences	Au & Kawakami, 1994; August, Artzi, Barr, & Francis, 2018; Calderón, 2007; Carlos et al. 2004; Echevarria, Vogt & Short, 2008; Gay, 2000; Hollie, 2012; Ladson-Billings, 1994; Linan-Thompson & Vaughn, 2007; Nieto & Bode, 2008; Paris, 2012; Sleeter, 2011
Language modeling and opportunities for practicing	Teacher models appropriate use of academic language, then provides structured opportunities for students to practice using the language in meaningful contexts	Dutro & Moran, 2003; Echevarria, Vogt, & Short, 2008; Gibbons, 2009; Linan-Thompson & Vaughn, 2007; Scarcella, 2003; Valdés, Poza, & Brooks, 2015
Use visuals and graphic organizers	Strategically use pictures, graphic organizers, gestures, realia, and other visual prompts to help make critical language, concepts, and strategies more comprehensible to learners	Brechtal, 2001; Echevarria & Graves, 1998; Haager & Klingner, 2005; Linan-Thompson & Vaughn, 2007; O'Malley & Chamot, 1990; Pang, 2013
Systematic and explicit instruction	Explain, model, and provide guided practice with feedback and opportunities for independent practice in content, strategies, and concepts	Calderón, 2007; Doabler, Nelson, & Clarke, 2016; Flagella-Luby & Deshler, 2008; Gibbons, 2009, Haager & Klingner, 2005; Klingner & Vaughn, 2000; Watkins & Slocum, 2004
Strategic use of native language and teaching for transfer	Identify concepts and content students already know in their native language and culture to explicitly explain, define, and help them understand new language and concepts in English	Carlisle, Beeman, Davis & Spharim, 1999; Durgunoglu, et al., 1993; Genesee, Geva, Dressler, & Kamil, 2006; Martinez, Harris, & McClain, 2014; Odlin, 1989; Schecter & Bayley, 2002

(Adapted from Sanford, Brown, & Turner, 2012, Table 1.)

explicitly on the needs of ELs at each tier of support, including ensuring ELD/ESL services are provided for all students who qualify, and ensuring EL student data are disaggregated to understand how they benefit from instruction as a group, and that their progress is compared to "true peers." Surrounding the triangle is the PLUSS framework to provide appropriate instruction at all tiers of instructional support. This is a global view, and the PLUSS framework should also be applied within individual lessons in the curriculum.

Although specifically designed as an overlay for instruction and intervention programs, teachers may also use the framework to analyze their own teaching or in peer observations to ensure lessons include the appropriate language and background supports. Identifying the number of PLUSS components evident within a lesson, as well as opportunities for language practice can be useful in determining whether instruction is supportive for EL students. Figure 3.13 is a PLUSS lesson plan template. To begin lesson planning, first identify the students' instructional goal (#1 on the lesson plan template) from the lesson and a language goal (#2) based on the language you need to teach students so they can comprehend the lesson. Then continue to follow the numbers in sequential order to plan your lesson for each component of the framework. While it may initially seem like these additional components to an intervention or instruction are time-consuming, once you begin to learn about EL students' lives and the types of instruction required to help them achieve, planning and executing PLUSS lessons becomes second nature. And there is no greater motivation than seeing children learn!

One way to apply the enhanced MTSS model is to analyze a typical intervention lesson to gauge whether vocabulary or language structures may be unfamiliar to the student(s) and need to be pretaught. Further, if content includes unfamiliar concepts, building background knowledge prior to the intervention lesson is also critical. To illustrate, a typical early reading intervention lesson might target distinguishing short vowel and vowel-consonant-silent e (VCe) words. In a story about a robe, one of us once observed a teacher asking for her group of EL students to define "robe." The young girl who raised her hand replied by making the motions for rowing. If the teacher had not stopped to ensure the students understood foundational content words the lesson quickly would have become incomprehensible for them.

SUPPORTING ALL STUDENTS

All students deserve to learn. All students deserve to be seen as capable learners with rich and unique individual experiences to grow from. With the burgeoning diversity in our student population across the nation, meeting the needs of all students requires educators to expand their skills. When an EL student experiences academic difficulties, school teams are frequently challenged to determine if their problem stems from language difference or an

Figure 3.12. MTSS elements triangle for English learner students.

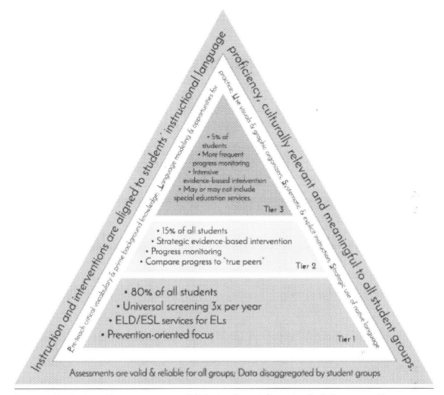

(Brown, Sanford, & Turner, 2018, unpublished; adapted from Sanford, Brown, & Turner, 2012, Figure 1)

intrinsic dis/ability. This determination becomes easier when schools have systems in place to ensure the provision of appropriate instruction for all student populations. One such systemic framework is a Multi-Tiered System of Supports (MTSS). MTSS is a prevention-focused model where all instruction is evidence-based, and increasingly intensive supports are implemented for students not meeting grade-level benchmarks. In this chapter, we examined the core features of MTSS, which include universal screening, progress monitoring, evidence-based instruction, data-based decisionmaking, and shared teaming and leadership along with the adaptations essential for the support of EL students. Ensuring appropriate support, however, is contingent upon understanding students' contexts. The EL student population is a heterogeneous group with differing native languages, proficiencies in English, educational backgrounds, and life experiences. Understanding students' unique contexts leads to specific supports that build on students' backgrounds to instruction in U.S. schools, including instruction aligned to their language

Figure 3.13. PLUSS lesson plan template.

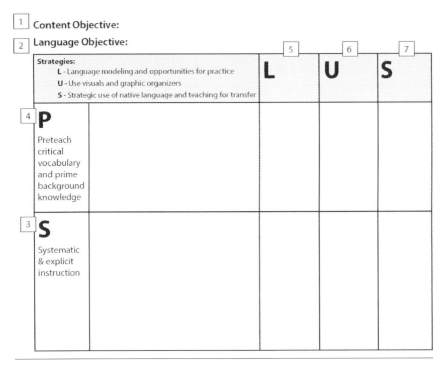

(Sanford, Brown, & Turner, 2012, Figure 2)

proficiency. Those students who are not responsive to targeted interventions may be referred for a special education evaluation.

Historically, school teams have struggled to appropriately distinguish difference from dis/ability when the student is an English learner. MTSS data, organized on a document such as the CPSF (see the Appendix), can enhance the data used for special education eligibility, enabling teams to make the most appropriate decisions within the law (see Chapter 7). Assessments and tests for EL students also require careful use to limit inherent bias. The next chapter examines in depth the continuum of assessment within MTSS. Ensuring that educational systems are responsive to the unique needs of EL students can be accomplished with the types of adaptations described here. It must be accomplished—all our students deserve to achieve their potential.

CHAPTER 4

Culturally and Linguistically Responsive Multi-Tiered Support Systems for English Learners
Assessment Across the Tiers

with Amanda K. Sanford

The purpose of a strong Multitiered System of Supports (MTSS) is to improve achievement for all learners. The MTSS process includes (1) universal screening, (2) progress monitoring, (3) evidence-based instruction, (4) evidence-based interventions, (5) data-based decisionmaking, (6) shared teaming and leadership, and (7) fidelity of implementation. Assessment data are used for all key decisions both on a program and individual student level. This chapter addresses assessment within the context of MTSS. First, it will describe how to evaluate basic principles of assessment: features like reliability, validity, and normative populations, especially in consideration of the unique needs of EL students. The chapter will then provide guidance on how to identify important educational questions and then use these questions to select appropriate assessment tools. These guiding questions are always focused on students' educational success and maintaining high standards for all learners. Finally, assessment across the tiers of instructional support will be described, including the process of special education referral and evaluation. All systems must recognize that EL students are a valuable part of our school system and communities, and that their success is vital to the success of our schools and our nation.

UNDERSTANDING ASSESSMENT AS A PROCESS: ASSESSMENT VERSUS TESTING

Assessment is the process of systematically gathering multiple sources of data, evaluating the data, using them to make instructional decisions, and planning future instruction. However, there is a long history of diverse individuals receiving inequitable treatment based on results from assessments. Thus, assessments and student scores on them have been called a form of cultural capital (Sternberg & Grigorenko, 2004). Assessments are critical to the iterative teaching and learning cycle, and can occur before, during, and after instruction. Testing and assessment are not identical: Narrower than assessment, "[T]esting is administering a predetermined set of questions or tasks for which predetermined types of behavioral responses are sought, to an individual or group of individuals to obtain a score" (Salvia, Ysseldyke, & Witmer, 2017, p. 5). Assessment is broad and may include testing as one tool. For EL students, results from both tests and assessments can be confusing because results are often confounded by issues of linguistic demands and cultural assumptions inherent in the tools. Additionally, EL students are often not represented in the comparison or norming groups when tests are developed, so educators must plan to compare the performance of EL students to students with similar backgrounds and educational experiences, rather than incorrectly assuming that EL students are appropriately included in testing samples. Throughout the process of assessment and testing, we must be clear in our purpose and constantly check for bias in our conclusions.

BASIC PRINCIPLES OF ASSESSMENT: WHAT PRACTITIONERS NEED TO KNOW

In order to ensure that fair and equitable decisions result from any assessment data, assessments must be (1) compared to a fair normative population (or normative sample), (2) reliable, and (3) valid. The following sections describe normative samples, reliability, and validity, so that these properties can be used in determining whether an assessment is being used fairly to support the learning and educational evaluation of EL students.

Criterion-Based and Norm-Referenced Assessments

Assessments can be criterion-based assessments or norm-referenced assessments. Criterion-based assessments compare a student's performance to a standard of performance—for example, what represents successful reading. These types of comparisons, which can be done with screening and progress monitoring tools, can address a question like, "How does the student's performance compare to grade-level expectations?" and make the comparison to established benchmarks. In this case, research may have shown that students need to read 90 words correct per minute (WCPM) by the end of 2nd grade to be on track for being a successful reader by 3rd grade and passing the state assessment the following year. If students perform below that level, they may require additional instructional support to be successful.

In contrast, norm-referenced assessments compare a student's performance to their same-grade or same-age peers to answer the question, "How does the student's performance compare to that of peers?" This is where student performance is compared to the normative population (described below, such as a national normative sample taken by the publishing company, or in the case of some schools and districts, a local normative population).

When determining whether an EL student has a dis/ability, a fair decision requires comparison to other EL students with similar backgrounds, not solely norms based on native English speakers. On the other hand, if we are determining instructional support, comparison to grade-level benchmarks can identify the need for intensifying the child's instructional support. Likewise, if an entire group of EL students is making less growth than their native English-speaking peers, it may be an indication that the school needs to reexamine its instruction to determine if it appropriately aligns to students' language proficiency levels and cultural backgrounds (Brown & Sanford, 2011; Kaminski, Cummings, Powell-Smith, & Good, 2008; Sanford, Brown, & Turner, 2012). This point is illustrated in the case study described later in this chapter.

Normative Samples: Making Fair Comparisons

Normative populations or normative samples are the groups of people that were assessed in order to determine what is "typical" or "normal" in that population. In order to make a fair comparison, the test scores must be compared to normative samples that are adequately representative of the individual being assessed (i.e., we want to compare mangoes to mangoes, not apples to mangoes). If we were to compare the performance of EL students to that of native English-speaking students, we would not be making a fair comparison because the background experience of these individuals is so different. Considering that there are about 5 million English learner students in U.S. schools (Kena et al., 2014) with a wide range of differences regarding language exposure and experience, cultural learning, types of education or lack thereof, socioeconomic status, and English language proficiency, it quickly becomes apparent that establishing an appropriate standard for comparison is no easy task.

Most standardized, norm-referenced tests include only English-speaking students in the normative sample or, at most, may include a representative sample by race. This means that a proportion of students may represent the population of interest, but the test is still like comparing mangoes to fruit salad rather than making a "mango to mango" comparison. Not including EL students or having an inadequate representation of EL students in the normative sample is a problem because the test will likely be systematically biased against EL students performing well on given items and the results will not be representative of how EL students should score. Research has found that when assessing EL students, the largest source of measurement error is unnecessarily linguistically complex test items (Abedi, 2006a; Solano-Flores, 2008). Examples include unfamiliar vocabulary, long phrases before a question, complex sentences, long noun phrases, and use of passive voice, to name a few (Abedi, 2006b). These sources of measurement error can result in EL students performing below their level of knowledge on the assessment, even if they have mastery of the content being assessed. Without a sufficient sample of EL students in the normative sample, these errors will likely go unrecognized.

However representative the sample is regarding race, it will not look exactly like the unique makeup of English learner students, and therefore is unlikely to ever be a fair or accurate comparison to a student who is a nonnative English-speaking student. What that means is that generally standardized norm-referenced assessments will underestimate the achievement, and more importantly the ability, of a nonnative English-speaking student. This is one reason why using local norms (and creating a "true peer" comparison group within those norms) that allow schools to compare students' performance to the performance of other children within that community may be a much fairer comparison than comparing to a nationally normed sample. Local norms can be obtained by assessing all the children in one class, school, or district, and creating standards for performance and growth based on the local population. These may be fairer and more accurate in terms of establishing what expected performance might be for a given population.

Reliability

The *Standard for Educational and Psychological Testing* (AERA, APA, & NCME, 2014) provide detailed guidance on the ethical use of educational and psychological assessments. In general, tests must be both reliable and valid for the individual being evaluated. Reliability is the consistency and precision of the measurement across repeated administrations of the test. For example, if I repeatedly weigh a 5-pound bag of flour on a scale, I should expect that bag (as long as I haven't opened it and used any flour) to weigh the same at each weighing using the same scale. Applied to assessments, reliability is the extent to which a student's performance or the performance of similar students, as reflected in the obtained standard score, remains about the same (with some acceptable degree of error) when measured multiple times.

Validity

Conversely, validity is more concerned with the accuracy of what is being measured. The *Standards* define validity as "the degree to which evidence and theory support the interpretations of test scores for proposed uses of tests" (p. 11). In other words, does the test actually measure the construct(s) it purports to measure? Having already established the reliability of a measure, test developers now gather evidence to demonstrate that what is being measured (the construct), is in fact, the thing that test is supposed to be measuring. For example, a test that is designed to measure a student's mathematical knowledge, but does so using word problems, may actually be measuring a student's reading or linguistic knowledge, rather than or along with their math knowledge. Or, if you repeatedly weigh yourself on a scale and it consistently reports that you weigh 200 pounds, the scale is reliable (consistent)—but not valid (accurate) if you actually weigh 150 pounds! If a test is valid, it must be reliable, but the converse is not true. A test can be reliable, but lack validity.

Validity and cognitive assessments. Validity is especially important to consider when examining cognitive abilities, or intelligence, where the individual's level must be inferred, as it cannot be measured directly. Consider, for example, a test designed to measure an individual's inferential ability using pictures of different sizes, colors, and numbers, where the response must utilize an accurate distinction between the use of *and* and *or* when multiple inferences are present. Imagine also that the instructions for such a task are verbal and rather lengthy and are administered to EL students with very limited English proficiency, and they consistently score very low. Would it be reasonable to expect that this test accurately measured EL students' inferential abilities as being deficient? Or is it more likely that the test merely reflected the EL students' limited proficiency in English? This is, of course, one of the fundamental dilemmas in distinguishing "difference versus dis/ability." Making the first inference may lead a team to conclude that the individual has a dis/ability and special education placement may ensue. If the latter inference is made, the individual would not be identified as having a dis/ability and any academic problems would rightly be ascribed to limited English proficiency—which is to say, the test's construct validity was lacking in that it measured English proficiency when it was supposed to measure inferential ability. The wrong construct was measured and the individual's score on the test is an invalid indicator of inferential ability.

Validity and academic assessments. The relationship between validity and academic evaluation is slightly different from that between validity and cognitive assessment. Academic skills are skills and strategies that develop over time and with instruction, as opposed to being latent like cognitive abilities. Thus, they are easier to measure, and reliability is rarely a problem. Likewise, using a parallel analogy to the one above, it would be accurate to say that giving an individual with limited English proficiency a test of reading comprehension in English may render a score that does not reflect the individual's total reading ability across languages but instead demonstrates their limitations only in English. Indeed, if the individual were able to read in their native language, it would be incorrect to suggest that the score represents a valid measure of their reading ability across languages (and is also a rationale for assessing a student's skills in their native language; see Brown & Sanford, 2011). It can be argued, however, that the score does in fact represent a valid measure of their reading ability in English. This is a very important point—if the question being addressed is in relation to a dis/ability, then the score lacks validity and should not be used to suggest a deficit in this area. On the other hand, if the question being addressed is in relation to instructional programming and intervention, the score does have validity in terms of evaluating how far behind the individual is compared to the grade-level standard, and how much support they may need to achieve reading proficiency.

Making fair and equitable decisions. The question of validity and its relationship to testing data and scores is inextricably linked to the specific question being asked in the evaluation (discussed below). This applies to any type of measurement that may occur in the educational setting and within the classroom. We must know what this question is and what standard should be applied to make fair and equitable decisions in the examination of any type of data and information. As we look at the different types of measures typically used within MTSS, we will reexamine these psychometric issues with particular emphasis on the reason and purpose of the assessment in determining the appropriate comparisons to ensure decisions for EL students remain as nondiscriminatory as possible.

DETERMINING ASSESSMENT TYPE:
WHAT'S THE QUESTION BEING ADDRESSED?

Whenever educational professionals embark on the assessment process, it is essential that they first identify the questions they are attempting to answer. These guiding questions assist in the selection of appropriate assessment tools and fair interpretation of the data collected. For example, if your guiding question is to determine what proportion of students require additional instructional support, you will select a different assessment tool (i.e., a screening tool) than if your question is to determine whether students have learned the content most recently taught in Unit 4 of the core literacy program (in which case you may use the end-of-unit assessment in the curriculum, a form of mastery measurement). Assessing a child in the absence of knowing the question one is trying to address is like asking "Which direction should I turn?" without specifying the location you want to reach.

Historically, educational decisionmaking has been focused around waiting until a student fails and then providing an intervention of some type. In the historic model, one of the questions that led to deeper investigation was, "Why isn't Johnny, Juanita, or Hans learning to read?" Within MTSS, however, instead of waiting until there is a problem, a proactive, prevention-oriented approach is taken. Within an MTSS model, we ask proactively, "What instructional supports do all students need to be successful?" When considering the needs of EL students, we must be especially mindful that different groups of learners may need different types of instructional supports. EL students will require consideration of their linguistic and cultural backgrounds as well as educational histories in order to provide the most appropriate instructional support.

The educational question to be addressed should match the purpose of the assessment and the type of assessment; it must consider the unique needs of EL students. Figure 4.1 summarizes the alignment between the purpose of assessment, questions that would be addressed by each assessment purpose, and the types of assessments that might be used to address these questions. Further, specific issues with respect to appropriately interpreting the assessment data for EL students are suggested.

Broadly speaking, there are two major purposes of assessment: *formative* assessment, which informs instructional planning and decisionmaking, and *summative* assessment, which evaluates students' or programs' performance after instruction is complete. Within these, there are several specific purposes. For example, screening, progress monitoring, and diagnostic assessment (i.e., diagnosing a students' instructional needs) are all specific purposes of formative assessment, whereas referral, classification, and outcomes evaluation are specific purposes of summative assessment. In the following section, we describe various types of assessments, including both formative and summative assessments. It will be helpful to reference Figure 4.1 as you read the following section to see the relationship of each of these purposes of assessment and types of questions they can answer and specific assessments or tests that might be used at each step.

Formative Assessment

Formative assessments provide information on how to plan or modify instruction and are generally conducted before beginning instruction (in the case of screening and placement tests) or periodically throughout instruction (as is in the case of mastery measures or progress monitoring assessments) (see, e.g., Fuchs & Deno, 1991; Gibbons & Silberglitt, 2008). A key feature of formative assessment data is that they are used to inform instruction to better meet the needs of students. Screening formative assessments are designed to answer questions like, "Which students need additional support to be successful and in what academic area(s)?" and "How many students are in need of more intensive support?" In contrast, progress monitoring types of formative assessment may address questions like, "Is a student or group of students growing at an appropriate rate to meet important grade-level benchmarks?" and "Is a change in instruction required to support students to meet their goals?" (see Good, Gruba, & Kaminski, 2001; Kaminski, Cummings, Powell-Smith, & Good, 2008). When using progress monitoring assessments for EL students, we must also ask questions like, "Is the student making appropriate growth compared to 'true peers,' or students with similar linguistic and cultural backgrounds?" (Brown & Doolittle, 2008), "Are EL students as a group growing at the same rate as their native English-speaking peers?", and in the case of dual language programs, "Are students responding to instruction in English? In their native language?" Finally, mastery measures can inform teachers about whether students have learned the content taught.

Figure 4.1. Using educational questions to guide assessment selection.

Purposes of Assessment	Questions to Guide Assessment	Types and Examples of Assessment Used	Key Issues for ELs
Screening	*Formative:* • What percentage of students are meeting benchmarks (how strong is our core)? • Which students need additional support to meet benchmarks and in what academic area(s)? • How many students are in need of more intensive support (Tier 2 and 3)?	CBMs (e.g., DIBELS, AIMSweb, Easy CBM) state assessments (e.g., SBAC) language proficiency tests (e.g., WIDA, ELPA 21) general outcome measures (e.g., STAR, DIBELS, AIMSweb)	Is scientifically based instruction in place for the target students and aligned to the students' cultural, linguistic, socioeconomic, and experiential backgrounds? Based on language proficiency data, what are students' current language support needs?
Instructional Planning	*Formative:* • Which skills do we need to focus on? • How much support do students need to meet grade level benchmarks? *Summative:* • Did the student master the objective or specific skill taught?	CBMs (DIBELS, AIMSweb, Easy CBM) language proficiency tests (e.g., WIDA, ELPA 21) program placement tests (e.g., Early Reading Intervention placement test) phonics inventories (e.g., Quick Phonics Screener) mastery measures (e.g., Accelerated Math) in-program end-of-unit assessments (core reading tests)	Do students currently have the language skills needed to access the instruction and demonstrate the target skills? If a large gap exists, what short-term goals will help students close the gap? Is the student having difficulty mastering the skills because of language or other barriers?

Figure 4.1. Using educational questions to guide assessment selection. (continued)

Purposes of Assessment	Questions to Guide Assessment	Types and Examples of Assessment Used	Key Issues for ELs
Monitoring Student Progress	*Formative:* • Is a student or group of students growing at an appropriate rate to meet key grade-level benchmarks? • If students are growing at a less than expected rate, how should instruction be intensified (e.g., increase time, reduce group size, increase instructional intensity)?	general outcome measures (e.g., DIBELS, AIMSweb, Easy CBM)	Are ELs as a group growing at lower than expected rates as compared to English-only students? Is the child responding to interventions in English? In native language? What specific supports (e.g., language, culture, experience) are needed to address gaps?
Referral	• Is there a concern that a child may have a disability?	comparing rate of progress	Is the student making lower than expected progress as compared to true peers?
Classification	*Summative:* • Is the student performing lower than expected compared to a norm-referenced peer group? • Does the student qualify for the _____ program?	standardized norm-referenced tests (Woodcock-Johnson Tests of Achievement and Cognitive Ability, WISC-V, WIAT)	Are data from standardized tests interpreted considering students' language proficiency and acculturation?
Program Evaluation/ Outcomes	*Summative:* • How did we do in getting most of our students to meet key benchmark goals at the end of a specified time frame? • What percentage of our students met state standards?	examine disaggregated state assessment (academic and by language proficiency) CBM data	How is our program meeting the needs of all students? Of each group? Do we need to provide intensive instruction for particular groups (e.g, ELs, Title 1) aligned to their unique needs?

Mastery measures. Mastery measures assess a specific skill or set of skills from the curriculum, and they can be used to answer questions like, "Did the student master the objective or specific skill taught?" (Fuchs & Deno, 1991; Kaminski, Cummings, Powell-Smith, & Good, 2008). An example of a specific educational question would be, "Can the student summarize a story, telling the character, setting, problem, and what happened at the beginning, middle, and end?" Mastery measures are often dependent on the curriculum and are usually not standardized measures. Mastery measures can include tests within a curriculum, teacher-generated assessments, and end-of-unit tests.

General outcome measures. Another type of formative assessment within an MTSS framework are general outcome measures (GOMs) that gauge students' general academic success in targeted skills and the growth they make. GOMs may also provide comparisons to benchmarks or normative age or grade peers. These normative comparisons could be to a national sample, local sample, or could be done according to student groups, depending on the purpose of assessment. Local norms can be especially helpful in ensuring fair comparisons for EL students, when the population of interest looks dramatically different from a national normative sample. Screening and progress monitoring measures are usually GOMs (Kaminski, Cummings, Powell-Smith, & Good, 2008; Shinn, 2008).

Curriculum-based measures. Curriculum-based measures (CBMs) are assessments that are linked directly to the curriculum and are meant to inform instruction. They often are GOMs and can be used within Tier 1 for benchmarking purposes, usually about three times per year (for example, screening in fall, winter, and spring), as well as for progress monitoring over the course of the year. Results are used to identify each student's instructional needs, to plan future instruction, and for progress monitoring instructional goals. CBMs date back to the 1970s (Deno, 1985, 1989, 2003) and ensure technical adequacy by specifying "what to measure, how to measure and how to score and interpret the data on student growth" (Deno, 2005, p. 28). CBMs were "developed to quantify student performance in reading, written expression, spelling, and arithmetic" easily and quickly in a standardized manner (Deno, 2005, p. 27).

Screening and progress monitoring across languages. Screening and progress monitoring assessments are most commonly CBMs and are useful in identifying both students who are at risk for not meeting academic benchmarks (screening) and progress monitoring their performance toward goals. Over time, research has provided evidence to support CBM use in making decisions for EL students across both English (Baker & Good, 1995; Fien et al., 2011; Domínguez de Ramírez & Shapiro, 2007; Fien et al., 2008; Riedel, 2007; Samuels, 2007; Vanderwood, Linklater, & Healy, 2008; Wayman, Wallace, & Wiley, 2007) and Spanish (Richards-Tutor, Solari, Leafstedt, Gerber, Filippini, & Aceves, 2013). Beyond

A CASE EXAMPLE

Figure 4.2 (Brown, Ortiz, & Sanford, 2016) compares the growth rate for words correct per minute (WCPM) for two EL students. In this case, there were two EL students, Chaseito and Panchito, who were referred to the individual problem-solving team at a school due to concerns about low reading performance and lack of adequate growth. Both students had been in intervention since the beginning of the school year (35 weeks) and neither student had made enough growth to get them on track for meeting the reading benchmarks by spring of 3rd grade. The team is meeting to address the question, "Does each of these students require a referral for a special education evaluation?" To address this question, the team knows one important question to address: "Is the student growing at a lower than expected rate compared to peers?" Figure 4.2 shows the growth rate for each student, as well as the growth of two peer comparison groups (*all students* and *EL students*).

In Figure 4.2, the line with long dashes represents the rate of progress for one EL student, Chaseito, and the line with dashes and dots represents that of the other EL student, Panchito. The line with short dashes represents the average growth of all the other students in Chaseito and Panchito's 2nd-grade class, a majority of whom are native English-speaking peers. In this comparison, if the evaluation question relates to growth and learning, use of the line with short dashes representing the classroom baseline drawn from mostly native English-speaking peers might lead erroneously to the conclusion that both Chaseito and Panchito are not making adequate progress and that perhaps there is some intrinsic dis/ability that is responsible, and therefore a special education referral and evaluation is appropriate.

The team recognized that a different standard of comparison was needed: "Is the student growing at a lower than expected rate compared to true peers (i.e., students with similar language and cultural backgrounds)?" They asked to look at the average performance of ELs in 2nd grade across the district. This line is represented by the solid line on Figure 4.2.

When the appropriate "true peer" (i.e., growth of other EL students in their school context) standard is applied (as denoted by the solid line), the impression is quite different. In Chaseito's case, it is clear that he is learning and acquiring reading skills at a rate and manner that is comparable to his true peers. The team concluded that Chaseito should not be referred for an evaluation for special education because he is growing at a rate comparable to peers. In this situation, the team realized the more appropriate questions to address are, "Why are EL students as a group making lower than expected progress when compared to their native English-speaking peers?" and therefore, "What instructional changes are necessary to accelerate the growth of EL students as a whole group?"

Figure 4.2. Reading trajectories of two EL students: Appropriate comparisons depend on questions being asked.

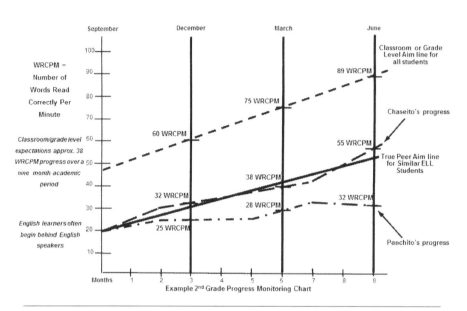

(Brown, Ortiz, & Sanford, 2016; original graph created for the referenced presentation)

their efficacy in Spanish and English, Deno (2003) suggests CBM oral reading measures can be used for phonetic languages such as Korean, and MAZE procedures (students silently read a passage where every seventh word is replaced with a choice of three) for iconic languages such as Chinese.

Summative Assessment

Summative assessments are given at the conclusion of instruction (Kaminski, Cummings, Powell-Smith, & Good, 2008) and can be used to answer broad performance questions like, "How did we do in getting most of our students to key benchmark goals at the end of a specified time frame?" or "What percentage of our students met state standards?" or "How did our students do compared to others of the same age or grade?" For the first two questions, criterion-referenced tests are used, while norm-referenced standardized tests are used for the third question. On the surface, such tests and the resulting assessment data appear ideal for accountability purposes and are administered to all students. Because of their use for accountability purposes, these can be high-stakes assessments. Another example of summative evaluation is when screening data are collected fall, winter, and spring; the spring data can be utilized as a summative assessment. Whatever assessment is being employed for

---

SUMMARY OF MAJOR PRINCIPLES OF ASSESSMENT
AND EDUCATIONAL QUESTIONS

Thus far, we have explained that assessment is a process, of which testing can be a part. The purpose of assessment within MTSS is to improve student outcomes. In order to effectively use assessment as a part of MTSS, assessments must be reliable, valid, and have an appropriate normative population for comparison. For EL students, an appropriate normative comparison is usually a local normative population of students with similar cultural and linguistic backgrounds (i.e., *true peers*). We have also described different major purposes of assessment, and their specific purposes: formative assessment (used for screening, instructional diagnosis and planning, and progress monitoring), and summative assessment (used for outcomes evaluation, determining whether to refer and place a student for special education). Within these purposes, several types of assessments have been detailed, including mastery measurement, general outcome measures, and curriculum-based measures, and their general use and specific application with EL students. We also provided a case example of utilizing formative assessment to determine whether a special education referral was warranted for two EL students, and discussed instructional implications at a group level. Below is a description of how these principles are used at each of the three tiers of support within MTSS.

summative purposes, the key is to determine to what extent a given individual or group is at the level of performance that is expected by the school, district, or state, and usually there is a consequence or grade attached to that determination (e.g., promotion to the next grade, designation for special education services, or a school performance grade).

ASSESSMENT ACROSS THE TIERS OF MTSS

Assessments are used across all tiers of instructional support within MTSS. At Tier 1, assessments should be shorter and more efficient and given to all students for global instructional planning purposes. At Tier 2, progress monitoring is more frequent to provide information for students who require strategic instructional support. At Tier 3, progress monitoring and teaming are more frequent and intensive according to students' more intensive instructional support needs. Figure 4.3 provides an overview of assessments at each tier, how goals are selected, how data-based decisionmaking is applied, and the teaming structures that support this process.

Figure 4.3. Overview of assessments examples by MTSS tier level.

Tier	Assessment	Setting Goals	Data-based Decision-making	Team
1	Screening CBM Language prof.	Benchmarks	Outcomes driven model (ODM)	Grade-level teams
2	Progress monitoring Program placement Phonics inventory	Growth norms	Standard treatment Group problem solving	Grade-level teams & specialists
3	Progress monitoring	Growth norms	Individual problem solving	Collaborative problem-solving team
Special Ed	Standardized assessment Developmental history	IEP	Eligibility IEP	Multidisciplinary team

ASSESSMENT AT TIER 1

Screening

Within MTSS, screening assessments with established reliability and validity for all student groups are administered at the beginning, middle, and end of each year in Tier 1 (Brown & Sanford, 2011). These assessments are brief and target specific skills known to be predictors of future reading or literacy achievement to determine which students are on track and which may need additional support. Results reveal which students may have difficulty meeting important literacy (or another academic area) benchmarks as well as providing a gauge of how all students perform in relation to benchmarks (Kaminski, Cummings, Powell-Smith, & Good, 2008). One common argument by bilingual and ESL/ELD teachers is that popular screening tools are biased because in the early grades, large numbers of EL students tend to score in the "at-risk" range. However, there is substantial evidence of the reliability and validity of screeners when used with EL students (Baker & Good, 1995; Fien et al., 2008;

Riedel, 2007; Samuels, 2007; Vanderwood, Linklater, & Healy, 2008; Wayman, Wallace, & Wiley, 2007). Given that the majority of EL students continue to be educated in English only, it is reasonable to conclude that screening assessments administered in English reliably indicate which students need additional support in English literacy. Learning to read in a language they are learning results in a double cognitive load (Goldenberg, 2008); EL students may need more intensive and explicit support in early literacy skills due to this double demand. The same needs may exist when instructed in Spanish, and scores on Spanish (or other native language) screeners may also be low if students have not had preschool experiences in either their native language or English. Low scores on screening assessments *do not* indicate low aptitude but rather are indicators of critical skills that students need to learn at particular developmental times to be on track to be a reader or to meet other literacy or subject matter content benchmarks.

Meaningful Instructional Goals

Establishing appropriate instructional goals for all students is an essential feature of MTSS. Some goals such as benchmark, progress monitoring, and grade-level standards are already established. A great deal of research has been analyzed to identify general grade-level norms for screening tools like Oral Reading Fluency in English (e.g. Hasbrouck & Tindal, 2017; see Figure 4.4, Compiled ORF Norms; Hasbrouck & Tindal, 2017). Further, most curriculum-based measurement tools have established empirically based benchmarks that can be used to determine whether a student is on track to meet later reading benchmarks, and some of this research includes EL students in their sampling and analysis (Brown & Sanford, 2011; Hasbrouck & Tindal, 2017). Predictive validity, or the ability of a measure to predict a student's future performance on a meaningful outcome measure, is an essential feature of these measures, and one of the features evaluated by the National Center for Intensive Intervention (intensiveintervention.org) when evaluating progress monitoring tools.

In the absence of established benchmarks or norms for a particular population, schools can also create local norms (described earlier in the section on normative samples) and examine what benchmarks at earlier points in time predict passing performance on the high-stakes outcomes assessments at the end of the year. This can be especially valuable when using curriculum-based measurement in languages other than English (especially Spanish when there is a large Spanish-speaking population at the school).

Maintaining rigorous academic standards for EL students is essential for ensuring their academic success (Brown & Sanford, 2011). In fact, for most EL students, more alignment between their instructional needs, benchmarks, and the instructional environment would likely prevent many of their difficulties (Francis, Rivera, Lesaux, Kieffer, & Rivera, 2006). For EL students, as with all

Figure 4.4. Compiled Oral Reading Fluency (ORF) norms.

Grade	Percentile	Fall	Winter	Spring
			WCPM*	
	90		97	116
	75		59	91
1	50		29	60
	25		16	34
	10		9	18
	90	111	131	148
	75	84	109	124
2	50	50	84	100
	25	36	59	72
	10	23	35	43
	90	134	161	166
	75	104	137	139
3	50	83	97	112
	25	59	79	91
	10	40	62	63
	90	153	168	184
	75	125	143	160
4	50	94	120	133
	25	75	95	106
	10	60	71	83
	90	179	183	195
	75	153	160	169
5	50	121	133	146
	25	87	109	119
	10	64	84	102
	90	185	195	204
	75	159	166	173
6	50	132	145	146
	25	112	116	122
	10	89	91	91

*WCPM: Words correct per minute (Hasbrouck & Tindal, 2017)

students, achieving benchmark goals should always be the long-term goal, but for students performing significantly below grade level, ambitious short-term goals may help them close the gap over time. For example, if you have a student who is 3 years behind their grade-level peers, it may be appropriate to set a goal for making 2 years progress in 1 year's time to catch them up. The student won't meet grade level standards at this rate by the end of the year, but could meet grade-level standards after 2 years.

Assess Across Languages: Dual Language Programs

In dual language programs, it is important to understand a student's achievement across both languages to create a complete understanding of a child's reading and literacy proficiency as their subject matter content knowledge. The goal of these programs is to produce biliterate individuals who express their content knowledge fluently in both languages, and research suggests that achieving literacy in one language confers a benefit on the second language (Steele et al., 2017). For example, it is essential to examine both English language and native language reading assessment data by placing the two scores side by side to determine a student's risk status (Figure 4.5). Figure 4.5 provides an example of a table summarizing (a) student performance on the fall DIBELS Next Oral Reading Fluency benchmarking, with (b) performance in Spanish Indicadores Dinamicos del Éxito en la Lectura (IDEL) Fluidez en la Lectura Oral, (c) EL status, and (d) special education status, to help educators create a side-by-side comparison of students' performance across languages. Light gray shading indicates students who were on track to meet later benchmarks; medium gray shading shows students who require strategic support to meet later reading goals, and darker (slate) shading indicate students who need intensive support to meet later reading goals. By including all this information in a single table, educators are better able to use and integrate this information in instructional planning.

In terms of instructional planning, students who are at the intensive level in both languages require intensive supports. When students require intervention, we recommend providing intervention in only one language, the stronger or dominant language (usually the home language; see Chapter 3 for discussion), especially in early grades like kindergarten and 1st grade. One reason is that intervening in two languages may be overwhelming for students, and once they learn the phonetic skills in one language, it will be easier to transfer them to the other language. In addition, providing more intervention than needed may disrupt a student's instructional day, which may hinder rather than support their academic progress in multiple areas. Along the entire instructional timeline, students should receive explicit instruction to support transferring their literacy skills to the second language. For example, teaching the phonics rules that are unique to the English language would be essential to help students develop grade-level English proficiency.

Figure 4.5. Example of Spanish-English side-by-side reading CBM results.

Student Name	DIBELs Next ORF*	IDEL FLO**	EL Status/ Proficiency Levels***	SPED/IEP
Student A	22	58	1	
Student B	36	35	2	Yes
Student C	43	65	3	
Student D	58	53	4	
Student E	64	90	2	
Student F	68	61	Native English speaker	
Student G	71	85	4	
Student H	85	88	4	
Student I	94	40	Native English speaker	
Student J	117	98	Native English speaker	
Student K	122	130	4	
Student L	132	152	4	

*Oral Reading Fluency

**Fluidez en la lectura oral (Spanish Oral Reading Fluency)

***Level 1 = Beginning English, Level 5 = Fluent English Proficiency

While it is not necessary to intervene in both languages, nontransferable skills should be taught through core instruction beginning relatively early in a students' academic program so that students can develop biliteracy, rather than being literate in one language and lacking sufficient reading skills in the second language to access the core curriculum. Even in a bilingual program that begins in kindergarten taught mostly in Spanish, students still benefit from instruction that begins to teach transferable skills, then begins to differentiate nontransferable skills (the different sounds vowels make across languages, and the different sounds consonants like j, h, and r make across languages) early in their academic program.

We recommend that interventions be provided in the stronger or dominant language and then explicitly taught for transfer. Because of the complexity of dual language development and the lack of empirical research, this is an experimental process. Progress monitoring, teaming, and data-based decision making are essential to this process, and if one approach isn't working, intervening in the opposite language and progress monitoring in both languages may be reasonable to try.

In monolingual programs, it is still valuable to assess EL students in their native language whenever possible to gain an understanding of their complete reading proficiency, especially when the children have prior literacy instruction in their native language. It honors the knowledge they bring in their native language and may make it easier to plan instruction (to either teach for transfer or intervene from a more foundational level) depending on the literacy knowledge in the child's native language.

Data-Based Decisionmaking for Instruction

Data-based decisionmaking follows screening or progress monitoring. Collaborative Planning Teams (CPT) that include all general and special educators, an ESL/ELD teacher, and other school professionals, review assessment data to plan instruction matched to the intensity of students' needs. These data-based decisionmaking teams often meet by grade level and should meet at least three times across the year to examine student screening data, plan instruction, and set goals for the entire student population. This process examines students' status in relation to benchmarks to determine the appropriate next steps. For EL students, data on their instructional language(s) proficiency also guides instruction and intervention to ensure the appropriate language supports are included.

Outcomes Driven Model

Data-based decisionmaking is most effective when it is used as a part of a systematic process for setting meaningful goals, planning instruction, and monitoring and evaluating student growth, while making adjustments as needed to help students meet meaningful outcomes. The Outcomes Driven Model (ODM; Kaminski, Cummings, Powell-Smith, & Good, 2008) was developed as a prevention-oriented model for planning and evaluating the effectiveness of instructional support, with the primary goal of improving the number of students who achieve meaningful reading (or other achievement) outcomes. This concept was built on the work of the development of the problem-solving model (see Deno, 1989; Shinn, 1995; Tilly, 2008), and it has been applied in the use of MTSS by data teams to make efficient and effective use of their assessment data. The steps of the ODM include: (1) identifying need for support, (2) validating need for support, (3) planning and implementing instructional support, (4) evaluating and modifying instructional support, and (5) reviewing outcomes. For a complete description and example of the application of this model, see Kaminski, Cummings, Powell-Smith, and Good (2008). The following is an overview of each step.

Identifying need for support. Identifying instructional support usually in-volves collecting screening data and asking the questions, "Which students are in need of additional instructional support? In what academic areas? How much support is needed?" For EL students, the questions must also include, "What are students' current language support needs?" and "What kinds of lin-guistic supports are needed to access key literacy content?" Answering these questions will require collecting additional data on students' language profi-ciency levels and talking with the English language development specialist to identify appropriate supports.

Validating need for support. Validating instructional support may require the collection of additional screening, progress monitoring, or diagnostic data, to determine if the student actually requires additional instructional support and, if so, what kind of supports. Screening tools are usually brief and can be subject to error if the student was sick or having a bad day, so collecting one or two additional progress monitoring points can confirm that there is actually a need for instructional support. Validating the need for support can also occur by checking if the students' risk status matches teacher perceptions about their performance in classroom literacy tasks. For EL students, including knowledge of their linguistic performance is essential at this stage to ensure the right kinds of support are provided.

Planning and implementing instructional support. Planning and implement-ing support involves the collection and analysis of data to be used for instruc-tional planning. This can be a combination of information collected at the level of identifying and validating the need for support, as well as additional diag-nostic data like phonics screening data, in-program assessment data, or more comprehensive examination of language proficiency data. In this case, the term *diagnostic data* refers to data that are used to diagnose instructional needs and plan instructional support according to students' instructional needs. This kind of information can be used to place students appropriately in an intervention program, or to identify key missing skills (e.g., phonics skills, vocabulary knowl-edge, comprehension skills and strategies, language structures needed to support learning) that can be taught in instruction and intervention.

Evaluating and modifying instructional support. Once interventions are im-plemented, support must be evaluated by progress monitoring at appropriate intervals according to students' instructional needs. If students are on track, interventions can be continued, whereas if students are not on track, interven-tions should be intensified. Further discussion of progress monitoring occurs in the following section.

Reviewing outcomes. Finally, reviewing outcomes involves evaluating whether individual students, as well as the students as a whole, were supported to achieve meaningful literacy outcomes. This can occur through reviewing end-of-year screening data, as well as state assessment and language proficiency data. The ODM provides a framework for ensuring individual students and the system of support as a whole is responsive to the instructional needs of the children.

ASSESSMENT AT TIER 2

Progress Monitoring

A central element within MTSS is to provide students with the appropriate intensity of support (interventions) and then monitor their progress toward instructional targets. Progress monitoring assessments should be: (1) available in multiple alternate forms that allow for frequent assessing to monitor students' growth rates, (2) valid and reliable for the population, (3) quick to administer, and (4) sensitive to student improvement, and should have (5) goals that link to reading outcomes (Mellard, McKnight, & Woods, 2009). Progress monitoring assessments may be similar to or the same as those used for screening (these assessments have multiple alternate forms so can be used for both purposes). CBMs, which are general outcome measures, are frequently used due to the longstanding evidence for their efficacy across student groups (Deno, 2003). Generally speaking, in Tier 2 progress monitoring is administered monthly, with weekly progress monitoring in Tier 3 (Kaminski, Cummings, Powell-Smith, & Good, 2008). Scores are graphed and teams analyze them to make decisions regarding the effectiveness of interventions for individuals or groups of students.

For EL students, there are some unique considerations. Brown and Sanford (2011) make four recommendations for progress monitoring EL students: (1) monitor student progress in all languages of instruction; (2) set rigorous goals that support students toward meeting grade-level standards; (3) evaluate growth frequently, increasing intensity of instruction when growth is less than expected; and (4) evaluate growth as compared to that of true peers.

Identifying Appropriate Growth Norms for True Peer Comparisons

The primary question when progress monitoring students is, "Is the student making adequate growth to meet meaningful grade-level benchmarks?" One way to work toward this is to set the instructional goal at the grade-level b3rd-grader who is 3 years behind in reading), the grade-level benchmark may not be a reasonable standard. In that case, educators may set a goal to try to make "catch-up" progress. A 3rd-grader who is reading at the kindergarten level may require a goal that catches them up to 2nd grade reading level by the end of 3rd grade, but then meets end of 4th grade benchmarks by the end of the following year.

Selecting goals based on growth norms is another option. Fuchs, Fuchs, Hamlett, and Walz (1993) established growth norms for students' oral reading fluency growth across 1st through 6th grade, providing an option for setting realistic or ambitious growth goals to help students catch up on their reading (see Figure 4.6). For a description of how to use growth norms to set instructional goals, see Hosp, Hosp, and Howell (2016). It is important to note, however, that these growth norms were not established with a population of ELs. To address this, some districts have created their own growth norms for EL students using locally normed information. Because differential growth rates with the EL student group may be due to differential levels of language proficiency, it is important to compare students to the greatest extent possible to "true peers," or students with similar linguistic and cultural backgrounds. This can be a powerful strategy to ensure the appropriateness of the growth norms for the local population. One caveat is that if instruction is ineffective, these growth norms may be insufficiently ambitious to help students catch up.

Data-Based Decisionmaking for Intervention

During the intervention process, data-based decisionmaking should occur regularly (i.e., at least monthly) in grade-level teams that also include expertise from ELD specialists, special education teachers, and reading specialists in addition to the building administrator. These teams should convene to review student progress data to determine whether students are making adequate progress toward their instructional goals. Decision rules should be utilized to determine when interventions are working and when they need to be adjusted. One example of a decision rule is "If students score three data points below their aimline, a change of intervention is needed" (Fuchs, Fuchs, Hamlett, & Ferguson, 1992; Fuchs, Fuchs, Hintze, & Lembke, 2007). Students who are on track should continue in their interventions. If students have already met benchmarks (e.g., three data points above the next benchmark goal), the team may consider discontinuing the intervention. If students fall three data points below their aimline, a change in intervention is necessary. Educators may consider intensifying the intervention by increasing intervention fidelity (or training of teachers), increasing time, or reducing group size (see Harlacher, Nelson, & Sanford, 2010, for additional options for intensifying interventions). For EL students, it is important to determine if entire groups of students are making inadequate progress. If a whole group of EL students is making less than expected progress, it may be because the intervention is not adequately addressing their cultural and linguistic needs. The ELD specialist can be a vital team member in sharing knowledge about the students' language development and instructional support needs. In this case, adjustments to the interventions, such as preteaching vocabulary and providing language supports should be made. Utilizing the PLUSS framework referenced in Chapter 3 may be useful in this situation.

Figure 4.6. Oral Reading Fluency (ORF) CBM weekly growth rates: Words read correctly (WRC).

Grade	Realistic Weekly Growth Rates of Words Read Correctly (WRC)	Ambitious Weekly Growth Rates of Words Read Correctly (WRC)
1	2	3
2	1.5	2
3	1	1.5
4	0.85	1.1
5	0.5	0.8
6	0.3	0.65

(Adapted from Fuchs, Fuchs, Hamlett, & Walz, 1993)

SECONDARY EL STUDENTS WITH INTERRUPTED FORMAL SCHOOLING

At the secondary level, ELs may enter the system with interrupted formal education; they may be reading at a 2nd-grade reading level, even as a 15-year-old sophomore in high school. In this case, it is important to meet students where they are in their reading level and utilize an intensive evidence-based intervention, setting ambitious goals to catch the student up and close the gap. Educators should still use progress monitoring tools at the students' instructional level (2nd grade in this case) until they meet each progressive benchmark and utilize an intervention program designed for catching up older students, such as Corrective Reading (Engelmann, 2008) with the PLUSS overlay to account for their cultural and linguistic backgrounds. Once students meet the current 2nd-grade benchmarks, they can advance through progressive grade levels' progress monitoring materials. It is noteworthy that many of the growth charts and progress monitoring materials only go up through 6th-grade reading level. In general, once students have reached a 6th-grade reading proficiency, interventions will focus less on the process of reading (like decoding, multisyllabic word reading, and accurate and fluent reading) and more on teaching vocabulary and comprehension strategies and the background knowledge needed to access content-area text. Vocabulary and comprehension should always be the focus of reading, and these supports may be necessary for EL students throughout their educational careers. However, the primary focus of the intervention may shift once students are reading at or above a 6th-grade level; therefore, progress monitoring tools and growth norms are most useful and necessary through this grade level, although some tools may be used through the 8th-grade reading level.

Standard Treatment and Problem-Solving Models

MTTS systems have been described as utilizing either a standard treatment or a problem-solving model for supporting students. Tilly (2008) has framed this a false dichotomy and indicated that effective systems utilize both.

Standard Treatment Protocol. Standard treatment protocols involve identifying planned research-based interventions for all students who meet inclusion criteria. For Tier 2 interventions, some systems identify specific intervention programs that have a strong research base and plan to implement these interventions with every child who fits a given instructional needs profile. This is known as a Standard Treatment Protocol because the options are predetermined within this model (see Figure 4.7 for an example). One benefit of the standard treatment protocol is that they implement research-based programs that have a higher probability of supporting students to meet grade-level reading expectations (or other literacy expectations). Further, they are efficient, and it is relatively straightforward to ensure standard implementation or fidelity to program implementation as well as to train a variety of school personnel (e.g., paraprofessionals, reading specialists, counselors, school psychologists) in the use of this treatment protocol because the research-based programs often utilize consistent teacher directions and are highly structured. It is also easier to deliver these small-group interventions efficiently to the relatively large number of students who may require them (in Tier 2, around 20% of the school population on average). This makes efficient use of limited resources in our schools to ensure maximum benefit to students.

Within a Standard Treatment Protocol, the interventions should be matched to student need in terms of using curriculum-based measurement data and program placement data, but they are not tailored individually to each child at this stage in the intervention process. As discussed in Chapter 3, one challenge with this model is there are significantly fewer intervention programs that included EL students in their research base; therefore, the interventions may partially address EL students' instructional needs while inadequately supporting language needs and not providing cultural links and background knowledge needed for EL students to succeed. For this reason, PLUSS adaptations to the Standard Treatment Protocol may assist in strengthening the effectiveness of these research-based programs for EL students, and they can be considered as a part of group problem solving, described next.

Problem-Solving Model. The problem-solving model involves analyzing student data at either the group or individual level. At the group level (for example, if a group of EL students is not responding adequately to an evidence-based intervention), the team may consider making enhancements to an intervention to address students' linguistic and cultural backgrounds. One potential option for responding to the linguistic, cultural, and experiential

Figure 4.7. Example of a Standard Treatment Protocol.

Core Program—90 Minutes Daily		Interventions		Time and Group Size
Grade	Curriculum Options (All Students)	Strategic (Below Benchmark)	Intensive (Well Below Benchmark)	
K	Reading Street *Calle de la Lectura* ECRI*	ERI (Early Reading Intervention by Scott Foresman) ECRI Tier 2	ERI Reading Mastery	**Tier 1** Maximum of 6 students per small group
1	Reading Street *Calle de la Lectura* Walk to Read**	ECRI Tier 2 Phonics for Reading Read Naturally (English and Spanish)	ERI Phonics for Reading Reading Mastery	**Tier 2** Core + 30 minutes of Intervention
2	Reading Street *Calle de la Lectura* Walk to Read ECRI	ECRI Tier 2 Phonics for Reading Read Naturally (English and Spanish)	Phonics for Reading Reading Mastery	
3	Reading Street *Calle de la Lectura* Walk to Read	Phonics for Reading Read Naturally (English and Spanish) REWARDS	Corrective Reading Phonics for Reading Reading Mastery	**Tier 3** Core + 45 minutes of Intervention
4	Reading Street *Calle de la Lectura* Walk to Read	Read Naturally (English and Spanish) Six Minute Solution	Corrective Reading Phonics for Reading Reading Mastery REWARDS	
5	Reading Street *Calle de la Lectura* Walk to Read	Read Naturally (English and Spanish) Six Minute Solution	Corrective Reading Phonics for Reading Reading Mastery REWARDS	

*Enhanced Core Reading Instruction is a multi-tiered program—Tier 1 and Tier 2—featuring a series of teaching routines designed to increase the efficiency and effectiveness of reading instruction in kindergarten, 1st, and 2nd grade. ** The process of grouping students in skill-alike groups for a small portion of the day. (Adapted with permission from Tigard-Tualatin School District, Oregon) needs of EL students and other diverse students, the PLUSS framework, provides a systematic enhancement to overlay intervention programs (see Chapter 3 for further description). Currently, the authors of this chapter are investigating the use of the PLUSS framework for EL students at risk for or with dis/abilities as part of a federal grant funded by the Office of Special Education Programs (OSEP). (See www.projectlee.org for further information and resources.) If most students are responding to the group interventions, but individual students are not responsive, individual problem solving may be needed to address their instructional needs (discussed in the following section).

ASSESSMENT AT TIER 3

Individual Problem Solving

Al Otaiba and Fuchs (2002) found that between 4% and 10% of students will not respond to high-quality, well-implemented interventions and need the most intensive interventions. These students may have difficulties developing phonemic awareness, visual perception skills, rapid automatic naming (RAN) ability, language, working memory, and executive functions (Fiefer, 2008). When students have received appropriate instruction and interventions aligned to their linguistic, experiential, and cultural backgrounds but are not making adequate progress when compared to their true peers, an Individual Problem-Solving Approach should be used. This is a part of the "planning, implementing and evaluating support" steps within the Outcomes Driven Model (described earlier). This approach recognizes that each student's contexts (as discussed in Chapter 3) must be considered in determining instruction, interventions, assessment, and in this case, adequate progress. Teams utilize four steps in this process: (1) define the problem, (2) analyze the problem, (3) set a goal and implement the plan, and (4) evaluate the success of the intervention (Shores, 2009).

Define the problem. Teams define the problem in observable, measurable terms (Batsche, Castillo, Dixon, & Forde, 2008) and write a clear description of the problem. Teams must consider and quantify the magnitude of the gap between the expected and actual performance. This can be done using curriculum-based measurement and comparing the student's performance to grade-level benchmarks, as well as the average performance of students with similar cultural and linguistic backgrounds.

Analyze the problem. The instructional setting is analyzed to determine why the problem is occurring and identify adjustments to instruction that may lead to improved outcomes. A process that includes ICEL/RIOT (Hosp, 2008) can be helpful for framing what and how to examine relevant factors affecting student learning and why the problem is occurring. ICEL stands for analyzing *Instruction, Curriculum, Environment*, and finally the *Learner*. RIOT frames how to go about collecting information: review *Records, Interview, Observe,* and *Test*. The first consideration for EL students is to determine that instruction is both comprehensible (e.g., through preteaching vocabulary, fast mapping [i.e., quickly defining] unknown words during oral reading, and ensuring appropriate language supports like sentence frames are in place) and culturally and experientially appropriate (e.g., background knowledge is not assumed, but taught, efforts are made to use materials inclusive of students' cultural group). Once these cultural and linguistic factors are supported, teams can evaluate other features of the intensity of the intervention and determine how to modify instructional support.

Set a goal and implement the plan. The new or adjusted intervention is clearly articulated in observable measurable terms, and delivered in a more intensive setting (i.e., duration, group size, and frequency). As in prior tiers, interventions for EL students, no matter the tier or intensity, must continue to align to their linguistic, cultural, and experiential contexts to rule out the possibility of inappropriate instruction.

Evaluate the success of the intervention. Progress monitoring data are used to determine if the intervention is effective for the target student. Again, progress for EL students must be considered both in relation to true peers as well as grade-level benchmarks.

If the initial interventions are not successful, the problem-solving process repeats and adjustments continue to be made until the student is successful (Howell & Nolet, 2000), or in some cases, students may be referred for a special education evaluation. Tier 3 interventions may include more than 100 individual sessions over more than 20 weeks at the intensive level (Kearns, Lemons, Fuchs, & Fuchs, 2014). As is true across all tiers, interventions must be adjusted to fit students' needs (Kearns, Lemons, Fuchs, & Fuchs, 2014) including their language needs (Brown & Doolitte, 2008).

Collaborative Problem-Solving Team (CPST)

At this stage, a CPST may meet again to analyze progress monitoring data and additional data that may include classroom work samples, teacher observations, and anecdotal records, to determine whether or not Tier 3 interventions have been successful. It is important to note that this team should continue to include expertise from the English language development or bilingual specialist to adequately understand the needs of EL students. Teams may form hypotheses as to the reason for the problem, create a written intervention plan, and adjust as necessary. When outcomes are lower than expected, teams may either: (1) recommend additional Tier 3 interventions, or (2) refer the student for a special education evaluation. If a referral is the chosen course of action, the student's progress must be compared to the performance of an appropriate comparison group (true peers).

EQUITABLE OPPORTUNITIES MEANS EQUAL STANDARDS

In this chapter we have reviewed the concept of Multi-tiered System of Supports (MTSS) and the continuum of assessments available to address specific educational questions regarding student performance, including possible eligibility for special education services. When the question centers on instructional need, the use of formative and summative assessment can generally address the issue by using the typical age and grade-level standards. For example, the questions "How does this student's performance compare to grade-level expectations and what are the appropriate supports they need to meet the benchmarks?" are as valid for an EL student as for a native English-speaking student since it is appropriate to use the same standard and expectations for both.

We must not lower standards for EL students. Certainly, many EL students and other students will have a long way to go toward reaching the standard (especially new high school EL students and other students with interrupted formal schooling), but that should remain the goal of instruction—to support the student to achieve at a level that is at least comparable to the average student of the same age or grade. In many ways, low assessment values for EL students in comparison to native English-speaking peers helps highlight the dire need for culturally and linguistically aligned intensive intervention and instructional programming to improve learning for an EL student in any meaningful way (Sanford, Brown, & Turner, 2012). Growth should be examined as compared to "true peers" and separately compared to native English-speaking peers and determine whether instruction is supporting both groups equitably (USDOE, 2016b). If not, specific conversations about how to intensify instruction for EL students to ensure it is meeting their unique cultural and linguistic needs, as well as their academic needs, as necessary.

When the question underlying the evaluation changes to be centered on the possible presence of a dis/ability—a condition that may prompt a referral for special education evaluation—a different standard for comparison must be used. For example, answering the question, "Does this student's low performance and relative lack of growth suggest the presence of some type of learning dis/ability?" in a valid manner will require comparison only to the individuals with similar cultural and linguistic backgrounds and experiences, i.e., their "true peers." Such a comparison provides the only legitimate and equitable standard for making this specific determination and to use anything else may result in a discriminatory outcome. Note that the fact that the EL student may not be identified as having a dis/ability does not change their instructional need. Indeed, a dis/ability determination and placement in special education do not alter the fact that instruction must still be intensive and appropriate if it is to be successful in helping the student succeed.

In summary, decisions regarding instructional need or intervention and possible dis/ability identification must be made separately and each must be based on the appropriate standard for comparison. Use of inappropriate standards or incorrect data is likely to perpetuate the disproportionate representation of EL students in special education. The real answer to such inequity is to ensure that any decision based on any type of comparison is made in accordance with the nature of the question being asked and the correct standard for making such a comparison. Only in this way is there likely to be any progress in ensuring that English learner students have the same opportunity to succeed in school as any of their same-age or same-grade peers, including those who are native English speakers.

CHAPTER 5

Effective Instruction for English Learner Students with Academic Challenges in General and Special Education

Collaborative Program Elements

Recent enrollment projections for public schools predict that by 2020 the percentage of White students will decrease by 1%, while Black students will increase by 1%, Latino students by 25%, Asian and Pacific Islander students by 36%, and American Indian and Alaskan Native students by 17% (Hussar & Bailey, 2011). Additionally, from 1980 to 2016, more than 3 million refugees (defined as persons fearing persecution in their country of origin because of race, religion, nationality, membership in a particular social group, or political opinion) have resettled in the United States (Krogstad & Radford, 2017). Since the U.S. Office of Refugee Resettlement (ORR) began keeping records of refugee arrivals in 1983, refugees from five countries have represented 77% of all such arrivals: the former Soviet Union (25%), Vietnam (23%), Cuba (13%), the former Yugoslavia (8%), and Laos (6%). Stepping into a public school classroom reinforces the fact that our students come from many backgrounds and represent many native languages and cultures. Of EL students, the majority speak Spanish as their native language (77.1%; U.S. Department of Education Statistics, National Center for Education Statistics, 2018) and the majority also were born in the United States. As we described in Chapter 2, as a group, EL students are heterogeneous; this group includes both students with limited formal education in their home language or interrupted formal education, and those with strong formal education and language foundation from their native countries. Some English learner students have languished in English as a Second Language (ESL)/English Language Development (ELD) programs for 6 years or more and are referred to as long-term English learners (LTEL) students. Additionally, they fall at all points on the socioeconomic continuum, but with more than 60% of EL students living in families who earn below the poverty line (Grantmakers for Education, 2013). These differences have important educational implications with each category of EL students requiring specific instructional and sometimes social–emotional supports. Within that population are EL students with true dis/abilities.

When EL students encounter academic challenges, too often educators' first response is to refer them for a special education evaluation. Instead, it is critical to look at instructional factors, particularly regarding the alignment or "fit" of instructional strategies to students' level of instructional language proficiency, their culture, and their previous educational and life experiences. To emphasize a point made in previous chapters, healthy and effective educational systems, especially those that use a Multi-Tiered System of Supports (MTSS) approach, identify which students need support early in the instructional process, provide interventions matched to the level of need, monitor progress toward instructional targets, ensure all instruction and interventions use strategies to make language comprehensible, use valid and reliable assessments for all student groups, and repeat the cycle as needed. Only after receiving this type of support, and using an appropriate comparison group, should students be referred for a special education evaluation. Using the appropriate comparison group is a key factor in identifying which students need a referral. This is done by compared to their "true peers" (defined in Chapter 3) to ensure the problem does not stem from instruction not aligned with EL students' unique needs. As straightforward as this support cycle sounds, to effectively develop and implement such a system requires strong leadership and a knowledgeable team of educators from multiple disciplines, including an EL/bilingual specialist. Such models of support are necessary to disrupt the historic disproportionate representation of EL students in special education and enable us to identify the right students for special education services. There will be EL students who truly have intrinsic dis/abilities and they have the right to special education services, but they should be represented in special education at a similar rate to native English-speaking students. We emphasize that special education is not a place, but a service (Kauffman, Hallahan, Pullen, & Badar, 2018), and those services can and should be provided alongside typical peers to the maximum extent possible (identified as "least restrictive environment" in IDEA; see Chapter 7 for more details). Further, these services must be reserved only for those with dis/abilities no matter the service location.

Appropriate decisions about referrals cannot be based on teacher judgment or gut feelings but must rather be made through an evidence-based data-driven decisionmaking process that ensures strong core instruction for all learners. Given the diversity of learners, teachers must use student-level factors to guide appropriate and effective instruction. To support educators in providing targeted instruction based on students' backgrounds, we will first identify and discuss characteristics within the EL student population and their instructional implications. Following that, we outline the steps to determine which EL students may benefit from a referral for a special education evaluation, emphasizing again that this decision rests on providing effective and appropriate core instruction and intervention prior to referral, in most cases. Next, the evaluation and eligibility process and a framework for interpreting scores from standardized testing that considers culture and language will be shared. Then, we define special education and describe service provision as well as components of the requisite Individual Education Plan (IEP) that outlines annual goals, services, and accommodations. Methods for developing culturally and linguistically appropriate IEPs and creating collaborative special education service models across the grades are included. Finally, this chapter concludes with the emerging policies regarding the use of differing standards or criteria for reclassifying EL students with learning dis/abilities as fluent English proficient (RFEP) and exiting EL programs (CCSSO, 2016a, 2016b). Our discussion will be especially relevant for administrators, general educators, and ELD/ESL teachers, who have less direct experience with special education students and for special educators with limited experience with EL students.

TYPOLOGIES OF ENGLISH LEARNERS: DIFFERENCES ACROSS THE POPULATION THAT IMPACT INSTRUCTION AND ACHIEVEMENT

Meeting the educational needs of EL students is increasingly challenging. One major factor is the heterogeneity of this group. Knowledge of student level factors such as the country of birth, types and consistency of education, proficiency in native language and English, immigration experiences, and socioeconomic status should all serve to shape instructional practices (Olsen & Jaramillo, 1999). One-size-fits-all educational approaches are not responsive to the diversity within the EL student group and often lead to low achievement as we continue to find in many systems. Below, we explore some additional details of the contextual factors described in Chapter 3 that educators should consider when planning high-quality, appropriate instruction.

Contextual Factors

Country of birth/Generation in the United States. Contrary to popular belief, recent demographic data indicate that the majority of EL students were born in the United States (77%) and thus only 23% are foreign born (Zong & Batalova, 2015). A student's birth country seems to have implications for schooling; research indicates that, unfortunately, as a group, U.S.-born EL students fare worse academically than foreign-born students (Connerty, 2009). One reason may be that teachers erroneously assume fluent English proficiency in U.S.-born EL students and conclude the root of any academic challenges to be lack of ability or a dis/ability (Roberge, 2002). Believing the problem resides within the student rather than within the system then limits educational opportunities. Evidence also suggests generational status bears on achievement with many third-generation students (U.S.-born students of U.S.-born parents) faring worse academically than second-generation (U.S.-born students of foreign born parents) ones (Rumberger & Larson, 1998). Whether born in the United States or not, many students live in households where a mixture of heritage language and English is spoken. This can lead to attenuated proficiency in both languages unless care is taken to fully develop as least one and preferably both languages.

Transborder students. Some EL students experience continuous border-crossing both in a literal and figurative sense (Cervantes-Soon & Kasun, 2018). For example, many children live in Mexico along the southern U.S. border and cross the border daily to attend U.S. schools. Some transborder students live with relatives in the United States during the week and see their parents only on weekends. By necessity, they engage in literacy, social media, and social experiences across two cultures and languages and exhibit sophisticated understanding of cultural nuances and bilingualism. These skills must be viewed and reinforced as assets, valued and built upon in school to further develop these linguistic, academic, and multicultural resources.

Formal education opportunities. Knowing the types and duration of educational experiences students have had in their home country, or during their immigration process, or in U.S. schools, is another significant factor in analyzing their success in school. Longstanding research documents the impact of strong native language and literacy skills on academic attainment (Cummins, 1984; Fillmore & Snow, 2000; Goldenberg, 2008; Thomas & Collier, 2002). Thus, students who experienced high-quality and consistent education in their home country generally can build on these experiences and transfer them to English in a relatively short amount of time. In fact, such prior experiences may serve to moderate the immigrant or refugee experience. On the other hand, students whose families have fled war- or famine-ravaged lands to refugee camps before coming to the United States may have experienced inconsistent and informal schooling, perhaps also in a second language. Such students are known as *students with interrupted formal education* (SIFE), and they may be overwhelmed by the myriad new experiences and expectations American schools bring. In other cases, there may be differences in the quality and frequency of schooling depending on whether they attended an urban or rural, public or private school. Opportunities for students also vary in this country with some communities establishing native language and culture after-school or weekend programs. Gathering information on these factors allows us to build on EL students' learnings from these multiple contexts and to better understand the gaps they may present with. We also know that parents' educational attainment, their experience with educational systems outside of the United States, and their knowledge of the U.S. educational system can also impact their children's achievement.

Long-term English learner students. Many of our EL students have been enrolled in English as a Second Language (ESL)/English Language Development (ELD) programs for more than 6 years and are known as long-term English learner (LTEL) students. Some LTEL students come from immigrant families or are immigrants themselves but most have been born in the United States or have lived in this country most of their lives (Park, Zong, & Batalova, 2018). LTEL students are most commonly seen at the secondary level and frequently struggle both academically and with English proficiency. In part, this struggle may be due to secondary content teachers who are not trained in and do not include literacy or language development activities for EL students in their content instruction. Typically, LTEL students exhibit adequate social language in both English and their home language but have difficulty with the deeper levels of academic language. LTELs require engaging programs and instruction that emphasize academic language, including talk, content development, and writing in most, if not all, of their classes.

The impact of low SES across all EL student groups. We know that socio-economic status (SES) impacts academic attainment across all student groups (Lara-Cinisomo et al., 2004; Neuman, 2008). Children with low SES often exhibit lower academic achievement than those with more financial capital (Harwell & LeBeau, 2010; Morgan, Farkas, Hillemeier, & Maczuga, 2009). Children from homes with low SES sometimes have less access to literacy experiences and books, computers, developmentally appropriate toys, and other resources (Bradley, Corwyn, McAdoo, & García Coll, 2001). Further, their neighborhood schools often lack the resources to boost learning trajectories. The good news is that Aikens and Barbarin (2008) report that school conditions and classroom environment play a more important role in school success than does home environment. This means that if systems focus on providing adequate resources for *all* schools, but particularly those serving less affluent communities, we can potentially mitigate the negative effects of poverty on outcomes. It should be further noted that low SES backgrounds appear to have greater impact in the early grades but high-quality programs, particularly in literacy, can neutralize the impact of poverty over time (Chetty et al., 2011; D'Angiulli, Siegel, & Maggi, 2004). Figure 5.1 provides a summary of the typologies covered above and some instructional implications.

All of the student contextual factors just described, as well as those described in Chapter 3, should be considered in determining the extent to which an EL student's struggles are due to less-than-high-quality instruction, a difference from other grade-level peers, and/or a learning dis/ability. Once a school team determines that the EL student's struggles may be due at least in part to a learning dis/ability, then a formal special education evaluation and placement determination process must begin.

EL Students with Disabilities

All the above factors can be barriers to achievement. Low achievement is often linked to dis/ability. Dis/ability or intrinsic learning difficulties will be true causes of diminished achievement in some cases, but instructional issues must

Figure 5.1. English learner (EL) student typologies.

Type	Description	Instructional Implications
Country of Birth		
U.S.-born ELs	ELs who are U.S.-born citizens account for the largest percentage of ELs in schools	Instruction should focus on developing strong oral language skills in both their home and second languages. Academic language and vocabulary must be taught explicitly.
Foreign-born ELs	ELs who were born outside of the United States	Foreign-born ELs tend to have stronger primary language skills than U.S.-born ELs depending on the length of time immersed in that language before immigrating. Instruction should bridge their native language and content knowledge to English. They may need support in bridging cultural differences.
Transnational ELs	ELs who frequently travel between the United States and their home country	Instruction should focus on academic language development across both languages. Support students in connecting their two languages and culture to school experiences. These students bring many assets that should be built upon and valued.
Newcomer ELs	ELs who have been in the United States for 1 or 2 years	Newcomers who have not developed oral and literacy skills in their primary language cannot build on "linguistic transfer." Such students need to learn functional words and terms and need support in bridging cultural differences. While it may be appropriate to instruct them with other newcomers for a short while, it is critical they be included with age peers and receive sheltered content instruction as soon as possible. Language instruction should not be emphasized over content instruction.

Figure 5.1. English learner (EL) student typologies. (continued)

Type	Description	Instructional Implications
Formal Educational Opportunities		
Highly schooled new-comer ELs	ELs who have been in the U.S. for 1 to 2 years, who attained a high-quality education in their primary language but have limited or no English skills	These students are able to build upon their strong primary language and academic foundations to transfer these skills to English with explicit instruction.
Students with interrupted formal education (SIFE)	Students who had limited to no access to school in their home country or whose education was interrupted; limited literacy in their native language and little or no English proficiency	To overcome critical academic gaps, language and content area instruction must be provided simultaneously rather than sequentially. Newcomer programs may initially help, but it is critical to assess students' existing skills to determine gap areas and plan instruction.
Time Enrolled in ESL/ELD Programs		
Long-term ELs (LTELs)	Students who remain classified as EL for 6 years or longer; these students generally have received all of their education in the United States	LTELs are often orally bilingual and sound fluent but often have not developed academic language or strong literacy skills in either language. Rather than providing remedial programs, instruction should be highly engaging, address content and language standards, and be engaging and rigorous enough to accelerate their academic and linguistic progress.
Reclassified ELs	Former ELs who have met their state's linguistic and academic criteria to be reclassified as fluent English proficient and exited from EL programs	The academic progress of students who have been exited from ESL/ELD services must be monitored for 2 years to ensure they continue to be provided meaningful access to grade-level core content instruction and provide support, if needed.

Figure 5.1. English learner (EL) student typologies. (continued)

Type	Description	Instructional Implications
Other		
ELs in special education	Students whose individual needs require specialized support and meet the eligibility requirements for special education services under one of the federal disability categories	Dual identified students should receive specially designed instruction and ELD services.

first be ruled out as a primary cause. When children have been identified with a true dis/ability and they need specialized support in school, they are served in special education programs under one of 13 federal disability categories outlined in the Individual with Disability Education Improvement Act (IDEA, 2004). IDEA (2004), formerly IDEA (1997), is the legislation that ensures students in special education are provided with a Free Appropriate Public Education (FAPE) tailored to each child's individual needs. Figure 5.2 lists IDEA's disability categories and their definitions. As is evident, it is easier to determine some disabilities than others and teams sometimes struggle with determining which category is the primary barrier to learning. Disproportionate representation of EL students occurs most often in the so-called "high incidence" categories (i.e., specific learning disability, speech or language impairment) where placement is based on a team's interpretation of data, rather than the "low-incidence" categories (e.g., intellectual disability, deafness, blindness) where decisions are much more straightforward. Once educators are confident that EL students have received appropriate and high-quality instruction and interventions across the tiers (that is, instruction is a good fit), or the disability appears to be one of "low incidence," then appropriate referrals of EL students for special education evaluations can be made with some confidence.

In summary, EL students require different instructional strategies and programs depending on their unique backgrounds and this need continues into any special education services provided.

SPECIAL EDUCATION

Kauffman, Hallahan, Pullen, and Badar (2018) describe special education as follows:

Although good general education is demanding, special education requires great-er control and precision along several dimensions of instruction: explicitness, sys-tematicness, intensiveness, relentlessness, pace, group size, curriculum, corrective feedback, duration, frequency, structure, reinforcement, monitoring, and assess-ment. Because all of these dimensions of teaching can vary from a little to a lot, education can differ in the degree of specialness, from sort of to very special. Ulti-mately, special education is only worthwhile if it improves instruction for students at the extremes of performance, low or high. (p. 92)

Making high-stakes decisions regarding "difference versus dis/ability" requires teams to examine the complex interaction between linguistic, cog-nitive, and academic development, and background factors, so it is not sur-prising that decisions often leans toward dis/ability, although both under- and overrepresentation is a concern nationally (USDOE, 2016b). Unfortunately, some local education agencies rationalize a decision to place an EL student in special education in terms of providing "extra help," especially after having exhausted the often limited general education resources in the school. Apart from the legal and ethical problems inherent in such default special educa-tion placement (USDOE, 2016b), offering additional educational assistance through special education to students with learning difficulties and not true dis/abilities rarely leads to successful outcomes for students. Rather, research indicates that there is a negative effect of such placement for any student (Hibel, Farkas, & Morgan, 2010) and such decisions may well have more significant adverse effects on EL students. It is hardly debatable that special education is simply not the answer to problems that may be rooted in mis-aligned or inappropriate general education instruction.

Students with True Dis/abilities Need Special Education

For students with dis/abilities, special education can be a lifeline because it pro-vides the Specially Designed Instruction (SDI) needed to meet the unique and individual needs of a child (IDEA, 2004) under the supervision of a licensed special educator. The curriculum used in special education varies. It may be curriculum different from that of same-grade peers without a dis/ability, the same general education curriculum with specific adaptations or modifications, or some combination of the two. Regardless of the program, *all* instruction must position *all* students as experts in their own unique learned knowledge. To reiterate, special education, as highlighted earlier, is the provision of services and not a place (Kauffman, Hallahan, Pullen, & Badar, 2018). Thus, special education services and instruction can be provided within the general educa-tion classroom (inclusive setting), through pull-out programs, special classes, special schools, in hospitals or other facilities, or at home. Service location and the amount of services is determined by the IEP team but must occur in the *least restrictive environment* (LRE) for that child, meaning instruction occurs as

Figure 5.2. IDEA federal disability categories.

Categories	Definition
Autism	Autism is a developmental disability that can have a significant impact on a student's communication skills, social interactions, and academic performance.
Deaf-blindness	Deaf-blindness under federal law means concomitant hearing and visual impairments, the combination of which causes such severe communication and other developmental and educational needs that they cannot be accommodated in special education programs solely for children with deafness or children with blindness.
Developmental delay	"Developmental delay" is the term that the IDEA (2004) uses for children aged 3 through 9 years who have delays in physical, cognitive, communicative, social– emotional, and/or adaptive development, and who, because of these delays, require special education.
Emotional disturbance	Students with emotional disorders are a very heterogeneous group with a wide range of issues that are unique to each individual.
Hearing impairment	The Individuals with Disabilities Education Improvement Act of 2004 includes "hearing impairment" and "deafness" as two of the categories under which children with dis/abilities may be eligible for special education and related service programming.
Intellectual disability	Intellectual dis/abilities are not an inherent trait of any individual, but instead are characterized by a combination of deficits in both cognitive functioning and adaptive behavior.
Multiple disabilities	The multiple dis/abilities category encompasses a variety of conditions that may impact a student's ability to learn and achieve success in an academic setting.
Orthopedic impairment	Orthopedic impairment is defined as a severe orthopedic impairment that adversely affects a child's educational performance.
Other health impairment	*Other health impairment* exists as an umbrella term encompassing hundreds of types of impairment that may result in a chronic condition limiting the individual's ability to effectively access the educational environment.

Figure 5.2. IDEA federal disability categories. (continued)

Categories	Definition
Specific learning disability	Specific learning disabilities (SLD) is defined as a disorder in one or more of the basic psychological processes involved in understanding or using language spoken or written.
Speech or language impairment	Speech and language impairment is defined as a communication disorder that adversely affects the child's ability to talk, understand, read, and write.
Traumatic brain injury	Traumatic brain injury (TBI) under federal law means a acquired injury to the brain caused by an external physical force, resulting in total or partial functional disability or psychosocial impairment, or both, that adversely affects the student's educational performance.
Visual impairment, including blindness	A visual impairment is any visual condition that impacts an individual's ability to successfully complete the activities of everyday life.

(Project IDEAL, n.d.)

much as possible alongside typical age-alike peers. Parents legally have a voice in all aspects of special education. For EL students in special education, ESL/ELD services that address the state ELD proficiency standards must continue to be provided. The instructional strategies used, however, should be the same specialized instruction described in their IEP. For dual identified students (EL and special education), instruction is best provided through a collaborative model taking into account students' dual program needs. Some teams erroneously believe that "special education trumps ESL/ELD." The truth is both are federally mandated programs for students who meet the criteria and students who qualify for both programs must receive both types of services.

High-Incidence Disability Categories

Misplacement of EL students generally occurs within two high-incidence categories—specific learning disability (SLD) and speech and language impairment (SLI). The eligibility criteria for each of these categories are based on the interpretation of data by the multidisciplinary team, rather than a medical determination. Here, we examine SLD and SLI more closely to better understand eligibility requirements in each as well as to understand the difficulty of teasing apart "difference from dis/ability" when the student is an EL student and is being considered under a high-incidence category.

Characteristics of students with a specific learning disability (SLD). IDEA (2004) defines SLD as:

> (j)—The term means a disorder in one or more of the basic psychological processes involved in understanding or in using language, spoken or written, that may manifest itself in an imperfect ability to listen, think speak, read, write, spell, or to do mathematical calculations. (34 CFR §§300.8(c)(10) and 300.309)

There are three prongs of eligibility based on the regulations: (1) documented academic skills below grade level, usually evidenced by standard scores in the below-average range (< 85 points or at least one standard deviation below the average, or mean, of 100), but it may also include low achievement on progress monitoring data; (2) a weakness in a basic processing area, or cognitive weakness, in the below-average range; and (3) a relative strength in some cognitive abilities.

To provide more clarity, the federal government issued further guidance in the Federal Code of Regulations (CFR) a. 300.534, that states:

> A child may not be determined to be eligible for services if the determinant factor is: (1) lack of instruction in reading or math, or (2) limited English proficiency . . . and the child does not otherwise meet the eligibility criteria under 300.7.

Accordingly, it is neither appropriate, nor legally defensible, to place students into special education programs solely because they struggle academically. That is why the first step in making a special education determination for SLD is to ensure opportunity to learn through instruction that aligns with a student's unique learning profile or typology.

Ensuring appropriate instruction for EL students and determining that their lack of progress is not a result of their learning English while learning content in English, however, can be complicated because characteristics of academic difficulties stemming from second language acquisition can mimic a learning dis/ability. Common characteristics of learning challenges for SLD and other dis/abilities can include these difficulties: following directions, distinguishing sounds in spoken words, learning sound–symbol correspondence, remembering sight words, retelling a story, understanding figurative language, processing language, and with concentration. Figure 5.3 provides a comparison of the characteristics of learners with SLD to the reasons EL students may also exhibit some of these behaviors.

Characteristics of students with speech or language impairment (SLI). IDEA (2004) defines speech or language impairment (SLI) as "a communication disorder such as stuttering, impaired articulation, a language impairment, or a voice impairment that adversely affects a child's educational performance" (Sec. 300.8 [c] [11]). In other words, SLI affects the child's

Figure 5.3. Comparison of characteristics of SLD and second language acquisition.

Characteristics Associated with SLD	Characteristics Associated with Acquiring a Second Language
Difficulty following directions	Difficulty following directions because the directions were not well understood; it can be harder to remember multistep directions in a second language
Difficulty distinguishing or separating the sounds of spoken words	Difficulty distinguishing among sounds not in one's first language
Slow to learn sound–symbol correspondence or failure to understand that letters represent units of speech	Confusion with sound–symbol correspondence when it is different than in one's first language; it is difficult to pronounce sounds not in the first language
Difficulty remembering sight words	Difficulty remembering sight words when word meanings are not understood; this creates a double cognitive demand
Difficulty retelling a story in sequence	Difficulty retelling a story in English without the expressive skills to do so; yet the student might understand more than s/he can convey (i.e., receptive skills in English might be stronger than expressive skills)
Confusion with figurative language	Confusion with figurative language, idioms, pronouns, conjunctions, and words with multiple meanings
Slow to process challenging language	Slow to process challenging language because it is not well understood
May have poor auditory memory	May seem to have poor auditory memory if sounds or words are unfamiliar or not well understood
May have difficulty concentrating	Learning in a second language is mentally exhausting; therefore, ELs may seem to have difficulty concentrating at times
Mispronounces words orally and when reading	Mispronounces words due to differences in letter sounds in languages

(Adapted from Sanatullova-Allison & Robison-Young, 2016)

ability to speak, listen, understand, read, and write. A child may experience speech impairments, language impairments, or both. SLI is the second largest disability category of EL students in special education behind SLD. Recent statistics show that while 17% of all students in special education had an SLI determination, 21% of EL students with a disability were qualified under SLI (USDOE, 2018). It is easy to understandable why the normal second language acquisition process can be confused with speech or language disorders. Difficulties in acquiring vocabulary, pragmatic use of language, and sound production can all be attributed to SLI, second language acquisition, or a combination of the two (Pieretti & Roseberry-McKibbin, 2016). In fact, language differences and disorders can and do coexist (Bedore et al., 2018). Common characteristics of EL students with SLI include difficulty in three cognitive processing areas: speed of information processing, working memory, and selective/sustained attention (Pieretti & Roseberry-McKibbin, 2016). These difficulties present across all of an individual's languages in SLI, rather than just in English. Readers familiar with second language acquisition will recognize that these characteristics can be exhibited by EL students. Thus, differentiating second language difference from disorder is complicated, even for a knowledgeable and experienced team. Figure 5.4 provides indicators of language difference and language disability, is divided into components of language, and compares characteristics of differences due to acquiring a second language and a language disorder, to help teams distinguish between the two.

PROCESS FOR APPROPRIATE SPECIAL EDUCATION REFERRALS

Here and in previous chapters, we have delved into the education of English learner students and we have emphasized that appropriate education is based on a full understanding of each student's life, cultural, and linguistic experiences and bridging those to instruction. Determining whom to refer and/or when to do so for a special education evaluation is not a single event but rather a process. Researchers have delineated several factors that lead to the disproportional referral of EL students that we want to avoid. They are: (1) teacher's fear of misidentification of EL students due to their English proficiency status; (2) lack of access to EL services; (3) poor understanding of their instructional needs; (4) lack of nondiscriminatory, reliable, and valid assessments; and (5) similarities between linguistic difference and dis/ability in addition to low SES (Artiles, Klingner, & Tate, 2006; Arzubiaga, Artiles, King, & Harris-Murri, 2008; Blanchett, 2006; Sullivan, 2011). Below, we delineate a multistep process across the MTSS tiers that can lead to appropriate referral of EL students to special education. Although the process is rather lengthy, each step helps lead to a more informed eligibility decision.

Tier 1

Identify students who are struggling academically. All students who have academic challenges should be provided support early in the educational process in order to determine the appropriate course of action. EL students, particularly those in the early stages of English language proficiency, may enter school with literacy experiences that have not given them what is considered school readiness. Understanding how a student responds to explicit instruction can help us begin to unravel difference from dis/ability.

Review student's records and interview the student and family (if this hasn't occurred earlier). In addition to reviewing school records, interviewing the student and/or family, guardians, or caregivers about the child's background information can be particularly helpful. Students who have immigrated here often have incomplete or even no school records. Sometimes, school records do not include prior health concerns, accidents, or trauma the child has experienced. Speaking with families also provides the opportunity to understand the many ways they do and can support their child's education within their cultural context.

Examine the quality of core instruction and appropriate fit. Based on individual student factors, ensure provision of access to grade-level core content aligned with students' proficiency level in the instructional language and experiential backgrounds. When instruction has been appropriate but the student is making less than expected progress, consider providing Tier 2 support.

Use valid and reliable assessments for EL students. Identify any academic gaps using assessment tools, such as curriculum-based measures with established validity and reliability for EL students.

Set long- and short-term instructional goals. Setting short- and long-term instructional targets that support students in closing the gap between performance and grade-level benchmarks is helpful when there are large gaps. Students are motivated by achieving goals and their progress must be celebrated.

Monitor progress toward grade-level benchmarks. Monitor the student's progress regularly, comparing growth to both grade-level benchmarks, state standards, and true peers. It is crucial to have high expectations together with effective supports for all students and the target should always address grade-level standards.

Compare progress to true peers. When a student's progress is lower than that of true peers who have received similar instruction or support, the student should be referred to the support or MTSS team.

Figure 5.4. Indicators of language difference versus language dis/ability.

Language Difference	Possible Language Dis/ability
Language performance is similar to other EL students who have comparable cultural and linguistic experiences (true peer; Brown & Doolittle, 2008).	Language patterns are unique to the student and unlike others in the student's cultural community (qualitative differences) or patterns are similar to others in the student's community but language performance is significantly lower (quantitative differences).
Limited vocabulary in the native language due to lack of opportunity to use and hear the native language.	Student demonstrates limited vocabulary even when there are rich language opportunities in the native language.
Student shifts from one language to another because code-switching is a typical way of communication in their environment.	Student shifts from one language to another because of evident word-finding problems.
Communication with unfamiliar listeners may be impeded by an accent or dialect.	Communication may be impeded even with familiar listeners due to deficits in expressive and receptive language.
Pragmatics—the contextually appropriate use of language, rules governing social interactions	
Age- and culturally appropriate behaviors in interpreting facial expressions, appropriate physical proximity, turn-taking, and use and interpretation of gestures.	Student demonstrates challenges in using and interpreting nonverbal language, often leading to social difficulties. May stray off topic even if they have sufficient topic-specific vocabulary.
Grammaticality (rules of language)—how the smallest meaningful units of speech (morphemes), individual words and basic meaningful units are combined to create phrases and sentences	
Negative transfer: Applying knowledge from one language to another language when rules are not the same in both languages. Grammatical errors due to native language influences (e.g., student may omit initial verb in a question—You like cake? (omission of *Do*).	Grammatical structures continue to be inappropriate in both languages even after extensive instruction (e.g., student cannot produce the past tense in either Spanish or English, indicating difficulty with grammatical tenses).

Figure 5.4. Indicators of language difference versus language dis/ability. (continued)

Language Difference	Possible Language Dis/ability
Grammaticality (rules of language)—how the smallest meaningful units of speech (morphemes), individual words and basic meaningful units are combined to create phrases and sentences	
Word order in L1 may differ from that of English (e.g., in Arabic sentences are ordered verb-subject-object while Urdu sentences are ordered subject-object-verb). Grammatical errors due to low-quality and/or quantity of experiences with a particular language. Not enough quantity of exposure to L2 yet and/or low quality of language and attrition in L1.	Grammatical structures continue to be inappropriate in both languages even after extensive instruction (e.g., student cannot produce the past tense in either Spanish or English, indicating difficulty with grammatical tenses).
Semantics—the ways in which a language conveys meaning, both surface and deep language meaning	
A student whose native language does not use pronouns may have difficulty using them, as they do not exist in his/her native language. A student knows the concept but has the label of the word only in one language. A student may use words from L1 in productions in L2 because of his inability or unfamiliarity of the vocabulary in L2 (e.g., "The car is muy rapido." In this case, the student knows the concept as well as the needed structure but cannot remember the vocabulary). A student does not know the concept in either language (vocabulary gaps) due to experience and is responsive to instruction—only needs additional time.	Student is demonstrating limited phrasing and vocabulary in both languages (e.g., his/her sentences in both languages demonstrate limited or no use of adjectives and adverbs and both languages are marked by a short length of utterance) and is not responsive to instruction.

Figure 5.4. Indicators of language difference versus language dis/ability. (continued)

Language Difference	Possible Language Dis/ability
Semantics—the ways in which a language conveys meaning, both surface and deep language meaning	
Student was learning the L2 when other students were using language as a tool to learn about that particular subject and was not being instructed in the stronger L1.	Student is demonstrating limited phrasing and vocabulary in both languages (e.g., his/her sentences in both languages demonstrate limited or no use of adjectives and adverbs and both languages are marked by a short length of utterance) and is not responsive to instruction.
Fluency—the flow of speech; rhythm and rate of speech that produces intelligible communication	
Student's language does exhibit more interruptions, interjections, and/or repetitions for his/her age, but there are no physical concomitants marking the speech (physical strain or repeated physical actions), and the student does not seem to exhibit a consciousness of his/her dysfluency.	Major reliance on gestures rather than speech to communicate in both L1 and L2, even after lengthy exposure to English.
Students learning L2 may exhibit interruptions, interjections, and repetitions as they are searching for words while speaking.	The student exhibits not only interruptions, interjections, and/or repetitions, but also demonstrates physical concomitants that accompany these behaviors such as facial grimacing, leg stomping, or blinking that indicates physical struggle in producing speech.
	In addition, these students may demonstrate recognition of their dysfluency and try to avoid specific sounds or words.
	These behaviors will occur in both languages.
Phonology—the patterns of basic speech units and the accepted rules of pronunciation	
Student may omit specific sound combinations or have difficulty producing certain sounds in the L2 that do not exist in the phonology of the L1.	Students will demonstrate a delay in the development of the age-appropriate sounds in both languages (e.g., a student may consistently have difficulty producing vowels in both language).

(Brown & Kapantzoglou, 2018, adapted table from Samora & Lopez-Diaz, 2010)

Tier 2

Support through MTSS using culturally and linguistically aligned interventions. The support or MTSS team plans culturally and linguistically aligned interventions. As in all instruction, interventions should match an EL student's level of instructional support and be culturally and linguistically appropriate. The PLUSS framework, described in Chapter 3, may be useful here.

Compare progress to true peers. When a student's progress is lower than that of true peers and they have been provided appropriate interventions, the team: (1) continues interventions but makes appropriate changes (i.e., increase the frequency and duration, decrease group size, provide more frequent progress monitoring, and/or changes the intervention) for a specified amount of time, or when the gaps are particularly large or a dis/ability other than SLD or SLI is suspected, may (2) refer the student for a special education evaluation.

Tier 3

Refer for special education evaluation when progress is insufficient. After determining the student is not making expected progress in Tier 2 and then again in Tier 3, the team (including an ELD specialist) refers the student for a formal special education evaluation. The student may receive more intensive interventions before the referral or throughout the referral and evaluation process.

Referral to Special Education

Adhere to the Standard Process and timelines for special education. The regular process and timelines for notice, referral, consent for assessment, eligibility, IEP development, and service delivery decisions that apply to all students must be followed for EL students.

Document developmental milestones. At the time of referral, a thorough developmental, language and education history is conducted, if it has not been done prior.

Include ELD specialist in decisions. Ensure the multidisciplinary team includes an ELD specialist or someone who can support the team in understanding the impact of second language acquisition on learning and achievement.

Include parents in decisions and assessment planning. The assessment team, including parents, identifies appropriate assessments and/or data necessary and decides on the language(s) of assessment used to determine special education eligibility. Many of these concepts may be unfamiliar to parents and families; thus, it is important to take the time to help them understand the concepts and make informed decisions in partnership with educators.

Use trained interpreters. Use trained interpreters at all meetings when parents have limited English proficiency, and when appropriate, during the student assessment process if assessments are conducted only in English and the student continues to qualify for ELD services (see below for some additional details and limitations on student assessment interpreters). Ensure that interpretation is available for the duration of all meetings involving parents with limited English proficiency. Interpreting jargon to another language remains jargon—be sure to clearly explain the ideas so the interpretation is clear and concise.

Interpret standardized assessment results considering students' linguistic and cultural contexts. If standardized cognitive or speech/language tests are administered, their results must be interpreted in a fair and defensible manner. One such approach is to use Flanagan, Ortiz, and Alfonso's Culture-Language Test Classifications and Culture-Language Interpretive Matrices (2013). These researchers recommend that assessment be conducted first in English. If all scores are within the average range, there is no further assessment needed; this confirms no dis/ability exists. If there are weaknesses in specific areas, the assessor should conduct testing in those areas in the native language to validate these weaknesses. If native language assessments are unavailable (i.e., in a language other than Spanish), validate weaknesses through additional English assessment, while continuing to consider the linguistic demands and cultural biases inherent in them.

Match background in instructional language(s) to achievement testing. Achievement testing should match the language(s) of instruction. If the student is currently in a dual language program currently or had received prior bilingual instruction, or received instruction in another country, it is important to evaluate their response to instruction in that language as well as English.

Eligibility Decisions

Use multiple data sources to make eligibility decisions. After all assessments have been conducted, reconvene the team to review the multiple data. This could include benchmark and progress monitoring data comparing progress to true peers and grade-level benchmarks in literacy, content areas, and language development in English and native language; classroom assessments and work samples, observations, and interviews from Tiers 1 and 2 and state achievement and English language proficiency assessments, as well as the special education assessment results.

Determine eligibility and the appropriate disability category. Use all assessment and test results to determine whether the student meets the eligibility requirements to receive special education services under one of the federal dis/ability categories and manifests a need for special education services. A student needs special education when it is clear that, without specialized support, the student's disability will prevent him or her from learning.

Determine that cultural and language differences are not the primary reason for academic challenges. If the student is being considered under the category of specific learning disability (SLD), the team must address IDEA's exclusionary clause and determine that a learning disability "does not include a learning problem that is *primarily* the result of visual, hearing or motor disabilities, of mental retardation, of emotional disturbance, or of environmental, cultural, or economic disadvantage" (34 CFR 300.8 [iii]). This means that teams provide evidence for the SLD determination showing the difficulties are not just the result of cultural and linguistic differences. The case study in Chapter 4 and Figure 4.2 outline such a process.

Develop culturally and linguistically appropriate IEP. Once eligibility is established, the team develops a culturally and linguistically appropriate Individual Education Plan (IEP), outlines present levels of performance, establishes measurable goals and any accommodations, and details the special education services.

Determine appropriate special education program and placement. A special education service delivery model is recommended based on the student's identified needs and the goals of the IEP.

Ensure continued ELD service provision. If the student continues to qualify for the ESL/ELD program, they must continue to receive ELD services *and* special education services. Services for both can be provided in a collaborative model and should not consist of just multiple pull-out services (e.g., only separately for special education and ELD).

Because of the many steps in this process, educators frequently complain about how long it takes for a child to qualify for special education services. Such a decision, however, can have lifelong implications and thus must be made judiciously. Therefore, a process such as highlighted here both ensures students receive support early in their instruction prior to falling too far behind and allows teams to make informed referral decisions. Once a referral is made, the data from this process equips the team with the complete information to guide special education decisions. Figure 5.5 summarizes the steps we have outlined above.

AFTER THE REFERRAL

Dis/ability decisions for EL students are inherently fraught with challenges ranging from a lack of requisite knowledge by assessment teams to differing philosophical and disciplinary stances (Klingner & Eppolito, 2014; Ortiz et

Figure 5.5. Steps in ensuring appropriate special education referrals for EL students.

Tier 1

Identify students who are struggling academically.

Review student's records (if this hasn't occurred earlier).

Examine the quality of core instruction and appropriate fit.

Use valid and reliable assessments for EL students.

Set long- and short-term goals.

Use culturally and linguistically aligned interventions across all tiers.

Monitor progress toward grade-level benchmarks.

Compare progress to true peers.

Tier 2

Support through MTSS using culturally and linguistically aligned interventions.

Compare progress to true peers.

Tier 3

Refer for special education evaluation when progress is insufficient. (Intensive interventions may be provided here before the referral or throughout the referral and evaluation process.)

Referral to Special Education[1]

Adhere to the standard process and timelines for special education.

Document developmental milestones (if this hasn't occurred earlier).

Include ELD specialist in decisions.

Include parents in decisions and assessment planning.

Use trained interpreters.

Interpret standardized assessment results considering students' linguistic and cultural contexts.

Match background in instructional language(s) to achievement testing.

Eligibility Decisions

Use multiple data sources to make eligibility decisions.

Determine the eligibility and appropriate dis/ability category.

Determine cultural and language differences are not the primary reason for academic challenges.

Determine appropriate special education program and placement.

Develop culturally and linguistically appropriate IEP.

Ensure continued ELD service provision.

al., 2011). With the reauthorization of IDEA in 2004, the process became even more complex. Until then, when students were referred for a special education evaluation, they were traditionally administered a cognitive (IQ) and achievement test and a discrepancy formula was used for eligibility purposes. The discrepancy formula meant that when teams found a discrepancy between ability and achievement that was equal to or greater than the benchmark set by a state (commonly 1.5 standard deviations or 22 standard score points), the student met the criteria for special education services under the disability category of specific learning disability (SLD). This method met with much criticism for enforcing a delay in placement until the student was significantly behind in order to observe this discrepancy, which then led to more student failure (Case, Speece, & Malloy, 2003; Donovan & Cross, 2002; Hallahan & Mercer, 2001; Lyon et al., 2001). In response, IDEA (2004) recommended a choice of two processes in lieu of a discrepancy formula for SLD eligibility. The first derives from MTSS (or RTI) where teams can determine eligibility based on multiple sources of data indicating insufficient progress even with increasingly intense, scientifically based interventions over a period of time.

> (2)(i) The child does not make sufficient progress to meet age or State-approved grade-level standards in one or more of the areas identified in paragraph (a)(1) of this section when using a process based on the child's response to scientific, research-based intervention. (§300.309)

Many districts utilize this MTSS-only model for eligibility. Teams collect screening and progress monitoring data across the tiers (work samples and other assessment data may be additional data sources). In this model, a combination of data, developmental history, and a review of other data assists teams in determining the need for intensive, specially designed instruction and eligibility for special education services under the category of SLD. Other districts use the second method identified in IDEA (2004)—determining a pattern of strengths and weaknesses (PSW). This is described in IDEA (2004) as follows:

> (ii) The child exhibits a pattern of strengths and weaknesses in performance, achievement, or both, relative to age, State-approved grade-level standards, or intellectual development, that is determined by the group to be relevant to the identification of a specific learning disability, using appropriate assessments, consistent with §§300.304 and 300. (§300.309)

For this model, results from standardized achievement and intelligence/cognitive tests are used along with progress monitoring data and work samples, for eligibility purposes. PSW, however, has met with criticism as well. One criticism concerns the use of standardized cognitive/IQ tests, where, when the referred student is an English learner, the issue of test bias becomes salient.

Longstanding research has consistently shown performance differences between racial or ethnic groups as well (Cummins, 1984; Jensen, 1974; Sanchez, 1934; Vukovich & Figueroa, 1992; Yerkes, 1921). There are two main reasons for these score differences: culture and language.

Culture. Standardized tests reflect the culture in which they were developed and are based on the cultural values and beliefs of the authors. It has been said that the very concept of intelligence is rooted in culture (Anastasi, 1937; Degler, 1991). When the test taker is not fully acculturated to the mainstream culture, resulting test scores may be attenuated simply because the full range of an individual's cultural knowledge is not accounted for in their performance (Cummins, 1984; Figueroa, 1990; Flanagan & Ortiz, 2001; Matsumoto, 1994; Valdes & Figueroa, 1994). The second attenuating factor, language, is inextricably linked to culture.

Language. The linguistic demands inherent in tests negatively impact an EL student's comprehension of test items. As described in Chapter 4, language may be a barrier to representing a student's ability to learn because the linguistic demands of a second language make it difficult to determine whether poor performance on the item is due to lack of skill, ability, or lack of linguistic knowledge (Abedi, 2006a, 2006b; Solano-Flores, 2008). Therefore, performance on nonnative language assessments consistently underrepresent an EL student's true abilities and threaten assessment validity. Additionally, norm samples are typically stratified by factors such as race, gender, and socioeconomic status and not by English learner status and proficiency level, falsely assuming homogeneity in this vastly heterogeneous population. "Comparing the performance of ELL students to appropriate norm groups (i.e., those with similar opportunities to learn) is critical for making valid inferences about the cognitive abilities of ELL students" (Lakin, 2012, p. 765). In other words, scores measure individual capacity *and* the ways development of that capacity have been limited or privileged (Skiba, Knesting, & Bush, 2002).

Many educators question the purpose of standardized testing as part of the special education eligibility process for the high-incidence categories (SLD and SLI). For some disability categories, such as intellectual disabilities, scores from a standardized cognitive test are one crucial component of eligibility decisions. For SLD and SLI decisions, we support the judicious use of standardized tests when the student is an English learner because determining difference from dis/ability is quite complicated and must be based on a convergence of multiple data sources. However, test scores must be properly interpreted in order to provide a fair and accurate portrayal of an EL student's abilities. There are a few approaches to using standardized tests with consideration of culture and/or language differences.

Test modifications and nonverbal tests. If assessors modify an assessment, by (for example) translating test administration directions, using an interpreter, or extending the testing time limits, they risk subverting test validity and reliability and altering the meaning of the results. As an alternative to modifying assessments, many assessors use nonverbal cognitive instruments. As "nonverbal intelligence" is not a construct, such tests are termed *nonverbal* because they measure broad abilities in a manner that reduces language demands, asking examinees to respond to items through "pointing, pantomime, and practice items" (Lohman & Gambrell, 2012, p. 3). McGrew and Flanagan (1998) hold that there is no such thing as nonverbal ability but that nonverbal tests measure abilities that can be expressed nonverbally. In other words, nonverbal tests were created to measure *general* cognitive ability absent the confounding factor of language. Nonverbal tests, however, do not measure the full range of abilities that are identified in modern theories of intelligence and consequently some inherent strengths or weaknesses may not be measured (Flanagan & Ortiz, 2001). Therefore, results from nonverbal cognitive tests can result in construct underrepresentation—a threat to score validity—and should be combined with other assessment batteries to assess the broad abilities not tested by nonverbal tests. For example, asking an EL student to point to pictures of words read aloud in English rather than reading and writing the words themselves can demonstrate some areas of vocabulary comprehension while not providing evidence of other reading and writing abilities.

Native language tests. When assessing EL students whose native language is Spanish, there are at least two Spanish cognitive tests available, WISC-V and the *Batería III Woodcock-Muñoz Pruebas de Habilidades Cognitivas* (the *Batería IV* should be on the market soon). Using native language assessments may not be a perfect option for assessing EL students. First, they require licensed bilingual assessors, who continue to be a rare commodity, and the normative population used in the norm samples must be carefully scrutinized. Little research exists on the use of native language cognitive tests with U.S. bilingual students. In one unpublished study, Brown (2008) found significant below-average performance in a sample of typically achieving EL students on the *Batería III Woodcock-Muñoz Pruebas de Habilidades Cognitivas*. More importantly, the results indicated that the degree to which performance was attenuated was related to language—the more a test tapped into the construct of language in its measurement, the lower the performance. Notably, this effect was observed in both students receiving native language instruction and those receiving English-only instruction.

This finding highlights the problems associated with the use of a test where the normative sample is comprised of Spanish-only speakers, some of whom are from the U.S. but most from other Spanish-only-speaking countries, which is the norming sample for the *Batería III*. U.S. bilingual and EL students are by definition not native language–only speakers and have a continuum of abilities in both English and Spanish. Younger children particularly often lack full proficiency in either their native language or English. The reliability and validity of native language test scores, as in all standardized tests, are dependent on the characteristics of the normative sample and whether the group of the individual being assessed is appropriately represented. Based on the limitations noted here and the limited research, assessors should carefully triangulate the data with other measures to confirm the validity of performance results.

    Addressing test score validity. Due to the limitations inherent in all current approaches routinely employed in the evaluation of EL students, the problem of test score validity for EL students remains unresolved. Apart from a single recent development in controlling for differential language exposure among ELs (e.g., Ortiz, 2018), practitioners cannot count on being able to administer a test and interpret scores, even with *extreme caution*, under the assumption that they are valid. So that educators can avoid using unvalidated procedures or tests with questionable psychometric properties with EL students or attempting to make meaning of results to which meaning cannot rightly be given, it has been recommended that research on EL testing in the United States in English be conducted in order to systematically investigate the impact of language differences on the validity of test performance (Ortiz, 2019).

    While that research is pending, the field needs a systematic and comprehensive approach to nondiscriminatory assessment. Fortunately, one such framework exists.

THE CULTURE-LANGUAGE TEST CLASSIFICATIONS AND CULTURE-LANGUAGE INTERPRETIVE MATRIX

Flanagan, Ortiz, and Alfonso (2007) developed a framework to assist practitioners in interpreting test results for EL students. They analyzed the available cognitive tests (and subtests), sorting them by three qualities: (1) the broad and narrow abilities they measure according to the Cattell-Horn-Carroll (CHC) theory of cognitive abilities; (2) their degree of cultural loading; and (3) their degree of linguistic demand. They then created the Culture-Language Test Classifications (C-TLC) using both the extant, though limited, research on the use of intelligence tests with diverse populations (Cummins, 1984; Jensen, 1974; Sanchez, 1934; Vukovich & Figueroa, 1992; Yerkes, 1921), and expert consensus. Since the original publication, they have refined the model using research on test performance of EL students when tested in English. They also developed a Culture-Language Interpretive Matrix (C-LIM) for each test battery based on the degree of cultural loading and linguistic demand inherent in each individual test. Together, the C-TLC and C-LIM provide a simple, evidence-based framework to assist practitioners in analyzing the extent of the

Figure 5.6. Classification of the WISC-IV subtests within the Culture-Language Interpretive Matrix (C-LIM).

Figure 5.7. Culture-Language Interpretive Matrix Main Graph with expected range for moderately different English learner.

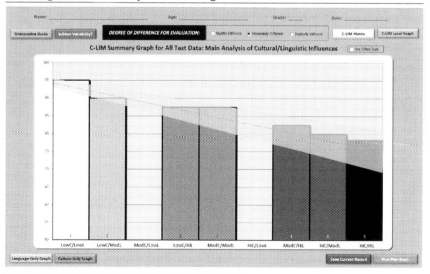

impact of linguistic and cultural variables on test performance of EL students tested in English. Figure 5.6 is an example of how the C-LTC were used to create a C-LIM matrix for the WISC-IV. Figure 5.7 is an example of a summary graph generated by the software indicating that the student's WISC-IV scores fall within the expected range of performance as compared to students with similar cultural and linguistic backgrounds. In other words, this profile would not suggest the student's scores indicated a disability.

Using the C-LTC and C-LIM is relatively simple. Tests from all of the major cognitive batteries (and more recently tests used by speech and language specialists) were ranked into the categories of low, medium, and high, depending on their degree of cultural loading and linguistic demand. They were then organized within the nine-celled C-LIM. Assessors use these classifications as a starting point to select a set of tests that may be better aligned to an EL student's cultural and linguistic background. After administering the tests, the scores are then placed into the appropriate cells on the C-LIM. The scores from each cell are averaged in order to view the performance pattern across the tests administered. A software program is available to graphically indicate whether an EL student's performance is typical of other EL students, which could suggest that any below-average scores are owed to the tests being in English, or atypical, meaning the low scores may in fact indicate inherent weaknesses. Then, to triangulate the results, assessors administer native language tests (or other English tests if native language tests are not available) in the areas of weaknesses. The final step is to analyze the multiple data sources gathered throughout the evaluation process. The C-LIM and C-LTC offer the field the first method to guide test selection and subsequent interpretation of test results that is systematic, logical, and theoretically defensible. To recap, Flanagan, Ortiz, and Alfonso (2007) recommend testing EL students in English first. If test scores are within the average range, there is no need for further testing since average performance in their second language should be sufficient evidence to support a finding of no dis/ability. On the other hand, if performance patterns are atypical as compared to other EL students, using the C-LIM and C-TLC, and native language tests (preferred when available) or other assessments in English on the identified weaker abilities provide additional support for special education eligibility. The reader is referred to the work of Flanagan, Ortiz, and Alfonso (2007, 2013) for further information as a more complete description of the model and process is beyond the scope of this chapter.

CREATING CULTURALLY AND LINGUISTICALLY APPROPRIATE INDIVIDUAL EDUCATION PLANS

Once an EL student is found eligible for special education services by a knowledgeable multidisciplinary team, a collaborative approach is central to creating an appropriate Individualized Education Program (IEP). Instruction within special education programs must continue to be linguistically and cultural-ly aligned. In January 2015, the U.S. Department of Education issued a *Dear Colleague* letter (Lhamon & Gupta, 2015) providing guidance to ensure that EL students, including those with dis/abilities, are able to participate mean-ingfully and equally in educational programs (U.S. Department of Education, 2016b). Specifically, this guidance reinforces the requirement of IDEA (2004) that IEP teams consider the language needs of a child with limited English proficiency as those needs relate to the child's IEP so students receive services that meet both their language and special education needs.

IEPs for EL students

The IEP is a comprehensive document describing the student's strengths and needs and setting measurable annual goals intended to advance toward age-and-grade appropriate standards. In 2017, the Supreme Court case *Endrew F. v. Douglas County School District* directed districts to ensure that a student receive an appropriate education and defined it as one that confers "*more than mini-mum benefit*" (Tran, Patton, & Brohammer, 2018, p. 1, emphasis added). The IEP provides the path to achievement. Developing a culturally and linguisti-cally appropriate IEP is essential for EL students to make maximum progress. Tran, Patton, and Brohammer (2018) define such an IEP as one that is "respon-sive to the student's curricular needs by capturing the cultural and linguistic features and skills that a student brings to the classroom" (p. 3). The mandated components are detailed below along with the specific additions for EL stu-dents. For EL students, the student's language proficiency and cultural assets should be documented and all IEP goals aligned to the student's proficiency level in the instructional language.

Present levels of academic and functional performance (PLAAFP). The PLAAFP details the student's current strengths and weakness in abilities (academic, physical, and social) and skills based on the assessment data. "PLAAFP is a statement that informs the IEP team precisely about the stu-dent's needs so the remainder of the IEP can address those needs" (Yell,

---

CREATING SMART GOALS

One common framework for writing goals is SMART (Doran, 1981). SMART stands for Specific, Measurable, Attainable, Results-oriented, and Time-bound. In the context of defining educational goals, they (1) specify the learner and the date by which the goal will be accomplished; (2) define the observable behavior; (3) state the condition under which the student will perform the behavior; (4) establish the performance level required to achieve mastery of the goal; and (5) identify the evaluation schedule or frequency of assessment.

Katsiyannis, Ennis, Losinki, & Christle, 2016, p. 34). Accurate and detailed data here lead to appropriate IEP goal setting. For EL students, current English language proficiency levels should be documented and, if possible, include data on native language proficiency. It is also recommended that teams document necessary cultural supports (e.g., the need to preteach unfamiliar concepts) as needed.

Measurable culturally and linguistically appropriate goals. The IEP addresses the educational needs related to the student's dis/ability. For some students, their goals may cover academic areas only. For others, the IEP may address multiple domains and require "specially designed instruction" (SDI) for the entire school day. All goals, however, should support the instructional relationship between language, literacy, and academic success. If the team determines a child needs a particular service, intervention, device, accommodation, or program modification related to the EL student's second language development needs in order to receive a free appropriate public education (FAPE), they must include a statement to that effect in the student's IEP. Specifically, IDEA (2004) mandates:

> In the case of a child with limited English proficiency, consider the language needs of the child as those needs relate to the child's IEP (§300.346[a][2][ii]) [and] in conducting a meeting to review, and, if appropriate, revise a child's IEP, the IEP team shall consider the factors described in paragraph (a) of this section. (§300.346[b] and [c])

IEP teams are charged with determining how the student's level of English language proficiency will impact special education and related services. Consequently, close collaboration between general education or content teachers, ELD specialists, and special education teachers is crucial, with each playing a specific, complementary role.

Roles of service providers. *General education and content teachers* plan instruction based on the Common Core Standards or other state standards, teach a broad continuum of students within the same environment by differentiating instruction, and facilitate developmentally appropriate socialization and behavior. *Language/ESL/ELD teachers* base their instruction on state English language proficiency standards. They generally provide explicit, systematic instruction of English in English for students to demonstrate annual growth. *Special education teachers'* instruction is guided by each student's IEP goals and generally attempts to remediate learning challenges. Together, the team creates culturally and linguistically appropriate and aligned IEP goals based on EL students' strengths, needs, and proficiency in their languages. IEP goals for EL students should include both content and language components. Based on PLAAFP data, content goals are developed in specified academic areas aligned to grade-level or appropriate standards. The students may not be at grade level, but goals must provide the plan for moving closer to meeting those standards. The language services the EL student needs to address the goal are identified and included in the goal.

A Model for Creating Culturally and Linguistically Appropriate Goals

The following is a model to create culturally and linguistically appropriate goals using the SMART framework (Brown & Turner, 2016). In the following examples, we also identify the linguistic demands of the standards in order to address both content knowledge or skill needs and language needs.

Consider the grade-level content and language proficiency standards for the student's grade or other appropriate standards (needs based on PLAAFP).

ELA Reading Standards: Literature
3.RL Key Ideas and Details
3.RL2 (Content Goal). Recount stories, including fables, folktales, and myths from diverse cultures; determine the central message, lesson, or moral and explain how it is conveyed through key details in the text.

Determine the linguistic demand (taken from the standards). In this case, the linguistic demand is "recount stories by making connections between story events."

Identify the language function (purpose), form, and key vocabulary needed to accomplish the task. The language function is to "recount" or "retell" a story. In order to retell stories, students will need to use past tense verbs and transition words. The key vocabulary will be taken directly from the story or stories used. Remember that second language acquisition is usually described by stages on a continuum, with most models identifying five to six stages. Stage 1 is students with no or very little English and Stages 5 and 6 identify fluency. Using the information above, here are three examples of potential goals for three different language proficiency levels—Stages 2, 3, and 4.

Examples of Goals Across Three Language Proficiency Stages

Goal for Language Proficiency Stage 2. By (date), after hearing a culturally relevant story along with three picture prompts, (student) will place the pictures in correct sequence and orally retell the story by stating at least one phrase per picture using past tense verbs for each picture (3 out of 3) as measured by teacher rubric.

Goal for Language Proficiency Stage 3. By (date), after hearing a culturally relevant story along with three picture prompts, (student) will place the pictures in correct sequence and orally retell the story using at least one complete sentence with past tense verbs for each picture (3/3) as measured by teacher rubric.

Goal for Language Proficiency Stage 4. By (_____), after reading a culturally relevant story at (____) reading level that has three picture prompts, (student) will place the pictures in correct sequence and orally retell the story using at least one complex sentence or two simple sentences per picture with past tense verbs and a taught transition word for each picture (3/3) as measured by teacher rubric.

Ideally, such goals are constructed collaboratively so that the IEP's goal addresses an EL students' content, instruction, and linguistic and cultural contexts.

Goals for ESL/ELD

"[I]n the case of a child with limited English proficiency," IEP teams are directed under IDEA (2004) to "consider the language needs of the child as those needs relate to the child's IEP" (34 CFR §300.324[a][2][ii]). This means that it would be appropriate for teams to develop a goal addressing English proficiency growth. One example of such a goal is: *By (date), (student) will demonstrate growth in English by one language proficiency level on the state's English proficiency test, administered with accommodations, if specified in the IEP, in three of the four language domains.* While in general EL students can progress by one level per year given a high-quality ESL/ELD program, it must be remembered that many dual identified students' language progress in any and all languages may be hindered by their dis/ability. Thus, teams should set the expected growth based on data from the PLAAFP, examining prior rate of English acquisition, and unique learning needs.

Reporting Progress Toward Goals

This section of the IEP addresses how and when a child's progress will be measured and reported. Current IDEA requirements are less precise than previous versions about how often progress must be reported, but common practice equates to the normal report card timelines. Consistent monitoring of measurable goals is essential so that if a child is not making adequate progress, adjustments can be made. For EL students, progress should be reported in the language of the parents' literacy, although this is not mandated in federal law but left to the discretion of states.

Related Services, Supplementary Aids, and Accommodations

A critical element of the IEP is a statement of the special education services plus the (1) related services, (2) supplementary aides and services, and (3) accommodation that will be provided to the child.

Related services. Related services are provided to students through their IEP to help them meet their annual goals, but they are not necessarily SDI. These can include speech and language therapy, interpretation (although specified in IDEA not for second language issues but rather for students with deafness), counseling, orientation and mobility, occupational therapy, music, dance or art therapy, transportation, and other services designed to address a student's individual needs. The particular types of services and amount are determined by the IEP team based on the student's evaluated needs. The language of service delivery should be specified. For EL students, native language services must be considered if the team determines the need. However, bilingual personnel capable of providing native language services continue to be rare.

Supplementary aides and services. These are aides, services, and support needed in any setting to enable the student to be educated alongside nondisabled peers to the maximum extent possible. They can include direct services or support and training for staff. An example would be training special education staff on the impact of the EL child's disability on their language acquisition in English and their native language.

Participation and accommodations on state assessments. IDEA (2004) requires that students with disabilities receive support on large-scale tests. Thus, any accommodations or modification needed for them to access a test must be provided. In some cases, the IEP team may determine a particular test is not appropriate for the student. Such exemptions are explained in the IEP along with a description of the alternate assessment to be provided. Also, the language of each state assessment should be documented on the IEP. These accommodations apply to state English language proficiency assessments as well. Educators are advised to become familiar with their own state's guidelines since some states allow exemptions on some, but not all, of the language domains (listening, speaking, reading, and writing).

Extent of Participation with Nondisabled Peers

The IEP must explain why the team has determined a child will receive education outside of the regular class or programs. Instructional placements must be based on the needs of the child and not for the benefit of the school or system and can include two-way immersion or other bilingual programs.

Transition Plan

Transition services to higher education or career are required beginning with the first IEP developed when the child turns 16 years old (or younger in some states). Transition planning must be documented and updated annually. Postsecondary goals are developed based on assessment data related to training, education, employment, and independent living skills, and services are determined to support the student in reaching the goals and reviewed annually. When working with diverse families, it should be noted that they may not share in the mainstream belief in the value of independence or other assumptions educators have. It is highly recommended that teams develop a relationship with families to fully understand their cultural beliefs about abilities and independence.

In summary, all facets of a dual identified student's IEP should consider their learning and language needs and relevant documents should be provided in the parents' language of literacy or native language so that they can be full partners in the development and implementation of the IEP.

Bilingualism and Students with Dis/abilities: What the Research Says

In the past, it was commonly recommended that students with dis/abilities from homes where non-English languages are spoken receive instruction only in English. Many claimed that such children would be confused trying to learn in two languages. They failed to consider that children living in an English-speaking country with families who do not speak fluent English need to navigate the world through two languages. Further, robbing children of the ability to communicate with their non-English-speaking family members fractures families. Fortunately, we can now refer to an ever-increasing body of research that clearly finds instruction in two languages and bilingualism are beneficial to *all* children (Duran, 1989, 1992; Rohena, Jitendra, & Browder, 2002; Scherba de Valenzuela et al., 2016; Spooner, Rivera, Browder, Baker, & Salas, 2009). Further, the same legal entitlements to bilingual programs where available and to federally mandated ELD services (*Castañeda v. Pickard*, 1981) holds for children with dis/abilities (Scherba de Valenzuela et al., 2016). Decisions regarding language of instruction are best determined in partnership with the family and should not be based solely on current available resources at a school or district.

Special Education for EL Students with Dis/abilities

We know that students with special needs benefit from explicit small-group instruction, but the optimal location of such instruction has been a topic of great debate. An increasing research base, however, attests to the growth in both academic and social skills that students in special education make when they are included with their peers (Fisher & Meyer, 2002; Ryndak, Ward, Alper, Storch, & Montgomery, 2010). Placement decisions are made by IEP teams who are mandated to use the principle of least restrictive environment. In considering placement, each student's strengths, challenges, and needed supports are weighed. Although we advocate for inclusive settings, there are times when teams determine that a student is best served in a special class or even special school. Regardless of setting, there are two important considerations specifically for EL students. For those who have not reached reclassification criteria for exit from ESL/ELD programs, they remain eligible and must receive ESL/ELD services. Also, decisions regarding language(s) of instruction must be determined by the IEP team based on a student's needs rather than school or district resources. The determination for choice of instructional language(s) is guided by the strengths and weaknesses identified in the special education evaluation and the PLAAFP. Title VI of the Civil Rights Act of 1964 requires that districts provide EL students with alternative language services to enable them to acquire proficiency in English, and give them meaningful access to the content of the educational curriculum provided to all students, including special education and related services.

Responding to EL Students' Language Needs in Special Education

Several factors should be taken into account when determining language(s) of instruction in special education services. First, an EL student's native language proficiency (receptive and expressive) and their family's language use in the home informs teams of the language(s) the student must navigate at home to receive supports from their family and caregivers. English-only instruction, particularly for students with innate communication challenges, may equate to the extinction of their home language, robbing EL students of the ability to engage with family, extended family, caregivers, and their cultural community.

Students' English language proficiency (receptive and expressive) guides their need for services through ESL/ELD so, regardless of special education status, they must be provided instruction addressing state English proficiency standards and the development of English in reading, writing, listening, and speaking as well as subject matter content standards.

In determining language provision, consideration of educational background and experiences is also necessary. How much formal instruction has a student received across their languages? Best practices and science tell us to build on students' strengths, meaning if a student has been in a dual immersion program prior to their special education determination, it may be difficult for them to be thrust into an English-only environment or even to decrease their access to native language instruction should all special education services be in English only. Whatever the language or location of instruction, teams must determine the optimal environment that will affirm students' and their family's cultural values, beliefs, and goals. To summarize, consider these factors when an EL student is deemed eligible for special education services: English language proficiency, native language proficiency and home language use; prior language(s) of instruction, and culturally responsive SDI.

SPECIALLY DESIGNED INSTRUCTION (SDI)—PROGRAM MODELS

The foundation of special education instruction, no matter the particular service delivery model, is specially designed instruction (SDI) that ensures students have access to the general education curriculum through the use of modifications. IDEA (2004) defines SDI as:

> adapting, as appropriate to the needs of an eligible child under this part, the content, methodology or delivery of instruction (i) to address the unique needs of the child that result from the child's disability; and (ii) to ensure access of the child to the general curriculum, so that the child can meet the educational standards within the jurisdiction of the public agency that apply to all children. (34 C.F.R. §300.39[b][3])

The goal is for students to have access to core curriculum, meet the same academic standards as peers, and progress toward meeting IEP goals. "SDI is the product of identifying the goals and objectives of intervention and, by definition, is individualized and will look different for students with different strengths, needs, and abilities" (Riccomini, Morano, & Hughes, 2017, p. 21). SDI addresses each student's needs by adapting content, methodology, or delivery of instruction to enable them to progress toward standards and goals and is planned by an appropriately certified special education teacher or service provider (e.g., speech language specialist, occupational therapist, adaptive physical education teacher). All instruction is linked to IEP goals, which, as has been discussed earlier, include an ESL/ELD goal.

Again, we emphasize that special education services should be provided alongside typical peers. For those cases where full inclusion is not the model, we highlight varying models that can be modified across the grade levels. The reader will note that in all models, for EL students who have not been reclassified and exited for EL services, they are legally entitled to services from both the ESL/ELD program and special education.

Native Language Models

Native language/bilingual SDI in an inclusive immersion setting. Two-way or dual immersion programs integrate language and academic instruction. Native English speakers and native target language students should be equally represented within the classroom. One general education teacher certified in two languages or two teachers who each provide content instruction in one of the target languages are required. Models differ by percentage of language use across the two languages with early transition models emphasizing a greater percentage of English as the grade levels increase. If either of the teachers also has a special education certification, they can provide SDI across both languages. ESL/ELD services can be provided within this setting if any of the teachers is appropriately certified.

Cotaught ESL/ELD. ESL/ELD services could alternatively be provided in an inclusive immersion setting through a coteaching model where an ESL/ELD teacher pushes into the general education immersion classroom to provide instruction, including to a dual identified student.

Native language/bilingual SDI in a resource room or learning center. A certified special education teacher who is fluent in the child's native language can provide SDI in the native language or a combination of that language and English in a resource room or learning center when IEPs direct that SDI is provided for less than 50% of the day. ESL/ELD instruction may be provided within this setting in a collaborative model that adapts SDI to the student's English proficiency level as well as teaching to the English proficiency standards.

Native language/bilingual SDI in a special education classroom. A certified special education teacher who is also fluent in the child's native language can provide SDI in the native language or a combination of that language and English in a self-contained classroom setting when IEPs direct that SDI is provided for more than 50% of the day. ESL/ELD instruction may be provided within this setting in a collaborative model that adapts SDI to the student's English proficiency level as well as teaching to the English proficiency standards.

Native language/bilingual SDI in related services. When related service providers are fluent in the child's native language, services may be provided in that language, in English, or a combination depending on what will best serve the EL student. For example, a bilingual speech and language specialist may develop language goals to support native language development that target one or more of the components of language. This is different from ESL/ELD instruction since these services must align with state English language proficiency standards.

ESL/ELD services through push-in, coteaching, pull-out. Requisite ESL/ELD services can be provided within any of the settings described here. The ESL/ELD specialist should also collaborate with all teachers and specialists in appropriately adapting students' SDI for their language proficiency level.

English-Only Models

English-only SDI in inclusive co-taught setting. A general education teacher who instructs in English only can collaboratively, along with or under the direction of a certified special education teacher, provide SDI in English. In this model, the EL student does not have the opportunity for native language instruction. If the child's stronger language, however, is not English, the team may consider bridging concepts through that language by assigning a bilingual instructional assistant to the classroom. Push-in ESL/ELD services within this setting or pull-out services in a different setting must be provided remembering that students who struggle with learning do not benefit from multiple pull-out programs that disrupt their learning experience.

English-only SDI in a resource room or learning center. A certified special education teacher provides SDI in English in a resource room or learning center when IEPs direct that SDI is provided for less than 50% of the day. If the child's stronger language, however, is not English, the team may consider bridging concepts through that language by assigning a bilingual instructional assistant to support the student in this setting. ESL/ELD instruction may be provided within this setting in a collaborative model or through separate ESL/ELD instruction.

English-only SDI in a special education classroom. A certified special education teacher provides SDI in English in a resource room or learning center when IEPs direct that SDI is provided for more than 50% of the day. If the child's stronger language, however, is not English, the team may consider bridging concepts through that language by assigning a bilingual instructional assistant to support the student in this setting. ESL/ELD instruction may be provided within this setting in a collaborative model or through separate ESL/ELD instruction.

English-only SDI in related services. When related service providers are not fluent in the child's native language, the team should consider the support of a bilingual instructional assistant if English is not the student's stronger language.

ESL/ELD services through push-in, coteaching, pull-out. Requisite ESL/ELD services can be provided within any of the settings described here. The ESL/ELD specialist should also collaborate with all teachers in appropriately adapting students' SDI for their language proficiency level.

UNIVERSAL DESIGN FOR LEARNING

Another powerful instructional framework used in special education but beneficial to all teachers in general education is Universal Design for Learning (UDL; CAST, 2016): the concept of designing learning environments to be accessible by all students. This concept originated in the architectural field in the 1970s. In education, UDL is a scientifically validated framework that

> (A) provides flexibility in the ways information is presented, in the ways students respond or demonstrate knowledge and skills, and in the ways students are

engaged; and (B) reduces barriers in instruction, provides appropriate accommodations, supports, and challenges, and maintains high achievement expectations for all students, including students with disabilities and students who are limited English proficient. (CAST, 2016, para. 7)

UDL has three core principles: to provide multiple means of (1) representation, (2) expression, and (3) engagement. Each core principle has three guidelines. Figure 5.8 identifies the principles and guidelines, provides examples, and provides connections for EL students.

POLICIES FOR RECLASSIFYING EL STUDENTS WITH DISABILITIES

All EL students, including EL students with a dis/ability, can be exited from ELD services only when they meet state definitions of English proficiency (USDOE, n.d.). Current federal laws do not allow IEP teams to exempt EL students with dis/abilities from state English language proficiency testing. Teams are, however, allowed to determine, via the IEP, an appropriate state accommodation that would not invalidate the test results (34 CFR §300.324[a][2][ii]). Accommodations can be provided for one or all of the language domains (listening, speaking, reading, and writing). An IEP team can also document the reason an EL student's dis/ability prevents them from participating in the regular state English language proficiency assessment. In this case, the student would need to take an alternative assessment (34 CFR §300.320[a][6][ii]). This alternative assessment could be administered via paper and pencil or other adaptive assessment (USDOE, n.d.; see also the discussion in Chapter 7 of Texas' use of alternative criteria for exiting dual identified students from ELD programs). In addition to determining whether or not a student should take an alternate ELP assessment, the IEP team may also determine that a student will not participate in one or more domains of the English language proficiency assessment due to the nature of their disabilities. If an

> English learner has a disability that precludes assessment of the student in one or more domains of the English language proficiency (ELP) assessment such that there are no appropriate accommodations for the affected domain(s), a State must assess the student's English proficiency based on the remaining domain(s) in which it is possible to assess the student. (34 CFR § 200.6[h][4])

As stated earlier, until EL students meet reclassification criteria, they must continue to receive ELD services designed to support them in meeting state standards in collaboration with special educators to identify appropriate instructional strategies.

Figure 5.8. Principles of Universal Design for Learning: Transforming accessible information to useable knowledge.

Principle 1: Provide multiple means of representation	Principle 2: Provide multiple means of action and expression	Principle 3: Provide multiple means of engagement
GUIDELINE 1: Provide options for perception *Examples:* Adjust presentation format; use multimodalities *EL Connections:* narrated slide presentations, podcasts, videos **GUIDELINE 2:** Provide options for language, mathematical expressions, and symbols *Examples:* Use multi-media, linguistic and nonlinguistic material, graphics and pictures, clarify syntax and structure of language, cultural connections *EL Connections:* Venn diagrams, tables, graphs, semantic webs **GUIDELINE 3:** Provide options for comprehension *Examples:* Prime background knowledge, scaffolds to ensure all learners have access to knowledge, graphic organizers connecting relationships *EL Connections:* audio books, frontloading concepts, explicit vocabulary instruction, cognate strategy	**GUIDELINE 4:** Provide options for physical action *Examples:* Use assistive technology, vary methods for response, provide materials that all learners can access *EL Connections:* total physical response, use real objects, role-play **GUIDELINE 5:** Provide options for expression and communication *Examples:* Provide alternative modalities for expression, use multi-media, build fluencies with graduated levels of support for practice and performance *EL Connections:* scaffold instruction, songs, role-play, readers theater **GUIDELINE 6:** Provide options for executive functions *Examples:* Expand executive function by scaffolding lower-level skills so they require less executive function and scaffold higher level skills and strategies so they are more effective and developed *EL Connections:* teach self-regulation, teach strategies using comprehensible language, help students look for patterns in learning as a way of making text more comprehensible	**GUIDELINE 7:** Provide options for recruiting interest *Examples:* Optimize choice, autonomy, and relevance; link to students' lives and cultures; provide social relevance *EL Connections:* create links to students' languages and culture; provide curriculum with relevance to their daily lives, families, and community **GUIDELINE 8:** Provide options for sustaining effort and persistence *Examples:* Remind students of final goal and why it is important, set long- and short-term goals, differentiate instruction *EL Connections:* allow students to partner in developing goals, provide examples of culturally reflective role models **GUIDELINE 9:** Provide options for self-regulation *Examples:* Develop students' intrinsic motivation; use prompts, guides, rubrics, and checklists; teach self-reinforcements; use of progress charts; provide clear, formative feedback *EL Connections:* ensure all rubrics, checklists, guidelines, and materials are comprehensible by students by reviewing them together; learn what motivates the students; provide external reinforcers and then fade them away

(Adapted from CAST, 2011)

DIFFERENTIATING LANGUAGE ACQUISITION FROM
LEARNING DISABILITIES

Every school needs robust systems that provide culturally and linguistically responsive instruction, interventions, and assessment. Every school needs educators who understand the impact of second language acquisition on learning new concepts through a language they are learning. It is with this grounding that fair and equitable decisions regarding support and educational programming for EL students will be made.

When EL students encounter academic challenges, too often the first response is to refer them for a special education evaluation. Instead, instructional strategies and services must be matched to students' levels of instructional language proficiency, cultural background, and educational experiences in order to provide adequate educational opportunity before any special education consideration. A PLUSS framework–adapted MTSS (see Chapter 4) can be an effective way to ensure that a school properly determines when an EL student should be referred for a special education evaluation.

As discussed in previous chapters, healthy and effective educational systems identify which EL students need support early on, provide interventions matched to the level of need, monitor progress toward instructional targets, ensure all instruction and interventions use strategies to make language comprehensible, use valid and reliable assessments for all student groups, and repeat the process as needed. Then students who do not make expected gains as compared to their "true peers" may potentially be referred for a special education evaluation (Brown & Doolittle, 2008). As straightforward as this process sounds, to effectively develop and implement such a system requires strong leadership and a knowledgeable team of educators from multiple disciplines, including an EL/bilingual specialist.

This chapter also shared the C-TLC and C-LIM framework for interpreting English language standardized test scores for EL students that has been used in the field of school psychology for more than a decade. It remains the only framework that considers the impact of culture and language on EL students' test performance. We also provided guidance on making essential decisions, such as language of special education service provision, culturally and linguistically responsive IEPs, and complementary ELD and special education program models. We concluded with current policies on standards and criteria for reclassifying EL students with dis/abilities as fluent English proficient (RFEP) and exiting EL programs (Council of Chief State School Officers, 2016a). Our goal is for educators to open their doors to their colleagues with varying expertise because meeting the needs of and making special education decisions for EL students is a complex process. However, working together, we will positively impact the outcomes for EL students.

CHAPTER 6

School-, District-, and Statewide Improvement

Lessons from State Manuals on Dual Identified Students

Whole schools and even entire districts can improve the learning environment for English learner (EL) students, including dual identified students, which will have both short-term and long-term positive impacts. This chapter builds on the earlier chapters, taking the improvement suggestions to the level of whole-system improvement. How do educators work effectively in multidisciplinary teams together with EL students, dual identified students, and their caregivers to accurately and consistently monitor, place, and teach them, along with former EL students and fluent English speakers? More specifically, how do educators implement best practices in MTSS, second language development, and special education system-wide in both individual classrooms and in collaborative teams that will enable high levels of EL and dual identified student success tomorrow and in the years to come?

For most teachers, principals, and district administrators, effectively implementing the best of MTSS, second language development, and special education requires substantive improvement on what they are currently doing. With this in mind, we draw on system improvement research in education (see, e.g., Fullan, 2001, 2005; Levin & Fullan, 2008; Orosco & Klingner, 2010) for guidance to help educators become better at being "system thinkers in action" (Fullan, 2006, p. 113). Educators who are system thinkers in action are those who understand the fundamental concepts for how to improve whole schools and even whole districts (a collective system of schools as systems) and how to use specific tools in everyday activities at the team, school, and district levels to make their new implementations effective system-wide (Fullan, 2006). Therefore, we describe both research-based conceptual underpinning of system improvement and resources for implementing some best practices for making it minnappen for EL and dual identified students within a system for educating all students.

Throughout this chapter, we focus on goals at three levels. At the highest level, we look for deep improvements in practice, in individual pedagogy and assessment, in small-team work, and collectively in system-wide activities, that are sustainable (Fullan, 2006). By sustainable, we mean that the school or district becomes a learning organization (Senge, 1990), such that its educators and administrators can continually understand their current situation and each of their roles in both making the situation what it is now and how it can be improved (Fullan, 2006). At the more specific level, we see these improvements occurring system-wide through three practical individual changes described by Fullan (2001). These changes occur through learning the following: (1) how to use new or revised materials or technologies; (2) how to implement new, research-based best teaching strategies and activities as well as collaborative work practices; and (3) how to examine, and likely change, how we understand our students, their learning, and our teaching, as well as the system of schooling in which it all occurs. And finally, at the collective level, we contend that these changes must occur simultaneously and the work of improvement must be continually supported and evaluated. Research has consistently shown that deep and lasting improvements in practice and results do not occur with piecemeal changes (Fullan, 2001).

OVERVIEW OF STATE DUAL IDENTIFIED STUDENT MANUALS

We open and anchor our suggestions for system-level improvements by describing practice manuals produced by seven states for improving the education of their dual identified students. We do this for three reasons. First, these manuals are publicly available and vary in content and style, so they can be valuable resources for anyone seeking to make their own improvements. (See the box below for the titles of the manuals and the reference section for the titles and links.) Second, the manuals contain and are themselves new materials involving new practices. Thus, they are direct examples of two of the specific individual changes that will need to occur. Third, they are comprehensive and thus are examples of state attempts to make (or at least document how they would like to make) simultaneous improvements in using new materials and new practices, and creating new understandings, in order for these improvements to occur system-wide across entire schools, districts, and states. Further, four of these manuals include specific discussions and materials for how to incorporate RTI or MTSS as part of their systemic change, with one of these states, Connecticut, including this discussion in an associated document. The description of the manual elements builds on a report by Burr, Haas, and Ferriere (2015), and we summarize the elements in Figure 6.1. In addition, we provide suggestions on implementation and extensions based on findings from the system improvement literature.

What did we learn from these manuals? First, nearly all required a lot of work. The three largest manuals, Minnesota's 323-page manual, Illinois' 167-page manual, and Oregon's 164-page manual, show contributions from multiple authors and stakeholders in several disciplines and with various types of experience. These manuals, and probably most of the seven manuals, took

Figure 6.1. Summary of elements of state manuals for dual identified students.

Topic	CT	IL	MI	MN	OK	OR	VT
Pages	38	167	93	323	25	154	52
Understanding and Belief							
Purpose and additional consideration statement	X	X	X	X	X	X	X
ELD-CLD-LD difference description	X	X		X		X	S
EL diversity statement				X		X	X
Stages of acculturation statement		X		X	X	X	
Second language acquisition description	X	X	X	X	X	X	
FAQs	X		X			X	X
Key terms defined	X		X	X		X	X
Case examples		X	X				
Practices							
RTI/MTSS approach	X		X		X	X	
Best pedagogy practices for pre- and/or post-Special Ed. referral, including modifications		X	X	X	X	X	X
Best assessment and/or monitoring practices, pre- and/or post-IEP referral	X	X	X	X	X	X	X
IEP, problem solve team guidance		X	X		X	X	X
IEP guidance		X	X	X	X	X	
Interpreter & cultural mediator use guidance		X		X	X	X	S
Guidance for working with EL families	X	X		X		X	X
Use of technology, including assistive		X					
Dual identification key questions & guidance (Process key questions)		X	X	X		X	X

Figure 6.1. Summary of elements of state manuals for dual identified students. (continued)

Topic	CT	IL	MI	MN	OK	OR	VT
Pages	38	167	93	323	25	154	52
Materials							
Sample forms	X	X	X	X		X	
Checklists, question lists	X	X	X	X	X	X	X
Evidence and/or instrument description and/or lists	X	X	X	X	X	X	
Personnel expertise descriptions, lists		X	X	X		X	X
Testing accommodation examples, description		X	X	X	X		X
Additional resources list	X	X	X	X	X	X	X
System-wide Practice and Improvement							
Over- and underrepresented guidance	X	X		X		X	
Effective program criteria		X	X	X	X	X	X
Legal guidance	X	X	X	X	X	X	X
System review guidance		X		x			X
Special ELD exit criteria							

Note: Connecticut has a second related document. It is listed in the box below.

many months to write and likely more months to conceptualize in meetings big and small across various stakeholder groups. This suggests that deep system improvements in English learner education that involve simultaneous changes in materials, practices, and understandings also require prework along these lines to develop the initial materials, practices, and understanding activities for effective implementation to occur. Educators should include the stakeholder meeting and resource preparation time as part of the improvement process.

Second, the manuals differ in style. Minnesota's manual, for example, is full of checklists, sample documents, and other resources and is written in a rather linear, step-by-step procedural style. Oregon's manual is more discussion-based, with a greater proportion than Minnesota's manual of written text describing the substance and background of key topics. Illinois' manual falls between those of Minnesota and Oregon, leaning more toward the Minnesota style. The other four state manuals are all shorter, with two less than 40 pages. They are produced by education systems that differ in quality and size, whose manuals are one piece of their education and improvement systems. We suggest that educators review these manuals as part of their improvement process. There is no need to start anew when you can get a jump-start by learning and borrowing from some leaders in the field.

SYSTEM IMPROVEMENT THEORY IN ACTION IN THE STATE MANUALS

We can also reflect on what system improvement theory looks like in practice by examining the patterns of content across the manuals. In our examination, we find five strengths in how the manuals operationalize systems improvement research: They state their beliefs, they suggest practical methods and scenarios for internalizing these beliefs, they offer a statement of purpose, they provide new materials, and they extensively discuss research and theory.

First, the manual authors explicitly state the beliefs and understandings that they want to guide their system and to have their stakeholders develop. Beliefs and understandings are the third set of ideas we need to examine and change (as suggested by Fullan, 2001), and the manuals consistently state the new understandings[1] in multiple ways. The manuals include in-depth descriptions of the understandings that support the practices they expect. For example, Minnesota's manual authors wrote a "set of operating principles" that guide the entire manual (Minnesota Department of Education, 2005, p. 106). They are statements of fundamental beliefs, written as an implicit challenge to the status quo:

> It is too simplistic to say that traditional assessment procedures are inappropriate or unfair for *all* students of a given race. Teams need to look at a student's background on a case-by-case basis and decide whether standardized instruments and traditional procedures are valid. Teams should use a variety of formal and informal strategies to gather information and determine whether an individual student has a disability and is eligible for special education services. Special education evaluations should yield information that will help to improve instruction and lead to greater success for the individual student. (p. 106, emphasis in original)

These principles begin the process of setting collective understanding—in essence, nonnegotiable starting points—for developing and implementing their dual identified education system.

The new understandings sections of the manuals of Oregon and Illinois also caught our eyes. These sections document some fundamental new concepts and language as part of the ways these states are setting expected common understandings for stakeholders, which likely involves changing some of their views as well. For example, Oregon's manual authors included "cultural

STATE MANUALS

Connecticut

Connecticut State Department of Education. (2011). *English language learners and special education: A resource handbook.* Hartford, CT: Author.

Connecticut State Department of Education. (2012). *Scientific research-based interventions for English language learners: A handbook to accompany Connecticut's framework for RTI.* Hartford, CT: Author.

Illinois

Illinois State Board of Education. (2002). *Serving English language learners with disabilities: A resource manual for Illinois educators.* Springfield, IL: Author.

Michigan

Michigan Department of Education. (2017). *Guidance handbook for educators of English learners with suspected disabilities.* Lansing, MI: Author.

Minnesota

Minnesota Department of Education. (2005). *The ELL companion to reducing bias in special education evaluation.* St. Paul, MN: Author.

Oklahoma

Oklahoma State Department of Education. (2007). *Identifying and assessing English language learners with disabilities: Technical assistance document.* Oklahoma City, OK: Author.

Oregon

Education Evaluation Center, Teaching Research Institute, & Western Oregon University. (2015). *Special education assessment process for culturally and linguistically diverse (CLD) students: Guidance and resources* [2015 update]. Salem, OR: Oregon Department of Education.

Vermont

Vermont Department of Education, New England Equity Assistance Center, Education Alliance at Brown University & Northeast Regional Resource Center, & Learning Innovations at WestEd. (2010). *English language learners in Vermont: Distinguishing language difference from disability: A resource guide.* Montpelier, VT: Author.

(Links to these documents are available in the References.)

humility" as a way of thinking that goes beyond the more familiar culturally responsive practices (Education Evaluation Center, Teaching Research Institute, & Western Oregon University, 2015, p. 11). In Oregon's manual, the authors describe cultural humility as

> a framework focusing on professionals' introspection and questioning of their preconceived ideas and biases and how they interact with their students and other individuals from language minority backgrounds. One of the goals of cultural humility is to mitigate the power imbalance between the professional and the client/student. Cultural humility development is a life-long learning and developmental process. Therefore, professionals are recommended to engage in continual introspection and professional development in this area. (p. 19)

Cultural humility is important for educating EL students, they write, because

> the starting point for all evaluation procedures is the education professional's introspection and examination of his/her cultural belief system and how it impacts his or her evaluation practices and interactions with students. . . . Therefore, an orientation to student factors should occur only after introspection and an evaluation of the professional's belief system has occurred. (p. 11, citing Chavez, 2012)

In Oregon, where, during the 2015–2016 school year, 91% of the teachers were White while 37% of the K–12 students were students of color (Chief Education Office, 2017), understanding and then practicing cultural humility is important. This cultural humility corresponds well with our discussion of transculturalism in Chapter 3.

In Illinois' manual, the authors present the concepts of a "holistic perspective" and "goodness-of-fit" from eco-behavioral psychology as a way to replace the ubiquitous label and deficit thinking of "at-risk" students (Illinois State Board of Education, 2002, pp. 2-4–2-5).[2] As Illinois' authors describe it, the label of "at-risk" students places the lack of fit or success predominantly with the students and their families. This is both unrealistic and inappropriate. Instead, any lack of fit occurs from a dynamic between the education system (beliefs, practices, and materials) that educators, administrators, and policymakers have created and implemented and the students who are required to participate in it. Thus, since educators, administrators, and policymakers have control over the structure and implementation of the education system, they have a primary and initial responsibility for ensuring student fit. As the Illinois manual authors state:

> [T]he concepts of holistic analysis and goodness-of-fit are critical to any successful intervention process. Members of the school community must be willing to look not only at themselves and other aspects of the instructional environment but

to work to make changes after problem areas have been identified. This is not a process for the meek; it takes courage to self-evaluate and adapt and to become an advocate for students when their needs are in conflict with hard-to-change attitudinal or organizational aspects of the school or district. (pp. 2–5)

Illinois' manual makes it clear that it will likely be hard work to change to thinking and acting in a holistic and goodness-of-fit manner, but it is the new required understanding in the state. This holistic, goodness-of-fit approach that starts with educators and schools fits with and is a well-stated summary of our description of high-quality MTSS education from Tier 1 core instruction through Tier 3 intensive interventions and special education identification and referrals for EL students.

Second, beyond stating understandings, all seven manuals provide multiple ways for readers to begin to internalize these likely new understandings. Four manuals (Connecticut, Michigan, Oregon, and Vermont) further challenge and enable readers' understandings with FAQs. Case examples were another interesting resource for improving understandings, especially for understanding best practices in working with dual identified students. Two manuals (Illinois and Michigan) include these best practice case examples. Michigan's manual has a "Case Studies and Scenarios" section (pp. 42–45) with three scenarios reflecting three different common issues for teachers of EL students who they think might have a learning difficulty. The final paragraphs of the scenarios include the educators' initial resolution, which implies that they followed some of the state's best practices. Illinois' manual contains two extended case studies and two shorter case studies that are similar to those in Michigan, though the extended case studies have more detail (pp. 4-11–4-16). In both manuals, the best practice discussion is short; however, the scenarios could be used as a resource for more in-depth small group or professional development discussions.

Key word lists are another means for promoting new understandings. Five states (CT, MI, MN, OR, and VT) have them. They are an easy resource for readers to check and recheck how they understand and state key concepts and terms. Through FAQs, case examples, and key word lists, likely common misconceptions or conceptual stumbling blocks can be illuminated and then resolved, which is a research-based best practice in constructing new ideas, especially those that contradict current ones that are deeply held (Brooks & Brooks, 2000; Donovan, Bransford, & Pellegrino, 2000; Haas, Fischman, & Brewer, 2014; Pelech & Pieper, 2010; Schermer, 2017; Stovall, 2004).

Third, all the belief and understanding resources above connect to each state's most comprehensive understanding: the purpose of the EL and dual identified education system that these manuals describe. All seven manuals have a purpose statement. Having a clear, succinctly phrased purpose aids cohesion in effort across a large system (Fullan, Cuttress, & Kilcher, 2005; Murphy & Louis, 2018). It can also enhance effort and engagement as a high moral purpose often motivates people to work harder (Pink, 2011). Further, each manual has what we describe as an "additional consideration" statement in its purpose section. This statement describes areas where educators should put emphasis and extra effort if EL and dual identified students are to be successful in school. The authors of Oregon's manual included a comprehensive yet succinct additional consideration statement in their "Closing Remarks:"

> We would be remiss if we did not acknowledge that in the real world the paucity of resources such as highly qualified bilingual school professionals, culturally responsive standardized assessment tools, culturally responsive research based instructional practices, etc. makes achieving successful outcomes for CLD [culturally and linguistically diverse] students an extremely challenging task. In the absence of ideal conditions, it is imperative that more intensive communication and collaboration occur among all stakeholders (parents, regular, bilingual and special education personnel); efforts are made to minimize cultural and linguistic bias through culturally responsive, nondiscriminatory assessment and instructional practices; and careful consideration is given to determine whether or not exclusionary factors exist, so that the team can appropriately arrive at decisions that lead to the best possible educational outcomes for CLD students .... [Further], school professionals are encouraged to embrace a culturally humble and responsive philosophy. Culturally humble and responsive education professionals are aware of their own biases and power differentials between their professional role and their students' role. Cultural humility and responsiveness equips [sic] school professionals with the knowledge, skills and sensitivity to make appropriate decisions regarding research based instructional, intervention and assessment processes, and helps them create a welcoming, safe and stimulating learning environment for all their students and their families. (Education Evaluation Center et al., 2015, p. 55)

In sum, the manuals include explicit statements of the purpose of their dual identification and support systems as well as foundational understandings (which also are often new understandings) that readers can access and work on in multiple ways.

Fourth, each manual is a new material that is itself full of more materials, many of which may be new to educators in that state. Learning to use new materials is a key element of systems change as described by Fullan (2001). The manual materials include sample forms (CT, IL, MI, MN, and OR), including IEP reporting forms (IL and MN) and sample parent letters (CT, MI, and MN). All five of these state manuals include lists to check their practice against, such as lists of evidence to collect before an IEP team meeting and lists of considerations when determining the likely causes of the struggles of an EL student. These new materials, of course, will require new practices, such as being, perhaps, more methodical in one's evidence gathering and decisionmaking process, as well as use of the forms themselves. They can also facilitate and reinforce other new practices, including everything from collaboration across multidisciplinary teams (because everyone uses the same forms and checklists) to promoting parent outreach and involvement through having parent communication templates (no need to start from scratch in an already busy profession). Further, all seven manuals include lists of resources, from organizations to web links, for accessing more resource materials.

The manuals include practice guidance, at the individual teacher, small-team, and whole-system levels, describing best practices and including system process diagrams. For example, Oregon's manual authors included hierarchies of best practices from most desirable to least desirable in the areas of fluency assessment personnel, dos and don'ts in English language assessment, and lists of best practice elements in a number of areas. In addition, six state manuals (IL, MI, MN, OK, OR, and VT) include system best practice criteria. Several of these states include one or more system process diagrams that set out the step-by-step actions and decisions for determining whether an EL student has a learning disability from pre-IEP through the IEP and ongoing postplacement reevaluations. Again, it is important that understandings, materials, and practice improvements occur simultaneously. Manuals and other improvement processes and resources must address all three of these areas at the individual, small-team, and school- and districtwide levels at the same time.

Finally, educators must not be satisfied with improving only in areas where they currently know they are weaker. Our schools and communities are continually changing so educators must begin to predict future areas of concern in order to proactively prepare for those challenges. Educators need to be effective today with the issues they know now and effective in the future with the issues they will likely confront. This is why the fifth strength of these manuals is so important: the extensive discussion of research and theory.

To be effective today and proactively prepare for the future, educators need to develop schools, districts, and even states that are learning organizations. Part of that process is for more and more educators to develop themselves into Fullan's "system thinkers in action." Educators must understand the underlying research and theory that supports the best practices they should be continually working to implement, both as individuals and as collaborative members of a system. It is not possible to have a proactive learning organization without this knowledge. We believe that the authors of all seven state manuals believed this too, for each manual contains extensive discussions of research and theory surrounding the key topics in accurately and consistently identifying which EL students have learning dis/abilities and differences and how to best support them. All seven state manuals have extensive discussions of research and theory related to one or more of the following: the stages of second language acquisition; the stages of acculturation; ways to recognize the different behaviors that manifest struggles due to learning English, acculturating, and having a learning dis/ability; the impact of parent engagement on student achievement and how to support it; and the strengths and limitations of various assessment measures. Further, all the manuals described the legal rights and responsibilities surrounding both EL students and students with learning dis/abilities, which provides the framework for how all of these decisions and actions must occur.

SYSTEM IMPROVEMENT BEYOND THE MANUALS

Having described the elements in these manuals that promote system-wide improvement, what more is needed? We see three additional elements that the system-improvement literature suggests are necessary: monitoring, professional development, and integration of educational subsystems. First, system improvement requires regular monitoring to illuminate areas of effectiveness and areas where improvement is needed. Some refer to this as accountability, and we strongly suggest that this accountability go in two directions. The systems we create must be accountable to the students and their caregivers as well as the educators who participate in it. Learning and teaching are hard work and so our schools, districts, and states must provide educators, students, and caregivers with the resources they need for high-level teaching and learning to occur. Only once we are sure that educational institutions are providing high-quality supports, including in the areas of teacher pedagogical skills, curriculum, family engagement, leadership, and technology, can educators hold students and their caregivers more accountable. Too often, in our view, we hold students, caregivers, and educators accountable for any lack of student success, without providing them the necessary resources to do the difficult learning and teaching needed to reach benchmarks we set for them. The path to success for EL and dual identified students will be both similar to and distinct from that of the stereotypical White, suburban, upper-middle-class, native English-speaking student. Therefore, system accountability must include additional resource and practice considerations for our diverse EL and dual identified students, as described above and in earlier chapters. Building off the discussions in the previous chapters, what do various EL and dual identified students, their caregivers, and their teachers need to enable their success? That is what we should provide.

We suggest that schools, districts, and states create accountability forms that include both types of accountability. Figure 6.2 is a template we have used in offering system-improvement technical assistance. Terms in brackets are possible areas of focus that should be adjusted to individual contexts.

The template includes traditional student and caregiver accountability or outcome areas of academic achievement and lifelong learning attitudes and behaviors. It also includes five common outcome areas for determining system quality and a sixth placeholder for any system area that is specific to an individual school or district or for any additional system-wide indicators. Inside each outcome area box, educators list the multiple measures they use (or will use) to determine the quality level of each area of each accountability level: student and caregiver, program, and overall system. For system improvement to occur, system quality and accountability must be explicit and made actionable.

Figure 6.2. System improvement template with sample headings and performance indicators.

If the goal is all learners being . . . **[Being COLLEGE and CAREER READY]**

Then all learners must be on the path of . . .

[Academic Achievement] **AND** **[Post–High School Trajectory]**

Performance Indicators	<ul><li>Score minimums on school or grade-level anchor assessments</li><li>Score minimums on state standardized tests</li><li>Teacher evaluation minimums</li></ul>	<ul><li>Graduation rate minimum</li><li>College enrollment rate minimum</li><li>Work-based learning participation rate minimum (e.g., Linked Learning, internships/mentorships)</li></ul>

And all learners must attain . . .

[Lifelong Learning Attitudes and Behaviors]

Performance Indicators	<ul><li>Minimum survey results from students</li><li>Teacher evaluation minimums on lifelong learning criteria</li><li>Attendance rate minimums</li><li>Discipline rate maximums</li></ul>

As a result of a K–12 program with quality indicators in the areas of . . .

	Pedagogical Skills	**Curriculum**	**Family Engagement**
Performance Indicators	<ul><li>Teacher observation scores</li><li>Teacher PD participation rates</li></ul>	<ul><li>Vetting of curriculum by educator team</li><li>Vetting of curriculum by outside group</li></ul>	<ul><li>Parent satisfaction survey</li><li>Participation rates</li></ul>

	Leadership	**Technology**	**Other**
Performance Indicators	<ul><li>Principal evaluation score</li><li>Parent, faculty, and student satisfaction survey</li><li>Administrator PD participation rates</li></ul>	<ul><li>Student, educator, and parent use rates</li><li>Parent, faculty, and student satisfaction survey</li></ul>	<ul><li>System-wide equity audits</li></ul>

We find the biggest stumbling blocks to system monitoring and account-ability for EL and dual identified student education is naming the system qual-ity measures and creating a set of data collection, analysis, review, and action step processes that will promote success. Earlier in this chapter, we described how the state manuals include criteria for a high-quality system of identifying and placing dual identified students, but how do you collect and analyze data on these criteria and then take improvement action steps based on what you learned? None of the manuals describe this type of monitoring system; how-ever, there are books full of research-based guidance on data-driven decision-making systems that can provide this guidance (see e.g., Datnow & Park, 2014; Mandinach & Gummer, 2016). Further, what system outcome measures and practical responses can educators use to understand the state of their current practice and then make improvements where needed? We list some common data examples in Figure 6.2, such as test scores, teacher grades, parent and stu-dent surveys, and program evaluations by educators and outside teams. These system-wide data-driven decisionmaking processes and teams can and should parallel, and thus reinforce, those teams and processes used in MTSS and IEP/504 decisions, described in previous chapters. Taken together, these mea-sures can offer formative insights into strengths and weaknesses of a program and integrated levels of data-driven decisionmaking, so teams can see and act on what they learn from continually examining these measures.

However, these measures, because they are taken of large groups of stu-dents, can mask the program and achievement weakness of specific subgroups of students, such as dual identified students. Therefore, we strongly suggest that educators seek out these areas of possible program weakness and relat-ed student underachievement. These subgroup specific aspects of a program evaluation are often labeled equity audits or as organizational change to pro-mote equity (Dowd & Liera, 2018; McKenzie & Scheurich, 2004). We find the practical guidance in McKenzie and Scheurich's (2004) article entitled "Equity Traps" to be a great starting place for probing for program weaknesses for EL and dual identified students as subgroups of large school, district, and state stu-dent populations. They offer measures to determine a program's equity quality, with a focus on "ways of thinking or assumptions that prevent educators from believing that their students of color can be successful learners" (pp. 601–602), which can be readily expanded and adapted to include other often marginal-ized subgroups. Then they provide action steps for making improvements if the equity audit outcomes show bias.

Their ideas can easily be extended for EL and dual identified students. For example, one can collect data on special education referral rates or care-giver participation rates both overall and by subgroups by race, gender, so-cioeconomic status, and English learner status to see if there are significant patterns of over- and underrepresentation. One could also do more in-depth qualitative studies, such as describing educators' talk about parents and stu-dents. These talk analyses can illuminate patterns of where educators avoid or are uncomfortable discussing race or English learner status as reasons for special education placement (or any other program or achievement measure) (McKenzie & Scheurich, 2004). Or in the opposite mindset, the analyses can illuminate where educators use essentialist language to lump, for example, an EL student's behavior incident as just what EL students do rather than what *this* EL student did in *that* moment (Gopnik, 2016). This type of action research, when conducted by educators and perhaps even caregivers too, can be thought- and behavior-changing in itself. Depending on the findings, follow-up activities could be conducted, from greater caregiver outreach to educator (and caregiver) reading circles to more equity audits. At the whole-system level, Fullan (2006) suggests adding a new measure to program quality that incorporates sustainability: counting the number of system thinkers in action who have been developed across the school or the district as a whole. Sustainable improvement will need to overcome turnover and promote extensive and diverse expertise—distributed leadership—which is essential for developing and maintaining a learning organization. Therefore, developing more system thinkers in action who act in various leadership roles should (or must) be an explicit goal with progress measures and action steps to accomplish it. Finally, a collaborative, distributed data-driven decisionmaking and improvement process as a form of regular action research inherently creates the system thinkers the learning organization needs.

Second, ongoing professional development and dissemination of manuals and similar resource materials are a common suggestion; however, it is also one that appears to be heeded less often than it should. Recent qualitative studies by Orosco and Klingner (2010) and Cavendish, Harry, Menda, Espinosa, and Mahotiere (2016) followed the new implementation of RTI/MTSS as related to EL students and to placement into special education, respectively. Both studies found the lack of professional development a key factor in the lack of high-quality implementation or fidelity of implementation of this new set of practices. Simply stated, both studies found that educators did not understand RTI/MTSS sufficiently to adapt their current English learner and special education monitoring and placement practices so that they fit into this new system. Improvement is learning and new programs that include substantive changes in practice usually take 3 to 5 years to reach effective levels of implementation (Fullan, 2001; Hall & Hord, 2001; Taylor, Getty, Kowalski, Wilson, Carlson, & Van Scotter, 2015). Further, teachers and other educators have a high turnover rate, so new teachers will continually be joining this new implementation. In short, ongoing training of teachers and other educators is imperative.

Much of the discussion in the middle chapters of this book focused on how educators can seamlessly integrate the monitoring, identification, assessment, and placement processes for dual identified students into their larger educational system. We focused on how to integrate these activities with MTSS and the specific adaptation of PLUSS for EL students. Thus, the third extension of the state manuals is consciously working to integrate what are often three separate systems—one for English learner students, one for special education services, and one for general education—into one cohesive system. With the exception of Oregon's manual, which has a lengthy discussion of fitting the dual identification system with the RTI/MTSS system in general education, the manuals do not explicitly discuss this integration process. We believe the integration must be explicitly and regularly discussed. Though RTI/MTSS and PLUSS and a dual identification system are complementary, there are some areas where they come into conflict, and educators and caregivers should know what to do in these moments. One of the central areas concerns when a parent or legal guardian can insist that the school convene an IEP team before the three-tier process of RTI/MTSS would typically call for one. Under IDEA, parents can require this "early" convening of an IEP team, even when the child's educators believe it is too soon. So, for these traditionally three systems to act as one, all educators, not just special education specialists and English learner specialists, must know their legal responsibilities under various federal and state laws. And they must know how to build trusting and collaborative relationships with caregivers and with other educators outside their primary discipline in order to manage the tensions between legal rights, responsibilities, and research-based best educational practices.

NEW ISSUES IN THE NEAR FUTURE

Finally, we look ahead to issues and actions that we expect to appear in the near future. Two come to mind: one, opening the possibility for modifications in ELD program exit requirements for dual identified students; two, fostering leadership in education for dual identified students. We must ask whether and when we should exit dual identified students from ELD programs, especially pull-out programs, when their inability to pass reclassification requirements is due to a learning dis/ability. In other words, if a native English speaker with a similar learning dis/ability would likely not pass the reclassification requirements for exiting an ELD program, are we doing a dual identified student a disservice by keeping them there as a long-term English learner? If the only or primary reason that a dual identified student remains in an ELD program is due to a learning dis/ability, is this a violation of the least restrictive environment (LRE) provision of IDEA? More fundamentally, what is the best learning environment for this subgroup of dual identified students?

We know of little guidance in this area. However, Texas explicitly permits exceptions to its ELD exit criteria for dual identified students, which can provide an initial point for discussion. During 2017–2018, Texas permitted an exception to their standard ELD exit criteria only when a student's inability to meet the exit criteria in a specific language domain (listening, speaking, reading, or writing) was directly related to the student's learning dis/ability (Texas Education Agency, n.d.). Further, Texas states directly that the exception can only be used on a case-by-case basis with individual students; it cannot be granted generally to groups of students (say, for example, all EL students diagnosed with a form of autism). The Texas regulations state that when a specific student is identified as potentially meeting the exception criteria, then a committee of educators, similar to an IEP committee, meets to determine if the student meets the criteria and whether the student no longer benefits from placement in an ELD program. The committee must provide a variety of evidence to support a decision to exit a dual identified student from an ELD program under this exception. We expect that these types of decisions will increase as the needs of dual identified students become more commonly understood.

Second, we wonder how to proactively promote expertise and leadership in high-quality education for dual identified students. Beyond developing these qualities through ongoing professional development and participation in data-based decisionmaking teams, we would like to see more explicit development of educators begin in the preservice preparation programs. We also wonder whether additional recognition of the knowledge and skills for identifying, placing, and teaching dual identified students through an additional certification might encourage more educators to seek this knowledge and these skills. Greater educator interest and a clear path to professional improvement might then facilitate greater distributed leadership in dual identified student education.

System-level improvement in educating dual identified students requires improvement in the larger general education system, too. It requires strong collaboration among teachers, specialists, administrators, caregivers, and students, of which the logistics alone can be difficult. It requires greater expertise in understandings, use of materials, and new best practices for many individual educators. And the improvements, if they are to be deep, sustainable, and system-wide, need to occur at multiple levels and in multiple areas simultaneously. This improvement can seem a daunting task. But it is possible. There are states, as well as districts and schools, that are leading the way. We described some of the work of seven states here. Learn from their work as a starting point for your own.

Using Legal Rights and Responsibilities to Promote Effective Programs and Practices for EL Students at Risk for or Having a Learning Dis/Ability

Established sets of legislation and case law separately support the rights of English learner students and students with dis/abilities to a meaningful free appropriate public education (see Haas, 2005; Individuals with Disabilities Education Improvement Act of 2004 [IDEA]; Powers, 2014; Rehabilitation Act of 1973; Title III of The Elementary and Secondary Education Act [ESEA], 2015). In addition, various federal and state laws and regulations require educators to perform specific activities to promote the education of EL students and students with dis/abilities. For example, pursuant to Title III of the most recent version of the Elementary and Secondary Education Act, currently named the Every Student Succeeds Act (ESSA), states must determine whether new students are English learners by administering a home language survey and then an initial English language fluency test if the student's parents or guardians report that a language other than English is spoken at home (see Haas, Tran, Linquanti, & Bailey, 2015). ESSA also made a number of changes in the progress reporting, identification, and exiting criteria of EL students, as well as requiring that districts and their states report specifically on the progress that dual identified students have made in English language proficiency (ELP) and their achievement on state content tests (Council of Chief State School Officers, 2016). In this chapter, we describe these rights for students (and their parents, guardians, and sometimes other caregivers) and educator responsibilities, including relevant definitions and federal guidance on required practices, and how they can (and should) be used to promote the effective practices previously described in this book (see, e.g., DeRuvo, 2010; Haas & Gort, 2009; Takanishi & Menestral, 2017).

We add one note of caution in reading the following sections on the rights of EL students and students who may or do have a learning dis/ability and the responsibilities of educators. We repeat here briefly what we stated initially in

Chapter 2 and an idea that permeates this book: Bilingualism and language diversity are resources that should be promoted; the success of each person contributes to the prosperity of their entire community and beyond (Haas, Fischman, & Brewer, 2014; Ruiz, 1984). Unfortunately, extended discussions of problems and rights can subtly promote the idea that EL students, students with dis/abilities, and dual identified students only have deficits that we need to fill or fix. This is neither our belief nor our intention. However, explicit and implicit biases and microaggressions, systemic racism, xenophobia, and ableism often force EL students, students with dis/abilities, and dual identified students, their caregivers, and their allies to focus on the lack of support for "problems." As a result, minoritized subgroups often must assert legal rights to the supports and processes they need to succeed, which are often ones that differ from those that the majority subgroups of native English speakers and abled students need to succeed. Properly understood, federal and state laws can be an effective tool for promoting best practices for identifying and supporting EL students with learning dis/abilities; however, like any policy, rule, or regulation, it is how people use them (or not) that determines their level of effectiveness. It is with this spirit that we present the following description of education policy, rights, and responsibilities.

ESSA AND THE CURRENT EDUCATION POLICY ENVIRONMENT

Both general education policies, such as adoption of the Common Core State Standards (CCSS) by 45 states (ASCD, n.d.) and the administration of standardized tests, including SBAC and PARCC in 23 states during the 2016–2017 school year (Gewertz, 2017), and targeted education policies, such as IDEA and Title III of ESSA, impact EL students, students with dis/abilities, and dual identified students. Sometimes the implementation of the general and the specific education policies interact, such as how accommodations required by IDEA and Title III are operationalized in the computer-based administration of adaptive testing in SBAC and PARCC. We describe the various policies in discrete sections, noting where they may impact other policies and practices.

ESSA, passed by Congress and signed by President Obama in December 2015, is the latest version of the Elementary and Secondary Education Act (ESEA), first signed into law by President Johnson in 1965. The version of ESEA just before ESSA was the No Child Left Behind Act (NLCB) of 2001. Each version of ESEA, however Congress names it, provides the overall blueprint of federal education policy and is administered through the U.S. Department of Education. ESSA continues the major education policies that existed under NCLB and many that existed under earlier versions. There are nine major policy areas or titles:

Title I. Improving Basic Programs Operated by State and Local Educational Agencies

Title II. Preparing, Training, and Recruiting High-Quality Teachers, Principals, or Other School Leaders

Title III. Language Instruction for English Learners and Immigrant Students

Title IV. 21st Century Schools

Title V. State Innovation and Local Flexibility

Title VI. Indian, Native Hawaiian, and Alaska Native Education

Title VII. Impact Aid

Title VIII. General Provisions

Title IX. Education for the Homeless and Other Laws

ESSA impacts dual identified students most directly through Titles I and III.

Overall, ESSA continues the basic federal education philosophy and policy actions of NCLB, though with more flexibility for states. Reading ESSA as whole, its philosophy looks to be that continuous school improvement should be founded on four main elements:

1. detailed, rigorous content standards (such as the CCSS) in at least math, English/language arts (ELA), and science that lead to students being "college and career ready";
2. annual standardized tests to measure student achievement progress toward meeting (or exceeding) these college and career ready standards;
3. accountability determinations and reporting requirements for how well LEAs and their educators have enabled their students to meet these standards; and
4. some support systems and federal funding for low-performing schools and certain programs, including preschool development, school counseling, physical education, and educator development (Education Counsel, 2015).

The underlying premise of ESSA appears to be that public data reporting will shine a light on the successes and failures of states, districts, and schools, and transparency will drive them to make evidence-based improvements. (Education Counsel, 2015)

States and their districts and schools are obligated to follow ESSA requirements as a condition for accepting federal education funding. Although federal education funding is only about 8% of all education funding, every state accepts ESSA funding and therefore must follow its required provisions (U.S. Department of Education, n.d.). However, many of the ESSA mandates are general or flexible in nature and there are specific limitations on the extent to which the U.S. Department of Education (USDOE) can regulate or review what states create in response to the ESSA mandates. For example, one ESSA mandate requires states to establish content standards but there is no requirement stating what they must contain, and the USDOE does not have the authority to judge their quality (see limitations in Title I on the secretary of education). Thus, ESSA's effectiveness in creating improvements in student achievement will depend on how each state, district, school, and educator utilizes its provisions.

ESSA's focus on standards, testing, and data reporting continues the general provisions of NCLB and these policy foci impact the everyday school experience of all public school students. In addition, ESSA more directly impacts dual identified students in three new ways. First, ESSA and the Individuals with Disabilities Improvement Act (IDEA, 2004) now have consistent language for defining *English learner* that includes both students born and not born in the United States whose environment includes a language other than English that is dominant or has a significant impact on their ability to understand English in an English-only instructional environment (20 USC §7801 [25]; 34 CFR §300.27). Second, ESSA requires states to create uniform processes and criteria for identifying EL students, placing them in EL support services, and exiting them from these EL support services as reclassified fluent English proficient (RFEP). In other words, each district and school in a state is supposed to follow the same criteria and rules.

Third, ESSA requires school districts or local educational agencies (LEAs) to report on the progress of dual identified students (EL students with dis/abilities recognized under IDEIA) in two ways. First, ESSA requires reporting of the number and percentage of currently dual identified students who are making various levels of progress toward their state's English language proficiency (ELP) requirements for reclassification as fluent English proficient (RFEP). Second, the number and percentage of reclassified or former EL students who met their state's academic standards (usually presented as passing scores on the state's academic content tests). Further, ESSA "encourages" similar reporting for dual identified students in other areas, including rates of reclassification as fluent English proficient (RFEP) (not just progress toward RFEP) and the rates at which dual identified students become long-term English learners (LTEL) students, who are defined under ESSA as EL students who have not reclassified after 5 years in their LEA's English language development (ELD) program.

ESSA requires districts and states to shine a light on the achievement progress of their dual identified students through required annual and biannual reporting (see U.S. Department of Education, 2016a), which could spur states and districts to improve their educational experiences (Barone & Lombardo, 2016; Gordon, 2017). However, illuminating the subgroup performance of dual identified students (or any other subgroup) will not necessarily happen and the reported results will not automatically lead to more effective teaching practices. What matters more than just the reporting is how each state and district, each school and educator, interprets the ESSA reporting requirements and then uses the reported results. The reliability and usefulness of subgroup reporting depend on the smallest subgroup size (in statistics, the "N") that is reported. If the minimum subgroup size is very small—say, five dual identified students in a grade or school—then the grades or schools at or near these small numbers of students will likely get big swings in the annual results as one very high or very low student score will dramatically change the group's average score.[1] This might lead to unhelpful program and practices changes in response to these unreliable average scores. Further, a small subgroup size also risks revealing the performance of individual dual identified students, which invades their personal privacy. If the minimum subgroup size is larger—say, 30 dual identified students in a grade or school—annual score averages are more consistent because each individual student's score will have a smaller impact on the group's average. However, with a 30-student minimum, many smaller schools, such as elementary schools or rural schools, will omit reporting on the progress of their dual identified students because they will have fewer of these students than the minimum required for reporting; no light is focused on these small-numbered subgroups of dual identified students and so there is less transparency and perhaps no action where improvement is needed. To balance these competing concerns, the U.S. Department of Education's National Center for Education Statistics has recommended that the minimum subgroup reporting size be 10 students (Institute of Education Sciences, 2010).

As a teacher, education leader, or policymaker, how might you use your state's minimum subgroup size to get a better understanding of how your dual identified students are doing and to promote best education practices if your school or district falls below the minimum? Gordon (2017) describes some nice examples of how this could be done based on how Oregon has set up its reporting and accountability requirements with a minimum subgroup size of 20, which we build off here. Imagine your state also has a minimum subgroup size of 20 and your K–5 elementary school has 40 dual identified students, but no more than eight in any one grade. What can you do? First, you can push your state to include aggregation options as part of the subgroup minimum. That is, if a grade level or school has fewer dual identified students than the minimum reporting size, then require some form of grouping to exceed the minimum. Forms of grouping could include multiyear groups (e.g., collect all the scores for 3rd-grade dual identified students over a 3-year period into one subgroup), multigrade groups (e.g., collect all the scores for grades K–3 [learning to read] and 4–5 [beginning to read to learn] into separate subgroups), or multischool groups based on some characteristic (e.g., group all K–5 schools based on geographic location clusters, percent of EL students, or percent of students eligible for free or reduced-price lunch into one subgroup), or a combination of groupings (e.g., 3-year K–5 and 4–5 subgroups or by grade level based on location clusters). Second, you can perform your own groupings in your school or in collaborative groups with other schools as part of your ongoing formative program reviews, even if your state does not require it. As we describe in Chapter 6, using system-wide data can be an effective way to guide reform.

The daily educational experience of EL students at risk for or having a learning dis/ability is directly impacted by the provisions of ESSA that affect all students and also by the student rights and educational agency responsibilities that come separately from English learner laws and special education laws. Each will be discussed in turn.

LEGAL RIGHTS OF EL STUDENTS AND RELATED EDUCATOR RESPONSIBILITIES

Generally, schools identify a student as an English learner prior to a determination that the student has a learning dis/ability. Under federal legislation and case law (see Haas, 2005; see also *Castañeda v. Pickard*, 1981; Every Student Succeeds Act, 2015b; *Lau v. Nichols*, 1974), schools must provide language support for students who are not native English speakers that is sufficient for them to meaningfully participate and learn until they are sufficiently fluent in English to participate in mainstream, English-dominant environments on their own (Hakuta, 2011; Hakuta, Butler, & Witt, 2000). This process of determining necessary minimum supports begins with an initial determination of whether a student's home language is one other than English and so the student might be learning English as their second language. Under Title III of ESSA, schools must administer a home language survey to determine whether a student is exposed to or uses a language other than English outside of school to such a degree that it could impact their ability to learn in an English-only school environment (Bailey & Kelly, 2013; Haas, Tran, Linquanti, & Bailey, 2015). Further, ESSA's Title III requires that each state have a uniform set of criteria and processes for identifying whether students should be classified as English learners, what their EL-related support services should be, and how and what criteria should later be considered for reclassification as fluent English proficient and being exited from any EL supports they are receiving. However, ESSA leaves it up to each state to create these criteria and processes.

When accurately done, this initial determination of whether students are sufficiently fluent in English to succeed in mainstream English-dominant classrooms will place them in the most appropriate learning environment. Students will receive additional supports if they are learning English as a second language, while students who are already fluent in English, including bilingual students, will not receive unnecessary and possibly detrimental language services (Haas, Tran, Linquanti, & Bailey, 2015). The first step in this determination is for parents or guardians of each new student to complete their state's home language survey. In California, for example, the home language survey has four questions:

1. Which language did your child learn when he/she first began to talk?
2. Which language does your child most frequently speak at home?
3. Which language do you (the parents or guardians) most frequently use when speaking with your child?
4. Which language is most often spoken by adults in the home (parents, guardians, grandparents, or any other adults)?

In California, if the student's parent or guardian answers any of the first three questions with a language other than English, including English and another language, then the student is considered to be a potential EL student. If the parent or guardian answers English to the first three questions and then a language other than English, including English and another language, for the fourth question, then the school or district has the discretion to decide whether the student should be considered a potential EL student (Haas, Tran, Linquanti, & Bailey, 2015). All states have basically similar process for determining whether a new student is a potential English learner.

Potential EL students must take the state's initial English language proficiency (ELP) screener test, which varies from state to state (Cook & Linquanti, 2015). Potential EL students who score at or above the minimum for reclassification as fluent English proficient are designated as initial fluent English proficient (IFEP) students, and they are placed full-time in mainstream English-dominant classes. Students who do not score at or above the minimum for classification as fluent in English are identified as EL students and placed in English language development (ELD) classes and/or provided other ELD supports until they demonstrate that they are fluent in English. EL students who later score at or above the minimum for English fluency are then reclassified as fluent English proficient (RFEP) and placed full-time in mainstream English-dominant classes without additional ELD supports.

English fluency is determined primarily by scores on the state ELP test (Bailey & Kelly, 2010, 2013), which can create problems for EL students who have a learning dis/ability, especially an undiagnosed one. On the initial ELP screener test, the difference between English fluency issues and dis/ability issues can be especially hard to sort out, as the ELP test is usually the only initial measure of the student's English proficiency. Further, most newly registering students are kindergartners, and therefore it is likely that many of the potential EL students have little to no experience with formal testing, have not been tested for learning dis/abilities, including non-visible disabilities like ADHD and dyslexia, and perhaps also have not been tested for other physical differences that can affect learning, such as hearing loss and weak eyesight. Thus, a potential EL student who does not pass the state ELP screener may have a low score due to having low levels of English proficiency, lack of test-taking experience, or a learning-related dis/ability, among other possibilities. Therefore, caregivers and educators who suspect that a newly registering potential EL student may have a dis/ability that affects their ELP screener results (and their learning in general) should seek out the required diagnostic services under IDEA, among other laws, which we describe in the next section. Educators must be responsive to these requests for diagnostic services as they have an affirmative duty to seek out students who might have a learning dis/ability (referred to as Child Find) and provide them services if they do (see IDEA, 2004, 34 CFR §§300.301[b], 300.309[c]). If a school does not act on the request for an evaluation, IDEA requires that it provide the requesting parent, guardian, or other appropriate ally with a written explanation of its refusal to act and a description of how to contest their decision (procedural safeguards).

Schools must provide all EL students language supports sufficient for them to meaningfully participate in class and learn both English and subject matter content knowledge. This right to a meaningful education was first set out by the Supreme Court in *Lau v. Nichols* (1974) and later in 1974, Congress passed the Equal Educational Opportunities Act (EEOA) with similar language. Seven years later, the Fifth Circuit Court of Appeals in *Castañeda v. Pickard* (1981) created a three-part test that courts now use as the standard for determining whether a given ELD support program meets the requirements of the EEOA and *Lau*. The three requirements are that the program must be

1. based on "sound educational theory";
2. have sufficient resources of personnel, instructional materials, and space to be implemented effectively; and
3. supported by evidence of effectiveness in overcoming language barriers once it has been implemented.

While these standards appear reasonable and can support the implementation of high-quality practices for EL students, including for dual identified students as described in this book, courts in subsequent cases have set the practical application of the standards so low as to make them nearly meaningless (Haas, 2005; Haas & Gort, 2009). For example, courts have consistently deferred to the judgment of the school districts on whether there is "sound educational theory" to support their ELD program. If a school district can find any "expert," however marginalized in their opinion, who will state that the supporting educational theory is sound, then courts have upheld it as appropriate against guardians and students who have their own experts who say it is not (Haas, 2005). Thus, like many of these other legal rights and responsibilities, the effectiveness of this test depends on how parents, guardians, and educators use it.

EL students who may have a learning dis/ability, potential dual identified students, have many additional legal rights under IDEA, Section 504 of the Rehabilitation Act of 1973, and the Americans with Disabilities Act (ADA). Under IDEA, every child with a dis/ability in the IDEA list (Figure 5.2) has the right to a "free appropriate public education" (FAPE). Further, these special education services must be provided in the "least restrictive environment" (LRE), which is generally interpreted as a mainstream classroom with fellow students their age, whenever possible. In addition, educators have a legal responsibility under IDEA to proactively seek out and assist students with learning disabilities (Child Find; see IDEA, 2004, 20 U.S.C. § 1412[a][3] and 34 C.F.R. § 300.111). Many states have also passed their own laws and regulations that parallel IDEA (see California Education Code Sections 56000 et seq.). These rights can be exercised by individual students and their parents and guardians, and the educator responsibilities require specific actions by individual educators, and students with dis/abilities, but who do not require specially designed instruction, can be provided accommodations through Section 504 and the ADA.

As described in Chapters 2–5, determining whether an EL student has a learning dis/ability begins with whether the student has been experiencing a high-quality education in their general education and ELD classes. Evidence-based teaching practices should include not only high-quality instruction but also incorporate ongoing formative evaluations of each EL student's progress using multiple forms of data (universal screening and progress monitoring), which should illuminate whether any struggles by an EL student may be due to a learning dis/ability. However, first having high-quality or appropriate instruction is not a requirement for conducting a dis/ability evaluation or providing special education services as required under IDEA (or even Section 504). Rather, the quality of instruction is a point of information in determining the cause of an EL student's struggles. Ironically, it may be determined that the EL student is struggling only because of poor-quality instruction, which, if extensive in the school or district, may limit the EL student's ability to improve their achievement.

Schools should not wait for a struggling EL student to fail before they begin to intervene with new and/or more intensive and focused supports (see IDEA, 2004). This is the philosophy behind MTSS and educators in schools using MTSS will likely proceed from Tier 1 to Tier 2 in the normal course of providing supportive services. Thus, many EL students whom educators suspect of having one or more learning dis/abilities would be in some type of Tier 2 placement or possibly a Tier 3 placement when a school believes it is time to begin a formal evaluation for a learning dis/ability as required by the IDEA Child Find requirements. However, under IDEA, an evaluation for any learning dis/ability does not have to wait until a school implements all the MTSS tiers. Even if a state were to require the use of MTSS data as part of a disability determination, a parent, guardian, other student ally, or educator can request a dis/ability evaluation prior to completion of the MTSS tiers under IDEA. As a federal law, IDEA supersedes state dis/ability laws and regulations where they overlap. The school must conduct the evaluation or explain in writing why it has refused to do so and describe the steps for contesting its decision. In other words, typical MTSS processes employed by the school, common district practices, and state laws and regulations cannot prevent a student ally from being an active participant in negotiating when an EL student receives a formal dis/

ability evaluation under IDEA (or possibly a learning-related impairment evaluation under Section 504 of the Rehabilitation Act of 1973) within an MTSS system of interventions. Once an evaluation determines that an EL student is struggling due to one or more dis/abilities, exclusive of or in addition to other factors, including poor instruction, then educators are required to proactively follow the requirements of IDEA to create the student's Individual Education Program (IEP) in addition to any services provided through the MTSS.

LEGAL RIGHTS OF STUDENTS AND RELATED EDUCATOR RESPONSIBILITIES

Once an EL student is identified as possibly having a learning dis/ability (IDEA) or a learning-related impairment (Section 504), whether by an educator, caregiver, or other student ally, IDEA or Section 504 will guide the criteria and procedures for the evaluation and receiving special education, accommodations, and related services (IDEA) or other support services and accommodations (Section 504). The main differences between IDEA and Section 504 derive from the specificity of the criteria for services, the flexibility of the procedures, individualized instruction versus accommodations, and the duration of services. In short, IDEA as compared to Section 504 has more specific eligibility criteria, more rigid procedural requirements, and a less demanding standard for appropriate education, but often more intensive required services, and applies for a more limited time frame (ages 3 to graduation or age 21). In addition, for educators, states receive federal funding for providing special education services under IDEA, but districts must pay for all services they provide under Section 504. Figure 7.1 presents the similarities and differences between IDEA and Section 504.

Within the list of IDEA provisions, there are several requirements that do or should include additional elements or considerations, as best practices, when the student is an English learner. Most of these requirements under IDEA are not specified under the less formal provisions of Section 504; however, they should likely be included as best practice additions to Section 504 proceedings as well. One requirement under IDEA is that the IEP team must be multidisciplinary, which includes some expertise in general and special education, and also familiar with the EL student. When the student is an English learner, recent federal guidance for IDEA also requires an IEP member to have expertise in the EL student's English language needs and suggests that someone on the IEP team have expertise in second language acquisition generally as well as how to differentiate between second language and dis/ability needs (U.S. Department of Education, 2016a). A second requirement under IDEA is that the school or district must provide parents and guardians of EL students, who often are nonnative English speakers themselves, with interpreters and some document translations to enable them to meaningfully participate in

Figure 7.1. Comparison of IDEA and Section 504 for EL students.

Component	IDEA	Section 504
Child Find	Yes	No
Eligibility for services	One or more of 13 specific disabilities categories and Dis/ability adversely affects educational performance	Handicapped as defined by a physical or mental impairment or even long-term illness that substantially limits a major life activity, including learning (this eligibility definition is broader than in IDEA)
Evaluation	Formal evaluation by a multidisciplinary team, which should include an expert in second language acquisition among the various required experts Evaluation includes multiple forms of data and formal written evaluation document Informed and written parental/guardian consent to the evaluation and assent to its results, which must include interpreters and translated documents Re-evaluation at least every 3 years or by parent/guardian request Re-evaluation not required for a significant change in placement or services Independent evaluations at district expense if parents disagree with initial evaluation	Includes information from a variety of sources that is documented in some manner (usually in writing, though can be informally) Decision made by knowledgeable persons, which does not require an expert in second language acquisition Parental/guardian notification but not consent to conducting the evaluation and to its decision Unspecified time period for periodic re-evaluations Re-evaluation required before a significant change in placement or services No requirement for an independent evaluation at the school's or district's expense

Figure 7.1. Comparison of IDEA and Section 504 for EL students. (continued)

Component	IDEA	Section 504
Child Find	Yes	No
Services (FAPE)	An individualized education program (IEP) is required that includes annual measurable goals related to academic, functional, and other needs that result from the disability "Appropriate" education means one intended to provide an "educational benefit" to the student, but the benefit does not mean educational outcomes equivalent to general education students or to fully meet the EL student's potential, such as potential for gifted-and-talented level success Placement in any combination of special education and general education classes, but the default is within the general education class under least restrictive environment (LRE) Other related services, if needed, such as physical therapy and transportation There are no special education service limitations due to cost	A plan (usually named a 504 plan) without formal requirements; it may not even need to be written "Appropriate" education means assistance to enable an equal opportunity to participate in school as compared to nondisabled or nonhandicapped peers. Further, the education is one that is comparable to the education provided to general education students, which therefore means it does not need to enable an EL student to reach their full potential, such as potential for gifted and talented level success Placement is generally within general education classrooms with support services and accommodations Services can be limited in scope if they are deemed to cause an undue financial burden on a school or district

Figure 7.1. Comparison of IDEA and Section 504 for EL students. (continued)

Component	IDEA	Section 504
Child Find	Yes	No
Due Process Rights of Students, Parents, and Guardians	Requires formal, impartial hearings when parent or guardian disagrees with school or district decisions on identification, evaluation, or placement and services Written notification and consent, including interpreters and translations as needed for knowing and active participation, including legal counsel Students "stay put" in current placement and with current services under IEP until hearings concluded Parents must receive written notice in a language they understand at a reasonable time prior to a significant change in placement or services	Requires impartial hearings when parent or guardian disagrees with school or district decisions on identification, evaluation, or placement and services Parents or guardians have an opportunity to participate in the hearing and can bring legal counsel No "stay put" provision; therefore an EL student's services or placement can change prior to the hearing conclusion Parents or guardians must be notified of a significant change in services or placement, but the notice can come after the change
Enforcement	Procedures enforced by the USDOE, Office of Special Education Programs	Procedures enforced by the USDOE, Office for Civil Rights
Funding	There are no costs to students or caregivers States receive additional federal funds for providing special education services to eligible students	There are no costs to students or caregivers Districts fund all 504-related services; there is no federal 504 funding

(Individuals with Disabilities Education Improvement Act, 2004; Ryder, 2016; Section 504 of the Rehabilitation Act of 1973; U.S. Department of Education, Office for Civil Rights, 2016, 2018) the IEP team's deliberations and in the eligibility, evaluation, and placement decisions as well as the implementation of their child's plan (see Equal Educational Opportunities Act, 1974; Title VI of the Civil Rights Act, 1964; U.S. Department of Education, 2016a, 2016b). However, these federal laws are also rather vague on the extent to which interpreters and translations must be provided when it is not convenient for the school or district to do so[2] and, in our experience, schools and districts often do not provide them or provide them in very limited ways.

Another, better practice example that goes to the spirit but not the letter of IDEA is to make an IEP plan "linguistically appropriate" by specifically tailoring the academic goals related to their dis/ability needs to the EL student's English fluency level and not just their general academic or cognitive developmental level as compared to native English-speaking students. These annual measurable goals, individualized for each dual identified student, would then include specific progress and accommodations in ELP as well as subject matter content, and these individualized goals could be informed by the progress of a true peer (see Chapter 4) who has the student's dis/ability as well. In the future, it might be possible to take these goals one step further. Someday, these IEP goals might include individualized measurement criteria and accommodations for determining reclassification as fluent English proficient and a transition out of ELD classes. Currently, what should be appropriate measurement instruments and activities and reclassification criteria for individual dual identified students is not well understood or practiced. However, some states are beginning to address this issue (see Texas Education Agency, n.d., discussed in Chapter 6), including not just accommodations but also differentiating reclassification criteria for exiting ELD support classes and services based on a dual identified student's dis/ability or difference.

One final area of potential promise and peril is how best to provide an appropriate education in the least restrictive environment in the intersection between the everyday tiers of MTSS and the individualized special education services required by IDEA or the generally more limited accommodations and services provided to individual students under Section 504. Under IDEA, special education requires "specially designed instruction" (SDI) for each individual student as developed and described in the IEP. However, in a well-designed and implemented MTSS system that includes culturally responsive general or core education classes and effective ELD supports, a school may be able to provide the type of services that meets a dual identified student's needs outside of the special education system in the best spirit of "least restrictive environment." Add regular, collaborative progress meetings that include educators and meaningful contributions and participation by caregivers (and students), and formal special education placements may be necessary for fewer dual identified students. However, we contend that it again comes down to best practice implementation that goes beyond mere compliance with statutory requirements. Even in the best system, we recommend that the caregivers and educators of EL students who may or do have dis/abilities know their legal rights and responsibilities to ensure EL students and dual identified students get the equitable educational services they deserve.

CHAPTER 8

Conclusion

Over the last seven chapters, we have addressed in some detail key topics about EL and dual identified students and high-quality educational practices to help them thrive. The question we now imagine is this: What should be done now? How do educators begin to make improvements in their own individual practices as well as systemically in collaboration with their colleagues, as well as caregivers and, ideally, students? What is the role of site administrators in this improvement process? And what should be expected of policymakers, whether at the district or state level? We suggest beginning this improvement process with a needs assessment conversation grounded in seven overarching questions in three areas of practice: Strengths and Weaknesses, Program Inputs and Resources, and System Checks. And, like in the system improvement template in Chapter 6 (Figure 6.1), we suggest that you provide specific data types and even specific data examples to support your answers to each question. In other words, the answer to every overarching question also answers another question: "How do we know?" We then suggest a set of complementary roles and actions for educators, site administrators, and policymakers that can make this improvement process lead to substantive, long-term change.

NEEDS ASSESSMENT: KEY QUESTIONS

We suggest that you start the needs assessment by determining your strengths and weaknesses. Ask directly: (1) "What are we doing now that we are proud of (as a school or district)?" and (2) "In which areas do we already know that we need to improve?" For program inputs and resources, start with (3) "Who makes up our community of students and families and what can they tell us about living and learning here?" (4) "Who are our educators and what can they contribute about second language development, subject matter content, special education, and evidence-based best instructional practices in literacy across the content areas?" and (5) "What is the quality of our program, including pedagogy and instruction, curriculum, family engagement, leadership, and technology, among other possible teaching and learning supports?" And to see the extent to which regular formative assessment is occurring, we suggest asking, (6) "How are we gathering, analyzing, and acting on data on a regular basis to proactively empower students to thrive?" and (7) "How are we checking our system to ensure that it is equitably meeting the needs of all our students?" Remember to include supporting data for each answer.

The answers to these questions can provide a foundation, an opening, for examining school and district programs in more depth, using the suggestions and resources throughout this book. This examination will likely lead you to consider deep changes in how you work to provide a rich, effective educational program for your EL and dual identified students, from the language you use to express new ways of thinking to new everyday structures that enable innovative, more evidence-based practices. However, deep changes like these require the concerted efforts of policymakers, site administrators, and educators in alliance with caregivers and students. Each has their roles and responsibilities.

COMPLEMENTARY ROLES AND ACTIONS

Policymakers should promote research-based systemic changes and enable stability through statutes and regulations. For example, they can enable case-by-case flexibility in reclassification criteria for dual identified students (see the Texas example in Chapter 7). They can promote dual language programs and the use of home languages in instruction (see, e.g., California's Proposition 58, approved in 2016). They can fund more bilingual schools and budget for hiring more bilingual teachers. They could also add a dual identified student certification to encourage this area of expertise. Further, policymakers can improve the working conditions of all educators, including reduced teacher instructional time to enable time and energy for individual pedagogical improvement, greater collaboration with colleagues, and improved relationship development with caregivers and students (see Sahlberg, 2015; Walker, 2017). Improved educator working conditions (including pay) can lead to the hiring of more highly qualified new educators (including those with expertise in dual identified students), expanding the professional development of current educators, and retaining these strong educators for decades.

Principals and other site administrators should promote increasing the number of system thinkers in action in their schools and then distribute authority to create effective educational structures. Some of the reduced instructional time should be repurposed both for individual professional development and collaborative activities, supported by changes in the daily school schedule to allow for these team activities. Creating an MTSS/PLUSS program across grades and classrooms will also benefit from new, more flexible daily schedules. In addition, formative data-based decisionmaking processes should become a regular part of school activity. Site administrators must initiate these changes if they are to happen.

Educators, most specifically teachers and certificated second language and special education experts, will need to embrace new learning, practices, and system thinker in action leadership roles. All teachers will need to embrace how to implement effective second language literacy pedagogies in all grades and all classrooms, especially in middle and high schools, where this is infrequently done. These new literacy activities, especially in middle and high school, will likely involve new models of authentic partnership and inclusion with students and their caregivers, as well as new media (see, e.g., Faltis & Coulter, 2008; Goodman, 2018; Nieto, 2010). Further, as the literacy, content, and pedagogy experts, teachers and certificated staff will need to organize, lead, and continually improve on these efforts. This distributed leadership will require teachers and certificated staff to organize work and professional development in often unfamiliar ways, such as in action research teams and in innovation teams in partnership with caregivers and students (see Anderson, Herr, & Nihlen, 2007; Fleischer, 2000).

FINAL THOUGHTS

To create consistently great educational experiences for dual identified students, we must be bold together. We must demand the social and school support for equity and social justice needed to make these deep, sustainable improvements in the education of dual identified students and all students. We must all seek out advice and guidance from others who are experienced in making these improvements. We describe the work of seven states. Make contact with them and others who are more local. There is more experience, expertise, and bold energy for improvement than we often realize. And usually it is right nearby.

Collaborative Problem-Solving Form (CPSF)

COLLABORATIVE PROBLEM-SOLVING FORM

Is student's screening data lower than that of "true peers?" If not, look closely at the efficacy of core instruction for that group of students. If yes, the collaborative team gathers the information on this form and determines the need for further intervention. ELD services continue across all tiers and is not considered an intervention; ELD is a core program for students who qualify. All instruction and Interventions must be linguistically and culturally responsive.

1. STUDENT'S BACKGROUND INFORMATION

Student:	Date:		Grade:	
Birthdate:	Typical Birthdate from this Grade is September 1, 20 ___ to August 31, 20 ___			
Student's L1:	Student's L2:		Student's L3:	
Teacher (L1):	Teacher (L2):		ELD Teacher:	
Core Reading Program	Eng:		Span:	
Concerns (circle all areas):	Reading	Writing	Math	Other:

What are the specific concerns regarding the areas circled above?

Team Members:

Attendance

Days Absent/Tardy Kinder	Days Absent/Tardy Gr. 1	Days Absent/Tardy Gr. 2
Days Absent/Tardy Gr. 3	Days Absent/Tardy Gr. 4	Days Absent/Tardy Gr. 5
Days Absent/Tardy Gr. 6	Days Absent/Tardy Gr. 7	Days Absent/Tardy Gr. 8
Days Absent/Tardy Gr. 9	Days Absent/Tardy Gr. 10	Days Absent/Tardy Gr. 11
Days Absent/Tardy Gr. 12		

Health ....

Hearing	Date	Results	Recheck needed
Vision	Date	Results	Recheck needed
Other			

Educational Background ....

Preschool: No	Yes	Language(s) of Instruction:
Early Intervention Program: No	Yes	IFSP Goals:
Kindergarten: Full-Day	Half-Day	Language(s) of Instruction:

Educational Experiences in Other Schools or Countries (include any concerns noted in file or shared by parents):

Was the school in an urban or rural setting:

| Was the student ever retained or grade-adjusted: | No   Yes | If so, when: |

Language Proficiency Assessments ....

Current English Proficiency Score/Level (state assessment)	Current Spanish Proficiency Score/Level
Prior Year's English Proficiency Score/Level (state assessment)	Prior Year's Spanish Proficiency Score/Level
Prior Year's English Score/Level (state assessment)	Prior Year's Spanish Proficiency Score/Level

Universal Screening-English

Universal Screening-Spanish

(or other language _____)

Fall . . . .

Measures	Score	Status

Measures	Score	Status

Winter . . . .

Measures	Score	Status

Measures	Score	Status

Spring . . . .

Measures	Score	Status

Measures	Score	Status

State Academic Assessments

Grade:	Grade:	Grade:
Name of Test:	Name of Test:	Name of Test:
ELA:	ELA:	ELA:
Math:	Math:	Math:
Other:	Other:	Other:
Grade:	Grade:	Grade:
Name of Test:	Name of Test:	Name of Test:
ELA:	ELA:	ELA:
Math:	Math:	Math:
Other:	Other:	Other:

Classroom Observation

Observation completed by:	Date:		
Is classroom instruction aligned to the student's language proficiency level?		**YES**	**NO**
Content Area:			
Observation:			

3. COLLABORATIVE PROBLEM-SOLVING TEAM MEETING

Problem Hypothesis (why does the team think the problem is occurring?):
How does this student compare to a true peer?
Is any other information needed prior to developing an intervention plan?
Team Decision:
Follow up date to review intervention progress monitoring data:

4. INTERVENTION PLAN
(DOCUMENT TYPE, FREQUENCY, DURATION AND LANGUAGE OF INTERVENTION)

Team Members . . . .

Intervention: (cirle one) PA phonics vocabulary fluency comprehension	Language of Intervention: (circle one) Spanish English	Tier (circle one) Tier 1/Benchmark Tier 2/Strategic Tier 3/Intensive	Who Will Provide Intervention?	How Frequently Will Progress be Monitored?	Learning Environment
Goal: Date to Review:					
Attach Progress Monitoring Data					

5. DATA REVIEW MEETING (ATTACH DATA)

Team Members:	
Consistent attendance? YES NO	Was goal met: YES NO
Was hypothesis validated?	
Does student need further intervention? YES NO	
If yes, begin intervention planning process again. Follow up date:	
Notes and comments:	

6. SPECIAL EDUCATION REFERRAL DECISION-MAKING

If the student has had appropriate interventions and is not making progress as compared to "true peers," determine if a referral for a special education evaluation is warranted.
Refer for special education evaluation: YES   NO
Team Members:

7. PARENT INTERVIEW

The following information should be gathered from parents through an interview.

Mother's L1:	L2	L3
Mother's birth country:		Highest grade mother attended:
What language(s) does mother read? Did the mother experience difficulty learning to read? Did any relatives experience difficulty learning to read?		
Father's L1:	L2	L3
Father's birth country:		Highest grade father attended
What language(s) does father read? Did the father experience difficulty learning to read? Did any relatives experience difficulty learning to read?		
Language primarily used when speaking to the student at home.		
Language family uses in the community:		
Describe the family's literacy practices in the home:		
Language student primarily chooses to speak at home.		
What was the language the student first spoke?		
When was the second language introduced?		

What are the child's strength's?
Does the child have any difficulties at home in behavior or communication?　　Yes　　　　No If yes, please describe.

Does the child have any household responsibilities? If yes, please describe.		Yes	No

Can the child follow one-step directions? YES NO	Two-step? YES NO	Three-step? YES NO

Does the parent have any concerns about their child? If yes, please describe.	Yes	No

What is their educational goal for their child?

How does the family celebrate and maintain their culture?

In what ways will the parents support their child at home?

How can school personnel help support the parents and child?

Comments:

8. STUDENT INTERVIEW – SECONDARY LEVEL

1. Were you born in the U.S? If not, how long have you lived here? Who do you live with?

2. How long have you attended this school? Where did you go before?

3. Are you involved in any special activities outside of school (e.g., sports, religious, volunteering, cultural groups)? If yes, what activities?

4. Do you read and write in your first language? If yes, a little bit or very well?

5. Is learning to speak English easy or hard?

6. Do either of your parents (or guardians) read and write in their first language? If yes, a little bit or very well?

7. What are you favorite subjects (or classes)?

8. What subjects or classes are the most difficult for you?

9. What is your educational goal?

What kind of help do you need from teachers and counselors to continue to succeed in school and reach your goals?

```



```

10. How would you rate your experiences in your classes?

☐ I understand **everything** I am supposed to learn in my classes?

☐ I understand most **everything** I am supposed to learn in my classes?

☐ I understand **about half** of what I am supposed to learn in my classes?

☐ I understand **a little bit** of what I am supposed to learn in my classes?

☐ I understand **none** of what I am supposed to learn in my classes?

11. Which of the following best describes how you feel about your reading skills?

☐ I can read **everything very well** in English.

☐ I can read **some things very well** in English, but not everything.

☐ I can read only read a **few things very well** in English.

☐ I cannot read **anything** very well in English.

12. Which of the following best describes how you feel about your writing skills?

☐ I can write **very well** in English.

☐ I can write **fairly well** in English, but not well enough for some assignments .

☐ I can write **at only a basic level** in English.

13. What responsibilities do you have at home?

```



```

14. Do you have a job?

```



```

15. What do you want to do after you graduate from high school?

```



```

16. What else do you want to share?

```



```

9. STUDENT INTERVIEW – ELEMENTARY LEVEL

1. What do you like about school?

2. What do you not like about school?

3. What is easy for you to do in school?

4. What is hard for you to do in school?

5. Is learning English easy or hard for you?

6. How can you help others in school?

7. How can others help you in school?

8. How can your teacher help you in school?

9. What do you like to do after school? At home?

10. What would you like to tell your teacher about yourself?

11. What do you want to do when you grow up?

12. Is there anything else you would like to tell me?

Notes

Chapter 1

1. The Individuals with Disabilities Education Act (1997) (IDEA) was reauthorized in 2004 as the Individuals with Disabilities Education Improvement Act (IDEIA). Despite the slightly different name, the reauthorization is still often referred to by its original acronym of IDEA. In this book, we will also refer to it by its original acronym of IDEA. A description of the differences between IDEA (1997) and IDEA (2004) can be found at Wright (2004).

2. There is discussion and concern among advocates and educators about whether it is better to use the term *learning differences* or *learning disabilities*. Proponents of using *learning differences* point to the deficit mindset of *learning disabilities* that can foster the isolation and "fixing" of students without recognizing and promoting how their thinking and learning differences contribute to classrooms and society. Deaf persons and deaf culture are prime examples of this phenomenon. Advocates of *learning disability* point to the fact that it is a term set in law that gives specific rights and supports to people who can benefit from them. The Individuals with Disabilities Education Improvement Act (2004) and the Americans with Disabilities Act (ADA) are two examples. A brief discussion by the Learning Disabilities Association of New York State (n.d.) describes both positions. In this book, we will use both terms: *learning disabilities* when we are discussing legal rights and responsibilities and *learning differences* or *learning dis/abilities* when we are discussing pedagogy and schooling.

3. In this book, we use the term *caregivers* to include parents, other adult family members who care for a child and may attend school meetings on the child's behalf, and legal guardians.

Chapter 2

1. We calculated the percent of non-EL students receiving special education services by subtracting the number of dual identified students from the numerator and denominator of all students receiving special education services as reported by NCES. According to NCES Table 203.20, for fall 2015, 6,677,000 students out of 50,484,900 total students received IDEA-based special education services. We subtracted the 713,000 dual identified receiving IDEA-based special education services from both total population numbers and calculated a non-EL special education rate of 11.9% (5,964,000/49,771,900).

Chapter 3

1. In the research literature and the practitioner literature, you will see *MTSS* and *RTI* both used interchangeably and distinguished one from the other. In this book, we will use *MTSS* as the name for a system where schools systemically provide ongoing monitoring of individual students and increasing levels of focused supports based on how each student responds to these supports, usually in three tiers or levels.

2. In this book, we will describe the three-tiered MTSS model in which a special education evaluation and referral typically occurs after the implementation of Tier 3 interventions, though they could occur at any time in any tier. In this model, after evaluation, special education services are treated as an integrated, parallel set of services that can occur at any level, but they generally occur in Tier 3.

3. As will be discussed later in this book and especially in Chapter 7, educators and caregivers do not have to wait until a student progresses through all three MTSS tiers before requesting and receiving a determination of eligibility for special education services and, depending on the results of this determination, receiving those services. Under IDEA, this determination and the receipt of services can occur at any time.

4. We realize that this "achievement gap" between EL students and EO students can be misleading: Once an EL student is considered fluent in English, they are reclassified (RFEPed) and no longer part of the EL student population used to make these comparisons. In other words, EL students are always only those who are still not fluent in English, so we would expect their achievement scores on English language content tests as a group to be lower than those of EO students as a group. However, the larger concern of whether our teaching methods are sufficiently sound to minimize this difference remains.

5. There is also consistent evidence that being fully bilingual can have academic advantages beyond language itself (see, e.g., ACTFL, n.d.). Thus, strong instruction for EL students that leads to fluency in English and another language can develop bilingual students who as a group can have greater academic achievement than monolingual English-speaking students as a group.

6. Prior to the No Child Left Behind Act (NCLB, 2001), while states were mandated to provide special language services to EL students, there was little guidance because there were no required ELP standards. NCLB directed states to develop ELP standards aligned with their content standards in English language arts, mathematics, and science in the four domains of reading, writing, speaking, and listening.

Chapter 5

1.   Also see the discussion in Chapter 7, which describes how special education referrals often occur after Tier 3 interventions have been implemented, but a special education referral can be requested and initiated during any MTSS tier.

Chapter 6

1. In the system improvement research literature, authors often use the terms *understandings* and *beliefs* somewhat interchangeably. For consistency, we will use the term *understanding* where many authors also use *belief.*

2. We admit that we have used the term *at risk* in this book as well, as it is a common term in schools and even the education literature. At the same time, we hope that we have sufficiently communicated that we see the primary responsibility for adjusting the fit of *at-risk* students with their educational experiences lies with educators and administrators within the schools they attend.

Chapter 7

1. Statistics classes often use the example of Bill Gates or an unemployed person coming to sit at a bar for a drink to illustrate how one person who is vastly different from everyone else in a small group will substantially and significantly change the group average. In this case, the average annual income of the, say, 10 people at the bar changes tremendously when an unemployed person (no income) or Bill Gates (hundreds of millions in income) shows up for a drink.

2. Federal laws provide less than clear messages on the extent to which interpreters and translations must be used. For example, the 1970 Memorandum states that some notices "in order to be adequate may have to be provided in a language other than English" and ESSA requires information be provided "to the extent possible, in a language parents can understand." On the other hand, IDEA (2004) § 300.304 (c) (1) (ii) specifically requires that key materials such as assessments and evaluation materials, parental notices, and parent consent forms, "are provided and administered in the child's native language . . . unless it is clearly not feasible to so provide or administer." Further, IDEA requires that interpreters be provided at IEP meetings "if needed."

References

Abedi, J. (2006a). Language issues in item-development. In S. M. Downing & T. M. Haladyna (Eds.), *Handbook of test development* (pp. 377–398). Mahwah, NJ: Lawrence Erlbaum Associates.

Abedi, J. (2006b). Psychometric issues in the ELL assessment and special education eligibility. *Teachers College Record, 108*(11), 2282–2303.

Abedi, J. (2008). Classification system for English language learners: Issues and recommendations. *Educational Measurement: Issues and Practice, 27*(3), 17–31.

Abedi, J. (2009). English language learners with disabilities: Classification, assessment, and accommodation issues. *Journal of Applied Testing Technology, 10*(2), 1–30. Retrieved from eric.ed.gov/?id=EJ865585

Aceves, T. C., & Orosco, M. J. (2014). *Culturally responsive teaching* (Document No. IC-2). Retrieved from ceedar.education.ufl.edu/tools/innovation-configurations/

Acosta, B., Rivera, C., & Shafer Willner, L. (2008). *Best practices in the accommodation of English language learners: A Delphi study.* Prepared for the LEP Partnership, U.S. Department of Education. Arlington, VA: The George Washington University Center for Equity and Excellence in Education.

ACTFL. (n.d.). Studies supporting increased academic achievement. Retrieved from www.actfl.org/advocacy/what-the-research-shows/studies-supporting

Adams, M. J. (1990). *Beginning to read: Thinking and learning about print.* Cambridge, MA: MIT Press.

Aikens, N. L., & Barbarin, O. (2008). Socioeconomic differences in reading trajectories: The contribution of family, neighborhood, and school contexts. *Journal of Educational Psychology, 100,* 235–251.

Al Otaiba, S., & Fuchs, D. (2002). Characteristics of children who are unresponsive to early literacy intervention: A review of literature. *Remedial and Special Education, 23*(5), 300–316.

Alton-Lee, A. (2003). *Quality teaching for diverse students in schooling: Best evidence synthesis.* Report from the Medium Term Strategy Policy Division. Wellington, NZ: Ministry of Education.

American Educational Research Association, American Psychological Association, & National Council on Measurement in Education. (2014). *The standards for educational and psychological testing.* Washington, DC: Authors.

Anastasi, A. (1937). *Differential psychology: Individual and group differences in behavior.* Oxford, UK: Macmillan.

Anderson, G., Herr, K., & Nihlen, A. (2007). *Studying your own school: An educator's guide to practitioner action research* (2nd ed.). Thousand Oaks, CA: Corwin Press.

Annamma, S. A., Connor, D., & Ferri, B. (2013). Dis/ability critical race studies (DisCrit): Theorizing at the intersections of race and dis/ability. *Race Ethnicity and Education, 16*(1), 1–31. doi:10.1080/13613324.2012.730511

Annamma, S. A., Morrison, D., & Jackson, D. (2014). Disproportionality fills in the gaps: Connections between achievement, discipline, and special education in the School-to-Prison Pipeline. *Berkeley Review of Education, 5*(1), 53–87. Retrieved from escholarship.org/uc/item/0b13x3cp

Artiles, A. J., Klingner, J. K., & Tate, W. F. (2006). Representation of minority students in special education: Complicating traditional explanations. *Educational Researcher, 35*(6), 3–5.

Artiles, A. J., Rueda, R., Salazar, J. J., & Higareda, I. (2005). Within-group diversity in minority disproportionate representation: English language learners in urban school districts. *Exceptional Children, 71*, 283–300.

Arzubiaga, A. E., Artiles, A. J., King, K. A., & Harris-Murri, N. (2008). Beyond research on cultural minorities: Challenges and implications of research as situated cultural practice. *Exceptional Children, 74*, 309–327.

ASCD. (n.d.). Common core state standards adoption by state [webpage]. Retrieved from www.ascd.org/common-core-state-standards/common-core-state-standards-adoption-map.aspx

Au, K. H., & Kawakami, A. J. (1994). Cultural congruence in instruction. In E. R. Hollins, J. E. King, & W. C. Hayman (Eds.), *Teaching diverse populations: Formulating a knowledge base* (pp. 5–23). Albany, NY: State University of New York Press.

Auerbach, E., & Paxton, D. (1997). "It's not the English thing": Bringing reading research into the ESL classroom. *TESOL Quarterly, 31*(2), 237–261.

August, D., Artzi, L., Barr, C., & Francis, D. (2018). The moderating influence of instructional intensity and word type on the acquisition of academic vocabulary in young English language learners. *Reading and Writing: An Interdisciplinary Journal, 31*(4), 965–989.

August, D., & Shanahan, T. (2006). *Developing literacy in second-language learners: Report of the National Literacy Panel on language-minority children and youth.* Center for Applied Linguistics. Mahwah, NJ: Lawrence Erlbaum Associates.

August, D., & Vockley, M. (2002). *From Spanish to English: Reading and writing for English language learners, kindergarten through third grade.* Washington, DC: New Standards.

Bailey, A. L., & Kelly, K. R. (2010). *The use and validity of home language surveys in state English language proficiency assessment systems: A review and issues perspective.* (Evaluating the Validity of English Assessments Project deliverable). Washington, DC: U.S. Department of Education. Retrieved from www.eveaproject.com/doc/Bailey%20%20Kelly%20HLS%20EVEA%20%20white%20paper%20July%20 2010%20revised%20Jan%202011and%20Sept%202011.pdf

Bailey, A. L., & Kelly, K. R. (2013). Home language survey practices in the initial identification of English learners in the United States. *Educational Policy, 27*, 770–804.

Baker, D. L., Cummings, K. D., Good, R. H., & Smolkowski, K. (2007). Indicadores dinámicos del éxito en la lectura (IDEL): *Summary of decision rules for intensive,* strategic, and benchmark instructional recommendations in kindergarten through third grade. (Technical Report No. 1). Eugene, OR: Dynamic Measurement Group.

Baker, S. K., & Good, R. (1995). Curriculum-based measurement of English reading with bilingual Hispanic students: A validation study with second-grade students. *School Psychology Review, 24*(4), 561–578.

Barone, C., & Lombardo, M. (2016, June 9). *ESSA implementation update: Shining a light on persistent disparities.* Retrieved from edreformnow.org/essa-implementation-update-civil-rights-data-collection-shines-a-light-on-disparities/

Bartolomé, L. I. (2000). Democratizing bilingualism: The role of critical teacher education. In Z. F. Beykont (Ed.), *Lifting every voice: Pedagogy and politics of bilingualism* (pp. 167–186). Cambridge, MA: Harvard Education Publishing Group.

Bartolomé, L. I. (2004). Critical pedagogy and teacher education: Radicalizing prospective teachers. *Teacher Education Quarterly, 39*(3), 97–122.

Bartolomé, L. I. (2008). *Ideologies in education: Unmasking the trap of teacher neutrality.* New York, NY: Peter Lang.

Batsche, G. M., Castillo, J. M., Dixon, D. N., & Forde, S. (2008). Best practices in linking assessment to intervention. In A. Thomas & J. Grimes (Eds.). *Best practices in school psychology* (5th ed., pp. 177–193). Washington, DC: National Association of School Psychologists.

Baumann, J. F. (2009). The intensity of vocabulary instruction and the effects on reading comprehension. *Topics in Language Disorders, 29*(4), 312–328.

Baumann, J. F., & Kame'ennui, E. (2004). *Vocabulary instruction: Research to practice.* New York, NY: Guilford.

Beck, I. L., McKeown, M. G., & Kucan, L. (2002). *Bringing words to life: Robust vocabulary instruction.* New York, NY: Guilford Press.

Bedore, L. J., Peña, E. D., Anaya, J. B., Nieto, R., Lugo-Neris, M. J., & Baron, A. (2018). Understanding disorder within variation: Production of English grammatical forms by English language learners. *Language, Speech, and Hearing Services in School, 49*, 277–291.

Begeny, J. C., Daly, E. J., III, & Valleley, R. J. (2006). Improving oral reading fluency through response opportunities: A comparison of phrase drill error correction with repeated readings. *Journal of Behavior Education, 15*, 229–235.

Bellocchi, S., Tobia, V., & Bonifacci, P. (2017). Predictors of reading and comprehension abilities in bilingual and monolingual children: A longitudinal study on a transparent language. *Reading and Writing, 30*(6), 1311–1334.

Bettini, E., Park, Y., Benedict, A., Kimerling, J., & Leite, W. (2016). Situating special educators' instructional quality and their students' outcomes within the conditions shaping their work. *Exceptionality, 24*, 1–18.

Blanchett, W. J. (2006). Disproportionate representation of African American students in special education: Acknowledging the role of White privilege and racism. *Educational Researcher, 35*(6), 24–28.

Blanchett, W. J., & Schealey, M. W. (2016). From the Editors: "We won't be silenced": Senior scholars in special education respond to *deficit* derived claims that "Minorities [students of color] are disproportionately underrepresented in special education." *Multiple Voices for Ethnically Diverse Exceptional Learners, 16*(1), 1–3.

Bradley, R. H., Corwyn, R. F., McAdoo, H. P., & García Coll, C. (2001). The home environments of children in the United States Part I: Variations by age, ethnicity, and poverty status. *Child Development, 72*, 1844–1867.

Brechtal, M. (2001). *Brining it all together: Language and literacy in the multilingual classroom.* Carlsbad, CA: Dominie.

Britton, J. (1983). Writing and the story of the world. In B. M. Kroll & C. G. Wells (Eds.), *Explorations in the development of writing: Theory, research, and practice* (pp. 3–30). New York, NY: Wiley.

Bronfenbrenner, U. (1991). "What do families do?" *Institute for American Values*, Winter/Spring, p. 2.

Brooks, J. G., & Brooks, M. G. (2000). *In search of understanding: The case for constructivist classrooms* (2nd ed.). Alexandria, VA: ASCD.

Brown, J. E. (2008). *The use and interpretation of the Batería III with U.S. bilinguals.* Unpublished dissertation. Portland State University, Portland, OR.

Brown, J. E., & Doolittle, J. (2008). A cultural, linguistic, and ecological framework for Response to Intervention with English language learners. *Teaching Exceptional Children, 40*(5), 66–72.

Brown, J. E., & Kapantzoglou, M. (2018). *Indicators of language difference and language disability.* Retrieved from www.livebinders.com/media/get/MTc0ODMyOTI=

Brown, J. E., & Ortiz, S. O. (2014). Interventions for English learners with learning difficulties. In J. T. Mascolo, V. C. Alfonso, & D. P. Flanagan (Eds.), *Essentials of planning, selecting, and tailoring interventions for unique learners* (pp. 267–313). Hoboken, NJ: Wiley.

Brown, J. E., Ortiz, S. O., & Sanford, A. (2016, September). *Collaborative evaluation model: What you must know before referring an English Learner.* Workshop presented at Northwest Educational Service District English Learner Conference. Hillsboro, OR.

Brown, J. E., & Sanford, A. (2011, March). *RTI for English language learners: Appropriately using screening and progress monitoring tools to improve instructional outcomes.* Washington, DC: U.S. Department of Education, Office of Special Education Programs, National Center on Response to Intervention.

Brown, J. E., Sanford, A. K., & Turner, M. (2018). *MTSS elements triangle for English learner students.* Unpublished.

Brown, J. E., & Turner, M. (2016). *Developing linguistically appropriate IEP goals in dual language programs.* Workshop presented at the annual meeting of the Massachusetts Dual Language Conference, Framingham, MA.

Burr, E., Haas, E., & Ferriere, K. (2015). *Identifying and placing English language learners with learning disabilities: Key issues in the literature and state practice.* (REL 2015-086). Washington, DC: U.S. Department of Education, Institute of Education Sciences, National Center for Education Evaluation and Regional Assistance, Regional Educational Laboratory West.

Butrymowicz, S., & Mader, J. (2017, November 4). *Almost all students with disabilities are capable of graduating on time. Here's why they're not* [webpage]. Hechinger Report. Retrieved from hechingerreport.org/high-schools-fail-provide-legally-required-education-students-disabilities/

California Department of Education. (2018). *Facts about English learners in California-CalEdFacts*. Retrieved from www.cde.ca.gov/ds/sd/cb/cefelfacts.asp

Calderón, M. (2007). *Teaching reading to English language learners: Grades 6–12*. Thousand Oaks, CA: Corwin.

Carlisle, J. F., Beeman, M., Davis, L. J., & Spharim, G. (1999). Relationship of metalinguistic capabilities and reading achievement for children who are becoming bilingual. *Applied Psycholinguistics, 20,* 459–478.

Carlos, M. S., August, D., McLaughlin, B., Snow, C. D., Dressler, C., Lippman, D. M., Lively, T. J., & White, C. E. (2004). Closing the gap: Addressing the vocabulary needs of English language learners in bilingual and mainstream classrooms. *Reading Research Quarterly, 39*(2), 188–215.

Case, L. P., Speece, D. L., & Molloy, D. E. (2003). The validity of a Response-to-Instruction paradigm to identify reading disabilities: A longitudinal analysis of individual differences and contextual factors. *School Psychology Review, 32*(4), 557–582.

CAST. (2011). *Universal design for learning guidelines version 2.0*. Wakefield, MA: Author. Retrieved from udlguidelines.cast.org/

CAST. (2016). *UDL in the ESSA?* Retrieved from http://www.cast.org/whats-new/news/2016/udl-in-the-essa.html#.XB0hl_ZFxgU

Castañeda v. Pickard, 648 F.2d 989 (5th Cir., 1981).

Cavendish, W., Harry, B., Menda, A. M., Espinosa, A., & Mohtiere, M. (2016). Implementing Response to Intervention: Challenges of diversity and system change in a high stakes environment. *Teachers College Record, 118*(5), 1–36.

Cervantes-Soon, C. G., & Kasun, G. S. (2018). Transnational learners and TESOL. In J. I. Liontas & M. DelliCarpini (Eds.), *The TESOL encyclopedia of English language teaching*. Hoboken, NJ: John Wiley & Sons. doi:10.1002/9781118784235.eelt0858

Chavez, V. (2012). *Cultural humility in community based participatory research & education* [video]. Retrieved from www.youtube.com/watch?v=SaSHLbS1V4w

Chetty, R., Friedman, J. N., Hilger, N., Saez, E., Schanzenbach, D. W., & Yagan, D. (2011). How does your kindergarten classroom affect your earnings? Evidence from Project STAR. *The Quarterly Journal of Economics, 126,* 1593–1660.

Chief Education Office. (2017, June). *2017 Oregon educator equity report*. Salem, OR: Author. Retrieved from www.oregon.gov/tspc/Documents/Educator_Equity_Reports/2017_Oregon_Educator_Equity_Report.PDF

Chu, S., & Flores, S. (2011). Assessment of English language learners with learning disabilities. *The Clearing House, 84,* 244–248. doi:10.1080/00098655.2011.590550

Civil Rights Act of 1964, Public Law 88-352, 78 Stat. 241 (1964).

Collier, C. (2005). Separating language difference from disability. *NABE News, 28*(3), 13–17.

Comeau, J. A. (2012). Race/ethnicity and family contact: Toward a behavioral measure of familialism. *Hispanic Journal of Behavioral Sciences, 34*(2), 251–268.

Connecticut State Department of Education. (2011). *English language learners and special education: A resource handbook*. Hartford, CT: Author. Retrieved from portal.ct.gov/-/media/SDE/English-Learners/CAPELL_SPED_resource_guide.pdf

Connecticut State Department of Education. (2012). *Scientific research-based interventions for English language learners: A handbook to accompany Connecticut's framework for RTI.* Hartford, CT: Author. Retrieved from https://portal.ct.gov/-/media/SDE/English-Learners/SRBI_ELL.pdf?la=en

Connerty, M. (2009). Variation in academic writing among Generation 1.5 learners, native English-speaking learners and ESL learners: The discoursal self of G1.5 student writers. (Unpublished doctoral dissertation). University of Birmingham, Birmingham, UK. Retrieved from etheses.bham.ac.uk/274/

Cook, H. G., & Linquanti, R. (2015). *Strengthening policies and practices for the initial classification of English learners: Insights from a national working session.* Washington, DC: Council of Chief State School Officers. Retrieved from https://eric.ed.gov/?id=ED565758

Cornoldi, C., & Oakhill, J. (1996). *Reading comprehension difficulties: Processes and intervention.* Mahwah, NJ: Laurence Erlbaum Associates.

Council of Chief State School Officers (CCSSO). (2016a). *English language learners with disabilities: A call for additional research and policy guidance.* Washington, DC: CCSSO.

Council of Chief State School Officers (CCSSO). (2016b). *Major provisions of Every Student Succeeds Act (ESSA) related to the education of English learners.* Washington, DC: CCSSO. Retrieved from www.ccsso.org/Documents/2016/ESSA/CCSSOResourceonESSAELLs02.23.2016.pdf

Counts, J., Katsyannis, A., & Whitford, D. K. (2018). Culturally and linguistically diverse learners in special education: English learners. *NASSP Bulletin, 102*(1), 5–21.

Crosson, A. C., & Lesaux, N. K. (2010). Revisiting assumptions about the relationship of fluent reading to comprehension: Spanish-speakers' text-reading fluency in English. *Reading and Writing: An Interdisciplinary Journal, 23,* 475–494.

Cummins, J. C. (1984). *Bilingual and special education: Issues in assessment and pedagogy.* Austin, TX: Pro-Ed.

D'Angiulli, A., Siegel, L. S., & Maggi, S. (2004). Literacy instruction, SES, and word-reading achievement in English language learners and children with English as a first language: A longitudinal study. *Learning Disabilities Research & Practice, 19*(4), 202–213.

Daniel, S. M., & Pacheco, M. B. (2017). Translanguaging practices and perspectives of four multi-lingual teens. *Journal of Adolescent and Adult Literacy, 59*(6), 653–663.

Datnow, A., & Park, V. (2014). *Data-driven leadership.* San Francisco, CA: Jossey-Bass.

Davis, L. J. (1995). *Enforcing normalcy: Disability, deafness, and the body.* London, UK: Verso.

Degler, C. N. (1991). *In search of human nature: The decline and revival of Darwinism in American social thought.* New York, NY: Oxford University Press.

DeMatthews, D., & Izquierdo, E. (2018). The importance of principals supporting dual language education: A social justice leadership framework. *Journal of Latinos and Education, 17*(1), 53–70.

Deno, S. L. (1985). Curriculum-based measurement: The emerging alternative. *Exceptional Children, 52,* 219–232.

Deno, S. L. (1989). Curriculum-based measurement and special education services: A fundamental and direct relationship. In M. R. Shinn (Ed.), *Curriculum-based measurement: Assessing special children* (pp. 1–17). New York, NY: Guilford Press.

Deno, S. L. (2003). Developments in curriculum based measurement. *Journal of Special Education, 37*(3), 184–192.

Deno, S. L. (2005). Problem-solving assessment with curriculum-based measurement (CBM). In R. Chidsey-Brown (Ed.), *Problem-solving based assessment for educational intervention* (pp. 10–40). New York, NY: Guilford Press.

Denton, C. A., Anthony, J. L., Parker, R., & Hasbrouck, J. E. (2004). Effects of two tutoring programs on the English reading development of Spanish–English bilingual students. *The Elementary School Journal, 104*, 289–305.

DeRuvo, S. (2010). *The essential guide to RTI: An integrative, evidence-based approach.* San Francisco, CA: Jossey-Bass.

Doabler, C. T., Nelson, N. J., & Clarke, B. (2016). Adapting evidence-based practices to meet the needs of English learners with mathematics difficulties. *Teaching Exceptional Children, 48*(6), 301–310.

Domínguez de Ramírez, R., & Shapiro, E. S. (2007). Cross-language relationship between Spanish and English oral reading fluency among Spanish-speaking English language learners in bilingual education classrooms. *Psychology in the Schools, 44*(8), 795–806.

Donovan, M. S., Bransford, J., & Pellegrino, J. (Eds.). (2000). *How people learn: Brain, mind, experience, and school* (Expanded ed.). Washington, DC: National Academy Press. Retrieved from www.nap.edu/catalog/9853/how-people-learn-brain-mind-experience-and-school-expanded-edition

Donovan, M. S., & Cross, C. T. (Eds.) (2002). *Minority students in special and gifted education.* Washington, DC: National Academy Press, National Research Council Committee on Minority Representation in Special Education.

Doran, G. T. (1981). There's a S.M.A.R.T. way to write management's goals and objectives. *Management Review, AMA FORUM, 70*(11), 35–36.

Dowd, A., & Liera, R. (2018). Sustaining change towards racial equity through cycles of inquiry. *Education Policy Analysis Archives, 26*(65). dx.doi.org/10.14507/epaa.26.3274

Duran, E. (1989). Functional language instruction for the student with moderate and severe handicaps and students who are culturally and linguistically different. *Reading Improvement, 26*(1), 33–36.

Duran, E. (1992). *Effective communication programming for language minority students with severe disabilities.* Paper presented at the Second National Symposium on Effective Communication for Children and Youth with Severe Disabilities, McLean, VA.

Durgunoğlu, A. Y., Nagy, W. E., & Hancin-Bhatt, B. (1993). Cross-language transfer of phonological awareness. *Journal of Educational Psychology, 85*(3), 453–465.

Dutro, S., & Moran, C. (2003). Rethinking English language instruction: An architectural approach. In G. G. Garcia (Ed.), *English learners: Reaching the highest level of English literacy* (pp. 227–258). Newark, DE: International Reading Association.

Echevarria, J., & Graces, A. (1998). Curriculum adaptations. In J. Echevarria & A. Graves (Eds.), *Sheltered content instruction: Teaching English language learners with diverse abilities* (pp. 121–149). Boston, MA: Allyn & Bacon.

Echevarria, J., Vogt, M., & Short, D. J. (2008). *Making content comprehensible for English language learners: The SIOP model.* Boston, MA: Pearson.

Education Counsel. (2015, December 10). *Summary analysis of the Every Student Succeeds Act (version 1.0).* Retrieved from ib5uamau5i20f0e91hn3ue14.wpengine.netdna-cdn.com/wp-content/uploads/2015/12/EdCounsel-Summary-of-ESSA-12-10-2015.pdf

Education Evaluation Center, Teaching Research Institute, & Western Oregon University. (2015). *Special education assessment process for culturally and linguistically diverse (CLD) students: Guidance and resources* [2015 update]. Salem, OR: Oregon Department of Education. Retrieved from 5c2cabd466efc6790a0a-6728e7c952118b70f16620a9fc754159.r37.cf1.rackcdn.com/cms/Special_Education_Assessment_Process_for_Culturally_and_Liguistically_Diverse_(CLD)_Students_with_logos_and_links_1489.pdf

Ehri, L. C., Nunes, S. R., Willows, D. M., Schuster, B. V., Yaghoub-Zadeh, Z., & Shanahan, T. (2001). Phonemic awareness instruction helps children learn to read: Evidence from the National Reading Panel's meta-analysis. *Reading Research Quarterly, 36,* 250–287.

Endrew F. v. Douglas County School District, 580 U.S.___(2017).

Engelmann, S., & Science Research Associates. (2008). *Corrective reading.* Seattle, WA: McGraw-Hill Education.

Equal Educational Opportunities Act. (1974). 20 U.S.C. 39.

Every Student Succeeds Act (ESSA). (2015a). Reauthorization of the Elementary and Secondary Education Act of 1965. Pub.L.No.114-9520 U.S.C.

Every Student Succeeds Act (ESSA). (2015b). Title III—Language instruction for English learners and Immigrant students. 20 U.S.C. §§3001–3004.

Faltis, C., & Coulter, C. (2008). *Teaching English learners and immigrant students in secondary schools.* Upper Saddle River, NJ: Pearson.

Feldman, K., & Kinsella, K. (2005). *Narrowing the language gap: The case for explicit vocabulary instruction.* New York, NY: Scholastic.

Fiefer, S. G. (2008). Integrating response to intervention (RTI) with neuropsychology: A scientific approach to reading. *Psychology in the Schools, 45*(9), 812–825.

Fien, H., Baker, S. K., Smolkowski, K., Mercier Smith, J. L., Kame'enui, E. J., & Beck, C. T. (2008). Using nonsense word fluency to predict reading proficiency in kindergarten through second grade for English learners and native English speakers. *School Psychology Review, 37*(3), 391–408.

Fien, J., Smith, J. L. M., Baker, S., Chaparro, E., Baker, D. L., & Preciado, J. (2011). Including English learners in a multitiered approach to early reading instruction and intervention. *Assessment for Effective Intervention, 36*(3), 143–157.

Figueroa, R. A. (1990). Assessment of linguistic minority group children. In C. R. Reynolds & R. W. Kamphaus (Eds.), *Handbook of psychological and educational assessment of children: Vol. 1: Intelligence and achievement.* New York, NY: Guilford.

Figueroa, R. A., & Newsome, P. (2006). The diagnosis of LD in English learners. Is it nondiscriminatory? *Journal of Learning Disabilities, 39,* 206–214.

Fillmore, L. W., & Snow, C.E. (2000). *What teachers need to know about language.* Washington, DC: Center for Applied Linguistics.

Fisher, D., & Frey, N. (2007). Implementing a schoolwide literacy framework: Improving achievement in urban elementary school. *The Reading Teacher, 61,* 32–45.

Fisher, D., Frey, N., & Rothenberg, C. (2008). *Content-area conversations: How to plan discussion-based lessons for diverse language learners.* Alexandria, VA: ASCD.

Fisher, M., & Meyer, L. (2002). Development and social competence after two years for students enrolled in inclusive and self-contained educational programs. *Research and Practice for Persons with Severe Disabilities, 27*(3), 165–174.

Flagella-Luby, M. N., & Deshler, D. D. (2008). Reading comprehension in adolescents with LD: What we know; what we need to learn. *Learning Disabilities Research & Practice, 23*(2), 70–78.

Flanagan, D. P., & Ortiz, S. (2001). *Essentials of cross-battery assessment.* New York, NY: John Wiley & Sons.

Flanagan, D. P., Ortiz, S. O., & Alfonso, V. C. (2007). *Essentials of cross-battery assessment* (2nd ed.). New York, NY: John Wiley & Sons.

Flanagan, D. P., Ortiz, S. O., & Alfonso, V. C. (2013). *Essentials of cross-battery assessment* (3rd ed.). New York, NY: Wiley.

Fleischer, C. (2000). *Teachers organizing for change: Making literacy learning everybody's business.* Urbana, IL: National Council of Teachers of English.

Fletcher, J. M., Shaywitz, S. E., Shankweiler, D. P., Katz, L., Liberman, I. Y., Stuebing, K. K., & Shaywitz, B. A. (1994). Cognitive profiles of reading disability: Comparisons of discrepancy and low achievement definitions. *Journal of Educational Psychology, 86*(1), 6–23.

Florit, E., & Cain, K. (2011). The simple view of reading: Is it valid for different types of alphabetic orthographies? *Educational Psychology Review, 23*, 553–576.

Francis, D. J., Rivera, M., Lesaux, N., Kieffer, M., & Rivera, H. (2006). *Practical guidelines for the education of English language learners: Research-based recommendations for instruction and academic interventions.* Houston, TX: Texas Institute for Measurement, Evaluation, and Statistics.

Fuchs, D., & Fuchs, L. S. (2006). Introduction to response to intervention: What, why, and how valid is it? *Reading Research Quarterly, 41*(1), 93–99.

Fuchs, L. S., & Deno, S. L. (1991). Paradigmatic distinctions between instructionally relevant measurement models. *Exceptional Children, 57*, 488–500.

Fuchs, L. S., Fuchs, D., Hamlett, C. L., & Ferguson, C. (1992). Effects of expert system consultation within curriculum-based measurement using a reading maze task. *Exceptional Children, 58*, 436–450.

Fuchs, L. S., Fuchs, D., Hamlett, C. L., & Walz, L. (1993). Formative evaluation of academic progress: How much growth can we expect? *School Psychology Review, 22*(1), 27–48.

Fuchs, L., Fuchs, D., Hintze, J., & Lembke, E. (2007). *Using curriculum-based measurement to determine response to intervention.* Powerpoint presented at the 2007 Summer Institute on Student Progress Monitoring, Nashville, TN. Retrieved from www.misd.net/mtss/ProgressMonitoring/progressmonitoring-rti2007.pdf

Fullan, M. (2001). *The new meaning of educational change* (3rd ed.). New York, NY: Teachers College Press.

Fullan, M. (2005). *Leadership & sustainability: Systems thinkers in action.* Thousand Oaks, CA: Corwin Press.

Fullan, M. (2006). The future of educational change: System thinkers in action. *Journal of Educational Change, 7,* 113–122. doi:10.1007/s10833-006-9003-9

Fullan, M., Cuttress, C., & Kilcher, A. (2005, Fall). 8 forces for leaders of change. *Leadership, 26*(4), 54–58, 64.

Garcia Coll, C. (1990). Developmental outcome of minority infants: A process-oriented look into our beginnings. *Child Development, 61,* 270–289.

Gay, G. (2000). Preparing for culturally responsive teaching. *Journal of Teacher Education, 5*(2), 106–116.

Genesee, F., Geva, E., Dressler, C., & Kamil, M. L. (2006). Synthesis: Cross-linguistic relationships. In D. August & T. Shanahan (Eds.), *Developing literacy in second-language learners: Report of the National Literacy Panel on language-minority children and youth* (pp. 153–174). Mahwah, NJ: Erlbaum.

Gersten, R., Baker, S. K., Shanahan, T., Linan-Thompson, S., Collins, P., & Scarcella, R. (2007). *Effective literacy and English language instruction for English learners in elementary grades: A practice guide* (NCEE 2007-4011). Washington, DC: U.S. Department of Education, Institute of Education Sciences, National Center for Education Evaluation and Regional Assistance.

Geva, E., & Zohreh, Y. Z. (2006). Reading efficiency in native English-speaking and English-as-a-second- language children: The role of oral proficiency and underlying cognitive-linguistic processes. *Scientific Studies of Reading, 10*(1), 31–57.

Gewertz, C. (2017, February 15). Which states are using PARCC or Smarter Balanced? An interactive breakdown of states' 2016–17 testing plans. *Education Week.* Retrieved from www.edweek.org/ew/section/multimedia/states-using-parcc-or-smarter-balanced.html

Gibbons, K. A., & Silberglitt, B. (2008). Best practices in evaluating psychoeducational services based on student outcome data. In A. Thomas & J. Grimes (Eds.), *Best practices in school psychology V* (pp. 2103–2116). Bethesda, MD: National Association of School Psychologists.

Gibbons, P. (2009). *English learners, academic literacy, and thinking: Learning in the challenge zone.* Portsmouth, NH: Heinemann.

Goe, L., & Stickler, L. M. (2008, March). *Teacher quality and student achievement: Making the most of recent research.* (Research & Policy Brief, National Comprehensive Center for Teacher Quality.) Retrieved from files.eric.ed.gov/fulltext/ED520769.pdf

Goldenberg, C. (2008). Teaching English learners: What the research does—and does not—say. *American Education,* 8–44. AFT publications and reports.

Goldhaber, D. (2016). In schools, teacher quality matters most. *Education Next, 16*(2), 56–62.

Gonzalez, N., & Moll, L. (2002). Cruzando el Puente: Building bridges to funds of knowledge. *Educational Policy, 16,* 623–641.

Good, R. H., III, Gruba, J., & Kaminski, R. A. (2001). Best practices in using Dynamic Indicators of Basic Early Literacy Skills (DIBELS) in an outcomes-driven model. In A. Thomas & J. Grimes (Eds.), *Best practices in school psychology IV* (Vol. 1, pp. 679–700). Bethesda, MD: National Association of School Psychologists.

Goodman, S. (2018). *It's not about grit: Trauma, inequity, and the power of transformative teaching.* New York, NY: Teachers College Press.

Gopnik, A. (2016). *The gardener and the carpenter: What the new science of child development tells us about the relationship between parents and children.* New York, NY: Picador.

Gordon, N. (2017, June 29). *How state ESSA accountability plans can shine a statistically sound light on more students* [report]. Washington, DC: Brookings Institute. Retrieved from www.brookings.edu/research/how-state-essa-accountability-plans-can-shine-a-statistically-sound-light-on-more-students/

Gottlieb, M. (2016). *Assessing English language learners: Bridges to educational equity: Connecting academic language proficiency to student achievement.* Thousand Oaks, CA: Corwin Press.

Gough, P., & Tunmer, W. (1986). Decoding, reading, and reading disability. *Remedial and Special Education, 7*, 6–10.

Grantmakers for Education. (2013). *Educating English language learners: Grantmaking strategies for closing America's other achievement gap.* Retrieved from edfunders.org/sites/default/files/Educating%20English%20Language%20Learners_April%202013.pdf

Graves, M. F. (2006). Building a comprehensive vocabulary program. *The NERA Journal, 42*(2), 1–7.

Greenberg Motamedi, J., Cox, M., Williams, J., & Deussen, T. (2016). *Uncovering diversity: Examining the representation of English learners in special education in Washington State.* Portland, OR: Education Northwest, Regional Educational Laboratory Northwest.

Griffiths, A., Parson, L. B., Burns, M. K., VanDerHeyden, A., & Tilly, W. D. (2007). *Response to intervention: Research for practice.* Alexandria, VA: National Association of State Directors of Special Education.

Gunn, B., Biglan, A., Smolkowski, K., & Ary, D. (2000). The efficacy of supplemental instruction in decoding skills for Hispanic and non-Hispanic students in early elementary school. *Journal of Special Education, 34*(2), 90–103.

Gunn, B., Smolkowski, K., Biglan, A., & Black, C. (2002). Supplemental instruction in decoding skills for Hispanic and non-Hispanic students in early elementary school: A follow-up. *Journal of Special Education, 36*(2), 69–79.

Haager, D. (2007). Promises and cautions regarding using response to intervention with English language learners. *Learning Disability Quarterly, 30*(3), 213–218.

Haager, D., & Klingner, J. K. (2005). *Differentiating instruction in inclusive classrooms: The special educator's guide.* Boston, MA: Pearson.

Haas, E. (2005). The Equal Educational Opportunity Act 30 years later: Time to revisit "appropriate action" for assisting English language learners. *Journal of Law and Education 34*(3), 361–387.

Haas, E., Fischman, G., & Brewer, J. (2014). *Dumb ideas won't create smart kids: Straight talk about bad school reform, good teaching, and better learning.* New York, NY: Teachers College Press.

Haas, E., Goldman, J., & Faltis, C. (2018). Writing practices for mainstream middle school teachers of English learners: Building on what we know works effectively with middle school English learners. *The Educational Forum, 82*(2), 208–226. doi. org/10.1080/00131725.2018.1420865

Haas, E., & Gort, M. (2009). Demanding more: Legal standards and best practices for English language learners. *Bilingual Research Journal, 32*, 115–135.

Haas, E., Huang, M., & Tran, L. (2014a). *The characteristics of long-term English language learner students and struggling reclassified fluent English proficient students in Arizona.* San Francisco, CA: REL West @ WestEd. Retrieved from ies.ed.gov/ncee/edlabs/regions/west/relwestFiles/pdf/REL_ELL3-2_Arizona_Report.pdf

Haas, E., Huang, M., & Tran, L. (2014b). *The characteristics of long-term English language learner students and struggling reclassified fluent English proficient students in Nevada.* San Francisco, CA: REL West @ WestEd. Retrieved from relwest.wested.org/resources/71

Haas, E., Huang, M., & Tran, L. (2014c). *The characteristics of long-term English language learner students and struggling reclassified fluent English proficient students in Utah.* San Francisco, CA: REL West @ WestEd. Retrieved from ies.ed.gov/ncee/edlabs/regions/west/Publications/Details/81

Haas, E., Huang, M., Tran, L., & Yu, A. (2016a). *The achievement progress of English learner students in Nevada* (REL 2016–154). Washington, DC: U.S. Department of Education, Institute of Education Sciences, National Center for Education Evaluation and Regional Assistance, Regional Educational Laboratory West. Retrieved from ies.ed.gov/ncee/edlabs/regions/west/pdf/REL_2016154.pdf

Haas, E., Huang, M., Tran, L., & Yu, A. (2016b). *The achievement progress of English learner students in Utah* (REL 2016–155). Washington, DC: U.S. Department of Education, Institute of Education Sciences, National Center for Education Evaluation and Regional Assistance, Regional Educational Laboratory West. Retrieved from ies.ed.gov/ncee/edlabs/regions/west/pdf/REL_2016155.pdf

Haas, E., Tran, L., & Huang, M. (2016). *English learner students' readiness for academic success: The predictive potential of English language proficiency assessment scores in Arizona and Nevada* (REL 2017–172). Washington, DC: U.S. Department of Education, Institute of Education Sciences, National Center for Education Evaluation and Regional Assistance, Regional Educational Laboratory West. Retrieved from ies.ed.gov/ncee/edlabs/regions/west/pdf/REL_2017172.pdf

Haas, E., Tran, L., Huang, M., & Yu, A. (2015). *The achievement progress of English learner students in Arizona* (REL 2015–098). Washington, DC: U.S. Department of Education, Institute of Education Sciences, National Center for Education Evaluation and Regional Assistance, Regional Educational Laboratory West. Retrieved from ies.ed.gov/ncee/edlabs/regions/west/pdf/REL_2015098.pdf

Haas, E., Tran, L., Linquanti, R., & Bailey, A. (2015). *Examining proposed and current home language surveys in California in relation to initial English language proficiency assessment results: An exploratory study.* San Francisco, CA: RELWest @ WestEd. Retrieved from eric.ed.gov/?id=ED564026

Hakuta, K. (2011). Educating language minority students and affirming their equal rights: Research and practical perspectives. *Educational Researcher, 40*(4), 163–174.

Hakuta, K., Butler, Y. G., & Witt, D. (2000). *How long does it take English learners to attain proficiency?* Stanford, CA: The University of California Linguistics Research Institute.

Hall, G. E., & Hord, S. M. (2001). *Implementing change: Patterns, principles, and potholes.* Boston, MA: Allyn & Bacon.

Hallahan, D. P., & Mercer, C. D. (2001). *Learning disabilities: Historical perspectives: Executive summary.* Washington, DC: U.S. Deptartment of Education, Office of Educational Research and Improvement, Educational Resources Information Center.

Harlacher, J., Nelson, N., & Sanford, A. (2010). The "I" in RTI: Research-based factors for intensifying instruction. *Teaching Exceptional Children Plus, 42,* 30–38.

Harry, B., & Klingner, J. (2006). The special education referral and decision-making process For English language learners: Child study team meetings and placement conferences. *Teachers College Record, 108*(11), 2247–2281. doi:10.1111/j.1467-9620.2006.00781.x

Harry, B., & Klingner, J. (2014). *Why are so many minority students in special education? Understanding race and disability in schools* (2nd ed.). New York, NY: Teachers College Press.

Harwell, M., & LeBeau, B. (2010). Student eligibility for a free lunch as an SES measure in education research. *Educational Researcher, 39,* 120–131.

Hasbrouck, J., & Tindal, G. (2017). *An update to compiled ORF norms* (Technical Report No. 1702). Eugene, OR: Behavioral Research and Teaching, University of Oregon.

Helman, L. (2009). English words needed: creating research-based vocabulary instruction for English learners. In M. F. Graves (Ed.), *Essential readings on vocabulary instruction* (pp. 124–141). Newark, DE: International Reading Association.

Hemphill, F. C., & Vanneman, A. (2011). *Achievement gaps: How Hispanic and White students in public schools perform in mathematics and reading on the National Assessment of Educational Progress* (NCES 2011-459). Washington, DC: National Center for Education Statistics, Institute of Education Sciences, U.S. Department of Education.

Herrera, S. G., Perez, D. R., & Escamilla, K. (2015). *Teaching reading to English language learners: Differentiated literacies* (2nd ed.). Boston, MA: Pearson.

Hibel, J., Farkas, G., & Morgan, P. L. (2010). Who is placed into special education? *Sociology of Education, 83,* 312–332. doi:10.1177/0038040710383518

Hollie, S. (2012). *Culturally and linguistically responsive teaching and learning: Classroom practices for student success* (2nd ed.). Huntington Beach, CA: Shell Education.

Hoover, W., & Gough, P. (1990). The simple view of reading. *Reading and Writing: An Interdisciplinary Journal, 2,* 127–160.

Hoover, J. J., Klingner, J. K., Baca, L. M., & Patton, J. M. (2008). *Methods for teaching culturally and linguistically diverse exceptional learners.* Upper Saddle River, NJ: Pearson.

Hosp, J. L. (2008). Best practices in aligning academic assessment with instruction. In A. Thomas & J. Grimes (Eds.), *Best practices in school psychology V* (pp. 363–376). Bethesda, MD: National Association of School Psychologists.

Hosp, M. K., Hosp, J. L., & Howell, K. W. (2016). *The ABCs of CBM: A practical guide to curriculum-based measurement* (2nd ed.). New York, NY: Guildford Press.

Howell, K. W., & Nolet, V. (2000). *Curriculum-based evaluation: Teaching and decision making*. Belmont, CA: Wadsworth Publishing Company.

Hussar, W. J., & Bailey, T. M. (2011). *Projections of Education Statistics to 2020* (NCES 2011-026). U.S. Department of Education, National Center for Education Statistics. Washington, DC: U.S. Government Printing Office.

Illinois State Board of Education. (2002). *Serving English language learners with disabilities: A resource manual for Illinois educators*. Springfield, IL: Author. Retrieved from www.isbe.net/Documents/bilingual_manual2002.pdf

Individuals with Disabilities Education Act (IDEA), 20 U.S.C. §§ 101 et seq (1997).

Individuals with Disabilities Education Improvement Act [IDEA], 20 U.S.C. §§ 1400 et seq. (2004).

Institute of Education Sciences. (2010, December). *Statistical methods for protecting personally identifiable information in aggregate reporting* (SLDS technical brief: Guidance for statewide longitudinal data systems [SLDS]). NCES 2011-603. Washington, DC: U.S. Department of Education. Retrieved from nces.ed.gov/pubs2011/2011603.pdf

Jensen, A. R. (1974). How biased are culture-loaded tests? *Genetic Psychology Monographs, 90*, 185–244.

Jiménez, R. T., García, G. E., & Pearson, P. D. (1996). The reading strategies of bilingual Latina/o students who are successful English readers: Opportunities and obstacles. *Reading Research Quarterly, 31*(1), 90–112.

Kaminski, R., Cummings, K. D., Powell-Smith, K. A., & Good, R. H., III. (2008). Best practices in using dynamic indicators of basic early literacy skills (DIBELS) for formative assessment and evaluation. In A. Thomas & J. Grimes (Eds.), *Best practices in school psychology V* (pp. 1181–1204). Bethesda, MD: National Association of School Psychologists.

Kauffman, J. M., Hallahan, D. P., Pullen, P. C., & Badar, J. (2018). *Special education: What it is and why we need it*. New York, NY: Routledge.

Kearns, D. M., Lemons, C. J., Fuchs, D., & Fuchs, L. S. (2014). Essentials of a tiered intervention system to support unique learners: Recommendations from research and practice. In J. Mascolo, D., Flanagan, & V. Alfonso (Eds.), *Essentials of planning, selecting, and tailoring interventions for the unique learner* (pp. 56–91). Hoboken, NJ: Wiley.

Keehne, C. N. K., Wai'ale'ale Sarsona, M., Kawakami, A. J., & Au, K. H. (2018). Culturally responsive instruction and literacy learning. *Journal of Literacy Research, 50*(2), 141–166.

Kena, G., Aud, S., Johnson, F., Wang, X., Zhang, J., Rathbun, A., Wilkinson-Flicker, S., & Kristapovich, P. (2014). *The condition of education 2014* (NCES 2014-083). U.S. Department of Education, National Center for Education Statistics. Washington, DC. Retrieved from nces.ed.gov/pubsearch/pubsinfo.asp?pubid=2014083

Kim, J. S, Vanderwood, M. L., & Lee, C. Y. (2016). Predictive validity of curriculum-based measures for English learners at varying English proficiency levels. *Educational Assessment, 21*(1), 1–18.

Klingner, J. K., & Edwards, P. A. (2006). Cultural considerations with response to intervention models. *Reading Research Quarterly, 41*, 108–117.

Klingner, J. K., & Eppolito, A. (2014). *English language learners: Differentiating between language acquisition and learning disabilities*. Arlington, VA: Council for Exceptional Children.

Klingner, J. K., & Vaughn, S. (2000). The helping behaviors of fifth-graders while using collaborative strategic reading (CSR) during ESL content classes. *TESOL Quarterly, 34*, 69–98.

Knight, J. (2013). *High-impact instruction: A framework for great teachers*. Thousand Oaks, CA: Corwin.

Komarraju, M., & Karau, S. J. (2005). The relationship between the Big Five personality traits and academic motivation. *Personality and Individual Differences, 39*, 557–567.

Kovelman, I., Baker, S. A., & Petitto, L. A. (2008). Bilingual and monolingual brains compared: A functional magnetic resonance investigation of syntactic processing and a possible "neural signature" of bilingualism. *Journal of Cognitive Neuroscience, 20*, 153–169.

Kovelman, I., & Petitto, L. A. (2002). Bilingual babies' maturational and linguistic milestones as a function of their age of first exposure to two languages. Poster presented at the conference for the Society for Neuroscience. Orlando, FL.

Krashen, S. (2004). *The power of reading*. Portsmouth, UK: Heinemann and Westport, CT: Libraries Unlimited.

Krogstad, J. M., & Radford, J. (2017, January 30). *Key facts about refugees in the U.S.* Pew Research Center. Retrieved from www.pewresearch.org/fact-tank/2017/01/30/key-facts-about-refugees-to-the-u-s/

Ladson-Billings, G. (1994). *The dreamkeepers: Successful teachers of African American children*. San Francisco, CA: Jossey-Bass.

Lakin, J. M. (2012). Assessing the cognitive abilities of culturally and linguistically diverse students: Predictive validity of verbal, quantitative, and nonverbal tests. *Psychology in the Schools, 49*(3), 756–768.

Lara-Cinisomo, S., Pebley, A. R., Vaiana, M. E., Maggio, E., Berends, M., & Lucas, S. R. (2004). A matter of class. *RAND Review, 28*(3), 10. Retrieved from www.rand.org/publications/randreview/issues/fall2004/index.html

Lau v. Nichols, 414 U.S. 563 (1974).

Learning Disabilities of America. (2018). *Types of learning disabilities*. Retrieved from ldaamerica.org/types-of-learning-disabilities/

Lenters, K. (2004). No half measures: Reading instruction for young second-language learners. *The Reading Teacher, 58*(4), 328–336.

Lesaux, N. K., & Siegel, L. S. (2003). The development of reading in children who speak English as a second language. *Developmental Psychology, 39*(6), 1005–1019.

Levin, B., & Fullan, M. (2008). Learning about system renewal. *Educational Management Administration & Leadership, 36*(2), 289–303. doi: 10.1177/1741143207087778

LeVine, R. A. (1977). Child-rearing and cultural adaption. In P. H. Leiderman, S. R. Tulkin, & A. Rosenfeld (Eds.), *Culture and infancy: Variations in the human experience* (pp. 15–28). New York, NY: Academic Press.

Lhamon, C.E., & Gupta, V. (2015, January 7). *Dear colleague letter.* Washington, DC: U.S. Department of Education, Office for Civil Rights.

Linan-Thompson, S., Vaughn, S., Hickman-Davis, P., & Kouzekanani, K. (2003). Effectiveness of supplemental reading instruction for second-grade English language learners with reading difficulties. *Elementary School Journal, 103*(3), 221–238.

Linan-Thompson, S., & Vaughn, S. (2007). *Research-based methods of reading instruction for English language learners, grades k–4.* Alexandria, VA: Association for Supervision and Curriculum Development.

Lingo, A. S. (2014). Tutoring middle school students with disabilities by high school students: Effects on oral reading fluency. *Education and Treatment of Children, 37*(1), 53–76.

Linn, D. (2011). Representation of English language learners in special education programs in Texas. *National Teacher Education Journal, 4*(2), 35–40.

Linquanti, R., & Cook, H. G. (2013). *Toward a "common definition of English learner": Guidance for states and state assessment consortia in defining policy and technical issues and options.* Washington, DC: CCSSO.

Lohman, D. F., & Gambrell, J. L. (2012). Using non-verbal tests to help identify academically talented children. *Journal of Psychoeducational Assessment, 30,* 25–44.

Lyon, G. R., Fletcher, J. M. Shaywitz, S. E., Shaywitz, B. A., Wood, F. B., Schulte, A., Olson, R. K., & Torgesen, J. K. (2001). Learning disabilities: An evidence-based conceptualization. In C. E. Finn, Jr., A. J. Rotherham, & C. R. Hokanson, Jr. (Eds.), *Rethinking special education for a new century* (pp. 259–287). Washington, DC: Fordham Foundation and Progressive Policy Institute.

Mancilla-Martinez, J., & Lesaux, N. K. (2010). Predictors of reading comprehension for struggling readers: The case of Spanish speaking language minority learners. *Journal of Educational Psychology, 102,* 701–711.

Mandinach, E., & Gummer, E. (2016). *Data literacy for educators: Making it count in teacher preparation and practice.* New York, NY: Teachers College Press.

Marchand-Martella, N. E., Martella, R. C., Modderman, S. L., Peterson, H. M., & Pan, S. (2013). Key areas of effective adolescent literacy programs. *Education and Treatment of Children, 36*(1), 161–184.

Martinez, R. S., Harris, B., & McClain, M. B. (2014). Practices that promote English reading for English learners (ELs). *Journal of Educational & Psychological Consultation, 24*(2), 128–148.

Matsumoto, D. (1994). *Cultural influences on research methods and statistics.* Pacific Grove, CA: Brooks/Cole.

Matsumoto, D. (1996). *Culture and psychology.* Pacific Grove, CA: Brooks/Cole.

McGrew, K. S., & Flanagan, D. P. (1998). *The intelligence test desk reference: Gf–Gc cross-battery assessment.* Boston, MA: Allyn & Bacon.

McIntosh, K., & Goodman, S. (2016). *Integrated Multi-Tiered Systems of Support: Blending RTI and PBIS.* New York, NY: Guilford Press.

McIntosh, P. (1989, July/August). White privilege: Unpacking the invisible knapsack. *Peace and Freedom,* 10–12.

McKenzie, K. B., & Scheurich, J. J. (2004). Equity traps: A useful construct for preparing principals to lead schools that are successful with racially diverse students. *Educational Administration Quarterly, 40*(5), 601–632.

Melby-Lervåg, M., & Lervåg, A. (2011). Cross-linguistic transfer of oral language, decoding, phonological awareness and reading comprehension: A meta-analysis of the correlational evidence. *Journal of Research in Reading, 34*, 114–135.

Mellard, D. F., McKnight, M., & Woods, K. (2009). Response to intervention screening and progress-monitoring practices in 41 local schools. *Learning disabilities practice, 24*(4), 186–195.

Michigan Department of Education. (2017). *Guidance handbook for educators of English learners with suspected disabilities.* Lansing, MI: Author. Retrieved from www.michigan.gov/documents/mde/ELs_with_Suspected_Disabilities_Guidance_Handbook_-_2017_558692_7.pdf

Minnesota Department of Education. (2005). *The ELL companion to reducing bias in special education evaluation.* St. Paul, MN: Author. Retrieved from www.asec.net/Archives/Manuals/ELL%20companion%20Manual%20020212%5B1%5D.pdf

Moll, L. C., Amanti, C., Neff, D., & Gonzalez, N. (1992) Funds of knowledge for teaching: Using a qualitative approach to connect homes and classrooms. *Theory into Practice, 31*(2), 132–141.

Morgan, P. L., Farkas, G., Hillemeier, M. M., & Maczuga, S. (2009). Risk factors for learning related behavior problems at 24 months of age: Population-based estimates. *Journal of Abnormal Child Psychology, 37*, 401–413.

Morgan, P. L., Farkas, G., Hillemeier, M. M., Mattison, R., Maczuga, S., Li, H., & Cook, M. (2015). Minorities are disproportionately underrepresented in special education: Longitudinal evidence across five disability conditions. *Educational Researcher, 44*(5), 278–292. Retrieved from eric.ed.gov/?id=EJ1068118

Murphy, J., & Louis, K. S. (2018). *Positive school leadership: Building capacity and strengthening relationships.* New York, NY: Teachers College Press.

Muyskens, P., Betts, J., Lau, M. Y., & Marston, D. (2009). Predictive validity of curriculum-based measures in the reading assessment of students who are English language learners. *The California School Psychologist, 14*, 11. doi:10.1007/BF03340947

Nassaji, H. (2003). Higher-level and lower-level text processing skills in advanced ESL reading comprehension. *Modern Language Journal, 87*, 261–276.

Nation, I. S. P. (2001). *Learning vocabulary in another language.* Cambridge, NY: Cambridge University Press.

National Reading Panel & National Institute of Child Health and Human Development. (2000). *Report of the National Reading Panel: Teaching children to read: An evidence-based assessment of the scientific research literature on reading and its implications for reading instruction: reports of the subgroups.* Washington, DC: National Institute of Child Health and Human Development, National Institutes of Health.

Neuman, S. (2008). *Educating the other America.* Baltimore, MD: Paul H. Brookes.

Nieto, S. (2010). *The light in their eyes: Creating multicultural learning communities* (10th anniversary ed.). New York, NY: Teachers College Press.

Nieto, S., & Bode, P. (2008). *Affirming diversity: The sociopolitical context of multicultural education,* (5th ed.). New York, NY: Pearson.

Odlin, T. (1989). *Language transfer: Cross-linguistic influence in language learning.* Cambridge, UK: Cambridge University Press.

Ogbu, J. U. (1981). Origins of human competence: A cultural-ecological perspective. *Child Development, 52,* 413–42

Oklahoma State Department of Education. (2007). *Identifying and assessing English language learners with disabilities: Technical assistance document.* Oklahoma City, OK: Author. Retrieved from sde.ok.gov/sde/sites/ok.gov.sde/files/SpecEd-IdentifyingELL.pdf

Olsen, L., & Jaramillo, A. (1999). *Turning the tides of exclusion: A guide for educators and advocates for immigrant students.* Oakland, CA: The California Tomorrow.

O'Malley, J. M., & Chamot, A. U. (1990). *Learning strategies in second language acquisition.* Cambridge, UK: Cambridge University Press.

Orosco, M. J., & Klingner, J. (2010). One school's implementation of RTI with English language learners: "Referring to RTI." *Journal of Learning Disabilities, 43*(3), 269–288. doi: 10.1177/0022219409355474

Ortiz, A. (2018, July 23). Personal communication.

Ortiz, A. A., Robertson, P. M., Wilkinson, C. Y., Liu, Y., McGhee, B. D., & Kushner, M. I. (2011). The role of bilingual education teachers in preventing inappropriate referrals of ELLs to special education: Implications for response to intervention. *Bilingual Research Journal, 3*(3), 316–333.

Ortiz, S. O. (2019). On the measurement of cognitive abilities in English learners [Special issue]. *Journal of Contemporary School Psychology, 23*(1), 68–86.

Pang, Y. (2013). Graphic organizers and other visual strategies to improve young ELLs' reading comprehension. *The NERA Journal, 48*(2), 52–58.

Paris, D. (2012). Culturally sustaining pedagogy: A needed change in stance, terminology, and practice. *Educational Researcher, 41*(3), 93–97.

Park, M., Zong, J., & Batalova, J. (2018). *Superdiversity among young U.S. dual language learners and its implications.* Washington, DC: Migration Policy Institute.

Pasquarella, A., Chen, X., Gottardo, A., & Geva, E. (2014). Cross-language transfer of word reading accuracy and word reading fluency in Spanish–English and Chinese–English bilinguals: Script-universal and script-specific processes. *Journal of Educational Psychology, 107*(1), 96–110.

Peregoy, S. F., & Boyle, O. F. (2000). English learners reading English: What we know, what we need to know. *Theory into Practice, 39*(4), 237–247.

Pelech, J., & Pieper, G. (2010). *The comprehensive handbook of constructivist teaching: From theory to practice.* Charlotte, NC: Information Age Publishing.

Petitto, L. A., Berens, M. S., Kovelman, I., Dubins, M. H., Jasinska, K., & Shalinsky, M. (2012). "Perceptual Wedge Hypothesis" as the basis for bilingual babies' phonetic processing advantage: new insights from fNIRS brain imaging. *Brain and Language, 121*(2), 130–143.

Pieretti, R. B., & Roseberry-McKibbin, C. (2016). Assessment and intervention for English language learners with primary language impairment: Research-based best practices. *Communication Disorders Quarterly, 37*(2), 117–128.

Pink, D. (2011). *Drive: The surprising truth about what motivates us*. New York, NY: Penguin.

Powers, J. (2014). From segregation to school finance: The legal context of language rights in the United States. *Review of Research in Education, 38*, 81–105.

Proctor, C. P., Carlo, M., August, D., & Snow, C. (2005). Native Spanish-speaking children reading in English: Toward a model of comprehension. *Journal of Educational Psychology, 97*(2), 246–256.

Proctor, C. P., Dalton, B., & Grisham, D. L. (2007). Scaffolding English language learners and struggling readers in a universal literacy environment with embedded strategy instruction and vocabulary support. *Journal of Literacy Research, 39*(1), 71–93.

Project ELITE, Project ESTRE²LLA, & Project REME. (2015). *Effective practices for English learners: Brief 3, Core and supplemental English as a second language literacy instruction for English learners.* Washington, DC: U.S. Office of Special Education Programs.

Project IDEAL. (n.d.). Disability categories. Retrieved from www.projectidealonline.org/v/disability-categories/

Quirk, M., & Beem, S. (2012). Examining the relations between reading fluency and reading comprehension for English language learners. *Psychology in the Schools, 49*(6), 539–553.

Rehabilitation Act of 1973, 20 U.S.C. §§ 701 et seq. (1973).

Riccomini, P. J., Morano, S., & Hughes, C. A. (2017). Big ideas in special education: Specially designed instruction, high-leverage practices, explicit instruction, and intensive instruction. *Teaching Exceptional Children, 50*(1), 20–17.

Richards-Tutor, C., Solari, E. J., Leafstedt, J. M., Gerber, M. M., Filippini, A., & Aceves, T. C. (2013). Response to Intervention for English learners: Examining models for determining response and nonresponse. *Assessment for Effective Intervention, 38*(3), 172–184.

Riedel, B. W. (2007). The relation between DIBELS, reading comprehension, and vocabulary in urban first-grade students. *Reading Research Quarterly, 42*(4), 546–567.

Roberge, M. M. (2002). California's generation 1.5 immigrants: What experiences, characteristics, and needs do they bring to our English classes? *The CATESOL Journal, 14*(1), 107–129.

Roberts, B. W., & DelVecchio, W. F. (2000). The rank-order consistency of personality from childhood to old age: A quantitative review of longitudinal studies. *Psychology Bulletin, 126*, 3–25.

Rohena, E. I., Jitendra, A. K., & Drowder, D. M. (2002). Comparison of the effects of Spanish and English constant time delay instruction on sight word reading by Hispanic learners with mental retardation. *The Journal of Special Education, 36*(3), 169–184.

Rueda, R., & Windmueller, M. P. (2006). English language learners, LD, and overrepresentation: A multiple-level analysis. *Journal of Learning Disabilities, 39*(2), 99–107. Retrieved from eric.ed.gov/?id=EJ757902

Ruiz, R. (1984). Orientations in language planning. *NABE Journal, 8*(2), 15–34.

Rumberger, R. W., & Larson, K. A. (1998). Toward explaining differences in educational achievement among Mexican American language-minority students. *Sociology of Education, 71*(1), 68–92.

Ryan, R. M., & Deci, E. L. (2010). Self determination theory and the facilitation of intrinsic motivation, social development, and well-being. *American Psychologist, 55*, 68–78.

Ryder, R. E. (2016, June 14). *Dear colleagues letter*. Washington, DC: Office of Special Education Programs, U.S. Department of Education. Retrieved from sites.ed.gov/idea/files/policy_speced_guid_idea_memosdcltrs_iep-translation-06-14-2016.pdf

Ryndak, D., Ward, T., Alper, S., Storch, J. F., & Montgomery, J. W. (2010). Long-term outcomes of services in inclusive and self-contained settings for siblings with comparable significant disabilities. *Education and Training in Autism and Developmental Disabilities, 45*(1), 38–53.

Saenz, L. M., Fuchs, L. S., & Fuchs, D. (2005). Peer-assisted learning strategies for English language learners with learning disabilities. *Exceptional Children, 71*, 231–247.

Sahlberg, P. (2015). *Finnish lessons 2.0. What can the world learn from educational change in Finland?* (2nd ed.). New York, NY: Teachers College Press.

Salvia, J., Ysseldyke, J. E., & Witmer, S. (2017). *Assessment in special and inclusive education* (13th ed.). Boston, MA: Cengage Learning.

Samora, S. C., & Lopez- Diaz, I. (2010). *Differentiation between language difference and language disability in Response to Intervention: Guidance for New York state school districts*. New York, NY: The University of the State of New York, State Education Department.

Samuels, S. J. (2007). The DIBELS tests: Is speed of barking at print what we mean by reading fluency? *Reading Research Quarterly, 42*, 563–566.

Sanatullova-Allison, E., & Robison-Young, V. (2016). Overrepresentation: An overview of the issues surrounding the identification of English language learners with learning disabilities. *International Journal of Special Education, 31* (2), 3–13.

Sanchez, G. I. (1934). Bilingualism and mental measures: A word of caution. *Journal of Applied Psychology, 18*, 765–772.

Sanford, A. K., Brown, J. E., & Turner, M. (2012). Enhancing instruction for English learners in response to intervention systems: The PLUSS model. *Multiple Voices for Ethnically Diverse Exceptional Learners, 13*(1), 56–70.

Scarcella, R. (2003). *Academic English: A conceptual framework*. Santa Barbara, CA: University of California Linguistic Minority Institute.

Schecter, S. R., & Bayley, R. (2002). *Language as cultural practice: Mexicanos en el Norte*. Mahwah, NJ: Erlbaum.

Scherba de Valenzuela, J., Bird, E. K. R., Parkington, K., Mirenda, P., Cain, K., MacLeod, A. A. N., & Segers, E. (2016). Access to opportunities for bilingualism for individuals with developmental disabilities: Key informant interviews. *Journal of Communication Disorders, 63*, 32–46.

Schermer, M. (2017, January 1). How to convince someone when facts fail: Why worldview threats undermine evidence. *Scientific American*. Retrieved from www.scientificamerican.com/article/how-to-convince-someone-when-facts-fail/

Senge, P. (1990). *The fifth discipline: The art and practice of the learning organization*. New York, NY: Doubleday.

Shafer Willner, L., Rivera, C., & Acosta, B. (2009). Ensuring accommodations used in content assessments are responsive to English language learners. *The Reading Teacher, 62*(8), 696–698. doi: 10.1598/RT.62.8.8.

Shanahan, T. (2016). Reading research: The importance of replication. *The Reading Teacher, 70*(4), 504–510.

Share, D. L., McGee, R., & Silva, P. (1989). IQ and reading progress: A test of the capacity notion of IQ. *Journal of the American Academy of Child and Adolescent Psychiatry, 28*, 97–100.

Share, D. L., & Silva, P. A. (1987). Language deficits and specific reading retardation: Cause or effect? *British Journals of Disorders of Communication, 22*(3), 219–226.

Shaywitz, S. E. (2003). *Overcoming dyslexia: A new and complete science-based program for reading problems at any level.* New York, NY: Knopf.

Shifrer, D., Muller, C., & Callahan, R. (2011). Disproportionality and learning disabilities: Parsing apart race, socioeconomic status, and language. *Journal of Learning Disabilities, 44*, 246–257. doi: 10.1177/0022219410374236

Shinn, M. R. (1995). Best practices in curriculum-based measurement and its use in a problem-solving model. In A. Thomas & J. Grimes (Eds.), *Best practices in school psychology III* (pp. 547–567). Washington, DC: National Association of School Psychologists.

Shinn, M. R. (2008). Best practices in curriculum-based measures and its use in a problem-solving model. In A. Thomas & J. Grimes (Eds.), *Best practices in school psychology,* (pp. 243–262). Bethesda, MD: National Association of School Psychologists.

Shores, C. (2009). *A comprehensive RTI model: Integrating behavioral and academic interventions.* Newbury Park, CA: SAGE Publishing.

Skiba, R. J., Knesting, K., & Bush, L. D. (2002). Culturally competent assessment: More than nonbiased tests. *Journal of Child and Family Studies, 11*(1), 61–78.

Skinner, C. H., Cooper, L., & Cole, C. L. (1997). The effects of oral presentation previewing rates on reading performance. *Journal of Applied Behavior Analysis, 30*, 331–334.

Sleeter, C. D. (2011). *The academic and social value of ethnic studies.* Washington, DC: National Education Association.

Solano-Flores, G. (2008). Who is given tests in what language by whom, when, and where? The need for probabilistic views of language in the testing of English language learners. *Educational Researcher, 37*(4), 189–199.

Spooner, F., Rivera, C. J., Browder, D. M., Baker, J. N., & Salas, S. (2009). Teaching emergent literacy skills using cultural contextual story-based lessons. *Research & Practice for Persons with Severe Disabilities, 34*(3–4), 102–112.

Stanovich, K. E. (1986). Matthew effects in reading: Some consequences of individual differences in the acquisition of literacy. *Reading Research Quarterly, 21*(4), 360–407.

Steele, J. L., Slater, R. O., Zamarro, G., Miller, T., Burkhauser, S., & Bacon, M. (2017). Effects of dual-language immersion programs on student achievement: Evidence from lottery data. *American Educational Research Journal, 54*(1), 282–306.

Sternberg, R. J., & Grigorenko, E. L. (2004). Why cultural psychology is necessary and not just nice: The example of the study of intelligence. In R. J. Sternberg & E. L. Grigorenko (Eds.), *Culture and competence: Contexts of life success* (pp. 207–223). Washington, DC: American Psychological Association.

Stovall, D. (2004). School leader as negotiator: Critical Race Theory, praxis, and the creation of productive space. *Multicultural Education, 12*(2), 8–12.

Stuart, M. (1999). Getting ready for reading: Early phoneme awareness and phonics teaching improves reading and spelling in inner-city second language learners. *British Journal of Educational Psychology, 69,* 587–605.

Sullivan, A. L. (2011). Disproportionality in special education identification and placement of English language learners. *Exceptional Children, 77,* 317–334.

Sullivan, A. L., & Bal, A. (2013). Disproportionality in special education: Effects of individual and school variables on disability risk. *Exceptional Children, 79*(4), 475–494.

Swanborn, M. S. L., & de Glopper, K. (1999). Incidental word learning while reading: A meta-analysis. *Review of Educational Research, 69,* 261–285.

Takanishi, R., & Menestrel, S. (Eds.). (2017). *Promoting the educational success of children and youth learning English: Promising futures.* Washington, DC: The National Academies Press. doi: 10.17226/24677. Retrieved from www.nap.edu/catalog/24677/promoting-the-educational-success-of-children-and-youth-learning-english

Taylor, J. A., Getty, S. R., Kowalski, S., Wilson, C. D., Carlson, J., & Van Scotter, P. (2015). An efficacy trial of research-based curriculum materials with curriculum-based professional development. *American Educational Research Journal, 52*(5), 984–1017.

Texas Education Agency. (n.d.). Process for considering special exit criteria from bilingual/English as a second language (ESL) services under 19 TAC Sec. 89.1225(k). Retrieved from tea.texas.gov/WorkArea/DownloadAsset.aspx?id=51539609138

Therrien, W. J. (2004). Fluency and comprehension gains as a result of repeated reading. *Remedial and Special Education, 25,* 252–262.

Thomas, W. P., & Collier, V. (2002). *A national study of school effectiveness for language minority students' long-term academic achievement.* Santa Cruz, CA, & Washington, DC: Center for Research on Education, Diversity & Excellence.

Thomas, W. P., & Collier, V. P. (2003). The multiple benefits of dual language. *Educational Leadership, 61*(2), 61–64.

Thompson, K. (2015). Questioning the long-term English learner label: How categorization can blind us to students' abilities. *Teachers College Record, 117*(12), 1-50.

Thorius, K. K., & Sullivan, A. (2013). Interrogating instruction and intervention in RTI research with students identified as English language learners. *Reading & Writing Quarterly, 29*(1), 64–88.

Tilly, D. (2008). The evolution of school psychology to science-based practice. In A. Thomas & J. Grimes (Eds.), *Best practices in school psychology V* (pp. 17–36). Bethesda, MD: National Association of School Psychologists.

Title III of The Elementary and Secondary Education Act [ESEA]. (2015). 20 U.S.C. § § 3001 et seq.

Title VI of the Civil Rights Act (1964). 42 U.S.C. § §; 2000 et seq.

Tran, L. M., Patton, J. R., & Brohammer, M. (2018). Preparing educators for developing culturally and linguistically responsible IEPs. *Teacher Education and Special Education, 41*(3), 229–242.

U.S. Department of Education (USDOE). (n.d.). *About ED. Overview. The federal role in education* [webpage]. Retrieved from www2.ed.gov/about/overview/fed/role.html

U.S. Department of Education (USDOE). (2016a). *Non-regulatory guidance: English learners and Title III of the Elementary and Secondary Education Act (ESEA), as amended by* the *Every Student Succeeds Act (ESSA)*. Retrieved from www2.ed.gov/policy/elsec/leg/essa/essatitleiiiguidenglishlearners92016.pdf

U.S. Department of Education (USDOE). (2016b). *Racial and ethnic disparities in special education*. Washington, DC: U.S. Department of Education.

U.S. Department of Education, Office for Civil Rights. (2016). *Parent and educator resource guide to section 504 in public elementary and secondary schools*. Washington, DC: Author. Retrieved from www2.ed.gov/about/offices/list/ocr/docs/504-resource-guide-201612.pdf

U.S. Department of Education, Office for Civil Rights. (2018, April 24). *Protecting students with disabilities*. Washington, DC: Author. Retrieved from www2.ed.gov/about/offices/list/ocr/504faq.html

U.S. Department of Education Statistics, National Center for Education Statistics. (2018, April). *The condition of education 2017 (2017-144): English language learners in public schools*. Available from nces.ed.gov/programs/coe/indicator_cgf.asp

U.S. Department of Health & Human Services. (n.d.). *U.S. federal poverty guidelines used to determine financial eligibility for certain federal programs: HHS poverty guidelines for 2018*. Retrieved from aspe.hhs.gov/poverty-guidelines

Vadasy, P. F., & Sanders, E. A. (2010). Efficacy of supplemental phonics-based instruction for low-skilled kindergarteners in the context of language minority status and classroom phonics instruction. *Journal of Educational Psychology, 102*(4), 786–803.

Valdés, G., Poza, L., & Brooks, M. D. (2015). Language acquisition in bilingual education. In W. E. Wright, S. Boun, & O. Garcia (Eds.), *The handbook of bilingual and multilingual education* (pp. 56–74). Hoboken, NJ: Wiley & Sons.

Valdes, G., & Figueroa, R. A. (1994). *Bilingualism and testing: A special case of bias*. Norwood, NJ: Ablex.

Vanderwood, M. L., Linklater, D., & Healy, K. (2008). Predictive accuracy of nonsense word fluency for English language learners. *School Psychology Review, 37*(1), 5–17.

Vaughn, S., Mathes, P. G., Linan-Thompson, S., & Francis, D. J. (2005). Teaching English language learners at risk for reading disabilities to read: Putting research into practice. *Learning Disabilities Research and Practice, 20*(1), 58–67.

Vellutino, F. R., Scanlon, D. M., Small, S. G., & Tanzman, M.S. (1991). The linguistic bases of reading ability: Converting written to oral language. *Text, 11*, 99–133.

Vermont Department of Education, New England Equity Assistance Center, Education Alliance at Brown University & Northeast Regional Resource Center, & Learning Innovations at WestEd. (2010). *English language learners in Vermont: Distinguishing language difference from disability: A resource guide*. Montpelier, VT: Author. Retrieved from education.vermont.gov/sites/aoe/files/documents/edu-federal-programs-distinguishing-language-difference-from-disability.pdf

Vukovich, D., & Figueroa, R. A. (1982). *The validation of the system of multicultural pluralistic assessment: 1980–1982*. Unpublished manuscript, University of California at Davis, Department of Education.

Wagner, R. K., Francis, D. J., & Morris, R. D. (2005). Identifying English language learners with learning disabilities: Key challenges and possible approaches. *Learning Disabilities Research & Practice, 20*, 6–15. doi: 10.1111/j.1540-5826.2005.00115.x

Walker, T. D. (2017). *Teaching like Finland: 33 simple strategies for joyful classrooms.* New York, NY: W. W. Norton.

Ware, J., Lye, C. B., & Kyffin, F. (2015). Bilingualism and students (learners) with intellectual disability: A review. *Journal of Policy and Practice in Intellectual Disabilities, 12*(3), 220–231. doi: 10.1111/jppi.12124

Watkins, C., & Slocum, T. (2004). The components of direct instruction. In N.E. Marchand-Martella, T. A. Slocum, & R.C. Martella (Eds.), *Introduction to direct instruction* (pp. 28–65). Boston, MA: Allyn & Bacon.

Wayman, M. M., Wallace, T., & Wiley, H. I. (2007). Literature synthesis on curriculum-based measures in reading. *Journal of Special Education, 41*(2), 85–120.

Yell, M. L., Katsiyannis, A., Ennis, R. P., Losinski, M., & Christle, C. A. (2016). Avoiding substantive errors in individualized education program development. *Teaching Exceptional Children, 49*(1), 31–40.

Yerkes, R. M. (Ed.). (1921). Psychological examining in the United States army. *Memoirs of the National Academy of Sciences, 1*, 252–259. Washington, DC: Government Printing Office.

Zehler, A. M., Fleischman, H. L., Hopstock, P. J., Pendzick, M. L., & Stephenson, T. G. (2003). *Descriptive study of services to LEP students and LEP students with disabilities (No. 4 Special topic report: findings on special education LEP students).* Arlington, VA: Development Associates, Inc.

Zong, J., & Batalova, J. (2015, July 8). *The limited English proficient population in the United States.* Washington, DC: Migration Policy Institute. Retrieved from www.migrationpolicy.org/article/limited-english-proficient-population-united-states

Index

Entries marked with *f* denote this is a figure.

About the Authors

Eric Haas is a professor and director of the educational doctorate in Educational Leadership for Social Justice program at California State University, East Bay. He is a former senior researcher at WestEd, where he directed the English Learner Alliance for the Regional Educational Laboratory West and was the principal investigator of an IES Goal 3 grant that examined the effectiveness of the WRITE Institute's writing program for middle school English learner students. He is also a former Peace Corps Volunteer and middle school teacher and principal. His previous book is *Dumb Ideas Won't Create Smart Kids: Straight Talk About Bad School Reform, Good Teaching and Better Learning* (with Gustavo Fischman and Joe Brewer).

Julie Esparza Brown is an associate professor in the Department of Special Education at Portland State University, where she specializes in working with culturally and linguistically diverse exceptional learners. After almost 2 decades in public schools as a special education and bilingual teacher, and school psychologist in California, Washington, and Oregon, she joined the faculty at Portland State University, where she has been the principal investigator on several federal grants to prepare diverse general and special educators. Currently, she is the principal investigator on a model demonstration project funded through the federal Office of Special Education Programs to examine the use of culturally and linguistically responsive frameworks in multi-tiered support systems (MTSS). Dr. Brown's publications include national briefs on MTSS for English learner students, district and university partnerships to prepare diverse teachers, and distinguishing language difference from disabilities in English learner students. Dr. Brown also serves as an elected school board member of a large, urban school district.